HERE IT IS, a case to challenge Sholto Lestrade of Scotland Yard.

Captain Orange and his nieces are killed in a carriage accident. The only clues? A tall man seen near the Captain's house shortly before the carriage left, and a broken mirror found in the Captain's breast pocket.

Next, Janet Calthrop of King's College tumbles to her death on the way to her lover's bedroom, the victim of a trip-wire across the stairs. The clue? A broken mirror found in said lover's boudoir.

So it is little surprise that, when a body is discovered in a ruined lighthouse, the only clue found is a broken mirror.

As the murders pile up, so do the mirrors… and the suspects.

"Mirror, mirror, on the wall," muses Lestrade, "who's the guiltiest of them all?"

He is to find out.

Lestrade and
the Mirror
of Murder

Other books in M.J. Trow's Lestrade Mystery Series

And coming soon!

Lestrade and the Mirror of Murder

Volume XIV in the Lestrade Mystery Series

M.J. Trow

A Gateway Mystery

REGNERY
PUBLISHING, INC.
Since 1947 • An Eagle Publishing Company

Cataloging-in-Publication Data on file with the Library of Congress

ISBN: 0-89526-233-9

Published in the United States by
Regnery Publishing, Inc.
An Eagle Publishing Company
One Massachusetts Avenue, NW
Washington, DC 20001
www.regnery.com

Distributed to the trade by
National Book Network
4720-A Boston Way
Lanham, MD 20706

Printed on acid-free paper
Manufactured in the United States of America
Originally published in Great Britain

10 9 8 7 6 5 4 3 2 1

Books are available in quantity for promotional or premium use. Write to Director of Special Sales, Regnery Publishing, Inc., One Massachusetts Avenue, NW, Washington, DC 20001, for information on discounts and terms or call (202) 216-0600.

The character of Inspector Lestrade was created by the late Sir Arthur Conan Doyle and appears in the Sherlock Holmes stories and novels by him, as do some other characters in this book.

Prologue

The dead man lay propped on his silk pillows, his shattered head thrown back, his right hand still clutching the silver-chased pistol which had ended his life. A small, neat, dark hole had punctured his right temple and the bullet had burst its way out of the other side of his head, taking most of the skull with it.

A photographer was crouching in one corner of the palace hall, his head buried under a black hood, trying to make the best of the poor Abyssinian light. At least his subject wasn't moving around much. The doors crashed back and the soldiery in the smoke-filled room clicked to attention.

'As you were, gentlemen,' the poppy-eyed general with the enormous sidewhiskers put them at their ease. 'Well, well, well.' He tugged off his forage cap and knelt beside the body on the dais. 'The Emperor Theodore, as I live and breathe. Staveley.'

A slim man of indeterminate years was at his elbow, 'Sir?'

'Anybody see this?'

'The 4th Foot got here first. I have the report of Sergeant Pepper, if it's of any interest.'

The general looked at his second-in-command with contempt. At least the man had his boots on this morning and hadn't stormed the gates of Magdala in his carpet slippers, but that cravat ... and that wideawake ... Had he no dress sense at all? All in all, bad form in front of the men. Deuc'd bad form.

'Out there,' said the general softly, 'I have thirteen thousand fighting troops, minus those we lost on the Arogee plateau and in today's assault. I have fourteen thousand, five hundred camp followers – at least eight of them, incidentally, have accused you of fathering their children, but we'll deal with that later. I have a clutch of scientists, thirty-six thousand pack animals and forty-four elephants. We have hired more than two hundred ships including seventy-five steamers. All of which has cost the British taxpayer in this Year of Our Lord 1868 alone, the appalling sum of two million pounds. "If it's of interest", you say. "*If* it's of interest!" *Everything* about this campaign is of interest to somebody, Staveley – politicians, military historians in the years to come, apologists of Empire; not to mention the families of those poor blighters who won't be going home. What does this man Pepper say?'

Staveley knew a dressing-down when he heard it. He stood up as his general did, 'Verbatim, sir?'

'Of course . . . No, wait a minute. Did you say Pepper of the 4th Foot?'

Staveley had.

'The same Pepper who brought that despatch last week from Charlie Speedy?'

'The same, sir.'

The general blanched. 'No. I was sitting there nearly an hour. The gist, man. Give me the gist.'

'The gist, s̶i̶r̶, is what you see before you. We must assume that the Emperor Theodore III took his own life while the balance of his mind was disturbed.'

'Hmm,' the general gazed on the pallid face on the pillow. 'Wife died. Ruler of three hundred and ninety-five thousand square miles of sand. Hot as buggery on the Red Sea Coast and wet as Lord Aberdeen for six months of the year. Then of course his people are Christians, Mohammadans, pagans and Jews and I don't even want to think about the admixture of races.'

'His people deserted him in the end, Pepper says,' Staveley commented.

'I'm not surprised,' the general unhooked his water-canteen and took a swig. His eyes swam and his throat locked. 'Apparently, our Lord suffered a man from Abyssinia to carry the cross.' He marched to the window and gazed down to see the men of the 4th Foot rounding up disarmed warriors and herding them into the square. 'Well, I don't suffer Abyssinians at all. Just imagine one of these fellows with their tightly-braided hair walking down the Strand of a Sunday afternoon. God, it doesn't bear thinking about. Where's Charlie Speedy?'

'Sir?' Staveley frowned.

'Speedy. Captain Speedy. Where is he?'

'Er . . . General Napier,' a muffled voice broke in.

'Who said that?' Napier whirled around.

'I did,' the photographer's tousled head appeared from the black hood, 'Charles Tenterden, sir. *London Illustrated News.*'

'Ah yes. Look, I've seen the work of that Matthew Brady chappie in America – lines of dead fellows at Chicamauga and so on. Not much of a war, the American Civil, but a deuc'd good collection of photographs. You'll have to go some to beat him, you know.'

'I'm not actually a photographer, General, I'm a journalist.'

'What? Some damned scribbler?'

Staveley crossed the darkening hall from a whispered conversation at the door. 'No one has seen Captain Speedy since last night, sir,' he said.

'I saw him then,' Tenterden said, 'at my campfire on the Arogee. He was helping me with an article for the *News.*'

Napier raised an eyebrow. 'An Intelligence Officer talking to a newspaperman? Deuc'd unprofessional. I hope he didn't divulge any secrets.'

'You know Charlie,' Tenterden said, 'the soul of discretion. As far as secrets go, I might as well have talked to the regimental goat. But he was going into the citadel.'

'When?' Napier and Staveley chorused.

'Last night,' Tenterden said, 'directly after he left me. We all knew the assault was planned for this morning. He said he had one or two things to do.'

Napier and Staveley exchanged glances. Then the general called his Number Two aside. '"One or two things to do"?' he whispered.

'You didn't . . .' Staveley frowned.

'Not my command,' Napier ground his teeth. 'What was he about?'

'You know Speedy, sir. Always a bit of a rogue male.'

'Loyal though.'

'To the core. But a maverick.'

'Trustworthy.'

'Through and through. But a loner.'

'What was he about? Always whistling that same damned tune.' Napier hooked his sword up to his belt. 'Well, well, he'll turn up. After all, you can't miss an Englishman who stands six foot five in his stockinged feet, can you?'

'Most of these Abyssinian chappies could, I'm very glad to say,' Staveley had found the bullet-hole in the brim of his wideawake. 'What'll we do with this place, sir?'

'Magdala?' Napier looked around him at the sumptuous fittings, the damask, the gold, the silver. 'Burn it,' he said, 'I've got despatches to write. You wouldn't care to help me with a few of the long words, Tenterden?'

Another enormous pair of sidewhiskers. Older. Greyer. Four thousand miles away. Mr Poulson had come a long way since his old man had a barrow in the Old Kent Road. Not that his brass shingle made any mention of that. No, his curriculum vitae spoke of Oxford and the Sorbonne, of Bologna and other famous Spanish centres of learning. And here he was on that wet April afternoon, seated in the study of his Academy for the Sons of Nearly Respectable Gentlefolk on windswept Blackheath, his formidable lips pursed behind two index fingers, both leather-stalled from years of inflicting child abuse.

And a most abused child stood before him, his badly polished boots squarely on the rather threadbare carpet where he was destined to remain, metaphorically, for the rest of his life.

'Sholto Joseph Lestrade,' the great man sighed, 'I do believe you have managed to find the end of my tether.'

The boy did not flinch, although the thought of Mr Poulson tied to a wall in some stable did appeal in a childishly sadistic way.

'How old are you now? Eighteen? Nineteen?'

'I was fourteen last January, sir.'

'Really?' Poulson's rugged eyebrows rose approvingly. 'Time to make your way in the world.'

'Sir?'

10

'You're the one whose father is a . . .' and he had to force his lips to it, '. . . a policeman, aren't you?'

'Yessir,' Lestrade stood an inch taller.

'And doesn't your mother take in washing? *Other people*'s, I mean?'

The boy sank again. 'She . . . did sir. She's dead now.'

Poulson was unmoved. 'Yes, well, these things are sent to try us, Lestrade. Let's leave the tear-jerkers to Mr Dickens, shall we? What of this?' He suddenly thwacked a short rattan cane down on an exercise book.

'It's an exercise book, sir,' the boy told him.

Poulson sat back in his chair. 'Such heights of levity may endear you to the Lower Fourth, Lestrade, but they do not impress me. Whose book is it?'

'Mine, sir,' the lad confessed.

'And to what subject does it pertain?'

'History, sir.'

'Quite. Quite. Very astute, Lestrade. It must be these letters H-I-S-T-O-R-Y on the front that gave you the clue. For there is nothing else I fear within its covers that would otherwise lead you to that answer. I had Professor Taylor in here yesterday, Lestrade. Standing . . . no . . . kneeling where you are now. The man is forty-six, Lestrade, I don't mind betraying a confidence. He is forty-six and he was sobbing. Do you know why, Lestrade?'

'Er . . . is it because Mr Gladstone has become Prime Minister, sir?'

The rattan cane bit the blotting paper on Poulson's desk and the dust jumped.

'No, Lestrade. It is because Mr Taylor cannot stand one more day of *you*.' He paused to let his blood pressure subside. 'Then there was the unfortunate affair of the Nativity Play.'

Lestrade frowned. 'That was five years ago, sir.'

'Do not presume to lecture me on the passage of time, sir. Were you or were you not cast by the late Mr Pritchard in the rôle of innkeeper?'

Lestrade knew what was coming, 'I was, sir,' he sighed.

'And what was the one line you had to utter?'

'Well, I . . .'

'The *one line*, Lestrade?' Poulson fumed.

11

'It was . . . er . . . "No, I'm sorry, traveller, the inn is full, what with the census and all, but I've got this stable at the back".'

'Precisely. And what did you say?'

Lestrade muttered something.

'What?' Poulson roared, his sidewhiskers lifting in the draught. 'Project, now, damn you! Did Mr Pritchard teach you nothing?'

'I said "Yes, of course, there's plenty of room. Business is surprisingly slack considering it's census time".'

'Exactly,' Poulson nodded, 'thereby throwing the whole production into the utmost confusion. Mary burst into tears. Miss Raverat, the prompter, had one of her turns . . .'

'You can't blame me for the donkey, sir . . .' Lestrade said.

'How dare you interrupt me when I'm lambasting you, Lestrade? The unfortunate beast was panicked by the screaming of Miss Raverat, which, as I have already established, was entirely due to you. That was an extremely expensive organ – and as for the stains on the robes of the Mayor of Blackheath, well . . .'

'I said I was sorry, sir.'

'Indeed you did,' Poulson had subsided a little, 'but not, I vowed then, as sorry as you were going to be. Then of course there was the tragic affair of the school cat.'

'I didn't see it, sir.'

'So you said,' Poulson nodded, 'after each gratifying swish of the cane. But I didn't believe it then and I don't believe it now.'

'But Mr Montfitchett . . .'

Poulson's right hand came upright, 'I will not hear it!' he thundered. 'I have heard the stories concerning Mr Montfitchett and I am disinclined to believe almost all of them. Anyway, I suspect that most of the slanders came from the diseased mind of that friend of yours – the one I expelled last year. What was his name?'

'Derbyshire, sir,' Lestrade hung his head. He missed him still.

'No, not him, the other one. Looked like a dung beetle.'

'Oh, Mellor.' He didn't miss him at all. Nobody did.

'Yes, that's the one. But this, Lestrade, this on top of all your other outrages comes as the last straw which you may accept has broken my over-generous back. On page sixteen of this . . .' he held the book by his fingertips, '. . . this lamentable excuse for scholarship; just about where Mr Taylor was attempting to instil into you Hammurabi's foreign policy, you have written . . .' he adjusted his spectacles, '. . . well, perhaps you'd like to tell me what you have written.'

'"General Napier is a B.O.F.", sir.'

'"A B.O.F.",' Poulson enunciated, 'and what does that signify?'

'Er . . . a brilliant officer fundamentally, sir.'

Poulson closed his eyes. 'Lestrade,' he said, 'in your time at this Seat of Learning, you have taken the ancient art of lying to unparalleled heights. I will ask you once more – what does "B.O.F." stand for?'

Lestrade took a deep breath. The little glass dangly bits on old Poulson's lamp were tinkling with the vibrations of their owner's voice. Time perhaps to come clean.

'Boring Old Fart, sir,' he blurted and watched the head-master's knuckles turn white.

'That is quite the filthiest word in the English language.'

'Chaucer uses it, sir,' Lestrade countered, 'Mr Chubb says that in the Miller's Tale . . .'

'"Mr Chubb says",' Poulson repeated viciously. 'Perhaps you'd care to rephrase that.'

'Er . . . Mr Chubb said . . .'

'When he was briefly with us, precisely. I sacked the man, Lestrade. His references were clearly written by a libertine. Did he not also use the word "Stocking" on one occasion?'

'I wasn't with Matron at the time, sir,' Lestrade informed him.

'Well, well,' Poulson cleared his throat, 'to the point, Lestrade. The point is not only that you are defacing an expensive exercise book – for which the National School down the road would give its eye teeth, may I remind you; not only are you doodling when your mind and soul should be riveted on ancient . . . wherever . . . but you have libelled one of Her Majesty's greatest soldiers, viz and to wit Lord Napier of Magdala. Did you not realize he has received a special vote of thanks from Parliament for his recent campaign? That the civilized world can rest easy in its bed because when the Heathen thundered at our gate, one man stood tall?'

'I . . . I hadn't thought of it quite like that, sir.'

'Of course you hadn't, Lestrade. And if you're unusually and meticulously honest with yourself, you'd admit that you don't *think* at all. Well, laddie, the time has come. How many strokes of the cat have you felt?'

'I told you, sir. I didn't see it. It was dark.'

'Not the *school* cat, you poltroon,' Poulson snarled, 'the leather one.'

'Oh, three hundred and twelve, sir. If you remember, you forewent the other three as it was my birthday.'

'Ah!' a leather-stalled finger shot skyward, 'charity. My first mistake. Well, there'll be no more, Lestrade. You will clear your locker by four of the clock. You will return all books to Mr Martinet, the Bursar and you will not cross these portals again on any pretext whatsoever.'

Poulson caught sight of something about the young reprobate before him that was untoward. 'What's that on your upper lip, Lestrade?' he asked, peering under the pince-nez rim.

'It's my nose, sir.'

'Let's not dabble in comparative anatomy, shall we? I'll have that abomination Professor Huxley writing to me again. That fuzz, man, that appears to be adorning, for want of the correct word, your face.'

'It's a moustache, sir.'

'A moustache, Lestrade? A moustache? An object of masculinity confined I believe to boxing clubs of certain public schools and officers of the cavalry. You are at the wrong school, young man and judging from the comments of Mr Piggott, the Riding Master, you will never make your mark in the mounted branch of the service. When you report to Mr Martinet, be sure you are properly tonsured. Clear?'

'Yes, sir. Thank you, sir.'

'Lestrade,' his headmaster's voice stopped him at the door, 'I don't want you to look on this as a mere hiccough in the peristalsis of life. I want you to look on it as terminal choking. You have failed, sir. Young as you are, callow as you are. There is no hope for you now.'

14

'Yessir,' the boy paused at the study entrance, gazing at its musty terrors for the last time. 'Please, sir, what's a poltroon?'

Poulson sighed. 'There you are, Lestrade. My very point. You don't listen, you see. I told you what a poltroon is – you are. Good afternoon, Lestrade. And goodbye.'

As the door clicked shut, another opened and a little oak panelling swung outward.

'Ah, it's you, Matron. Good Lord, is that the time?' The headmaster rummaged with his fly buttons.

'Why didn't you tell him, Poulsey-Woulsey?' She curled what was left of his hair.

'Tell him what? Damn Mrs Poulson, she's been heavy with the starch again. Can't seem to get my . . .'

'Why didn't you tell Lestrade that his dad can't afford the fees any more?'

Poulson looked pale. 'Matron, please. I couldn't be that unpleasant. Had to let the lad down gently. Don't want him topping himself like those three last term. Oh, lock the door, will you, Gladys – and make sure the blotting paper's wedged securely in the keyhole. I've been getting those threatening letters again.'

1

'Bee?' the chief inspector said, checking the sheet, 'how are you spelling Bee?'

'B-e-e, sir, as in the thing that flies.'

'How long on the Force?'

'Three years, sir, L Division.'

'Ah yes, how is old Marrion?'

Bee looked a little shocked. 'No ladies in L Division, sir: oh, unless you're talking about Sergeant Clary and he underwent a medical to scotch the rumours.'

'No, Chief Inspector Marrion – Ned Marrion.'

'Dead, sir.'

'Ned? Dead?' the chief inspector looked horrified. A little of his own mortality confronted him. Ned Marrion and he had grown up together, copper and boy. Inseparable they were at one time – Walter Dew and Ned Marrion – the terrible twins. Went together like Castor and Oil.

'Last March, sir, 1905. Went of the influenza.'

The chief inspector shook his head, greying now around the temples. His hair was on the turn, too. 'Well, well. You must be . . . how do you say this – Querks?'

'Queue, sir,' the other constable said, his regulation bowler firmly in the crook of his arm, 'spelt Q-u-e-u-x. Pronounced Queue. The x is silent, as in xenophobia.'

'Well, of course it is,' the chief inspector observed. 'Those plant names are always peculiar, aren't they? Is that right, you've spent the last year in Accounts?'

'It is, sir. Before that the Chelsea Polytechnic.'

'For eight years?'

'Double-entry bookkeeping, sir – it's a long course.'

The inspector leaned back at a rakish angle in his battered old chair. 'Bee and Queux,' he mused, 'a total of three years' experience – and the ex is bloody loud in that word, Queux.'

'Four years, sir,' the constable corrected him. Clearly those nights sweating away at evening classes had left their mark.

'I don't count Accounts, Queux,' the chief inspector told him flatly. 'There's no substitute for the pounding of leather on pavement, the rain dripping off your helmet-brim, your night-stick chafing your unmentionables. And then, there's the Yard. Look around you, gentlemen. There's no finer institution in the world. On the ground floor we've got drawings of every conceivable shape of ear known to man – loads of lobes. We've got eyes, noses, teeth, aliases, fingerprints. Remember the Stratton brothers?'

The new constables didn't.

'Well, last year they burgled a property. Only thing was they left their dabs all over the safe. Quick as a flash, we were on to 'em. Case made history – the first time that fingerprints were used to seal the fate of felons. On the second floor, we've got criminal records as long as your arm. Wall to wall shoe boxes – all the latest in technology. On the fourth floor, transport. Marias, horses, drunk carriages, horseless vehicles.' He closed to his men. 'There's talk – nothing concrete yet, mind you – that we're to get motorized vehicles this year. That'll slow down Joe Felon a bit, I can tell you.'

'What's on the top floor, Chief Inspector?' Queux asked.

'That's Special Branch, lad,' the senior man told him. 'You needn't go worrying your not-particularly-pretty little head about them. Coppers in name only. No, it's here. Here on the third floor that things happen. This is the nub. The gist. The very heart of criminal detection. And you know what makes a great detective, gentlemen?'

The door crashed back before either of them could answer, and a ferret-faced man with parchment skin hurried in, throwing his bowler to a hat-stand and caution to the winds. 'The ability to make a decent cup of tea.'

The detectives, old and new stood to attention. 'Good God, Walter,' the newcomer said, unbuttoning his Donegal, 'as you were, as you were. You'll be polishing your shoes on the backs of your trousers next. Who are these?'

'New recruits, sir, Constables Bee and Queux. This is Superintendent Lestrade, gentlemen – the guv'nor.'

They looked at him and he at them. A man easily the wrong side of fifty-two, his face like a crumpled copy of Magna Carta. A man who looked as though he had been expelled from a third-rate crammer, somewhere in the wilds of Blackheath. One look at them told him all he needed to know – two more idiots at the Yard. When, oh when were they going to set examinations for these people?

'A word in your ear, Walter,' Lestrade said and took his man into the inner sanctum, even more littered with shoe boxes than the outer one. 'The memorandum from the Miserable Major?'

Dew slapped his macassared forehead with his open hand. 'Hellfire, guv,' he hissed, 'it went right out of my head.'

'It's only that I got another one this morning which had words like "disciplinary action" and "never in all my born days" in it. Nothing to worry about, of course; it's just that if I ever *do* retire, I'd like to decide when it is I get the watch.'

'God, guv,' Dew shook his head, 'I don't know what to say. Look,' he rummaged in his pocket, 'here it is,' and held up the tatty piece of paper. 'Oh, no, that's Mrs Dew's list.'

Lestrade raised an eyebrow, 'I'm very sorry to hear it, Walter,' he said, 'try the liniment, tell her. In the meantime, I'll be on the carpet on the floor above. If you hear a loud noise, it'll be me, grovelling to the Mournful Major. Check those two out, will you? I'm not sure either of 'em could dunk a decent Bath Oliver,' and he swept out.

He took the lift. Well, he was fifty-two and his old trouble had been getting to him recently. He only jammed his fingers once in the moving machinery, those metallic murderers known at the Yard as the Gates of Hell. But, as he could have told you as the tears cleared, once was enough.

Then he was there, the frosted glass burnished before him, his knuckles resounding on it.

'Come,' the Melancholy Major called from within.

When Edward Henry had this office, it spoke volumes about the man. It was bright, spick and almost span. Framed pictures

18

of the ends of people's fingers were all over the walls and here and there was the odd Indian objay dar to remind him of the early days, in India. Now, it was gloom itself. That awful painting, known colloquially as Whistler's Mother, by Whistler, hung none too well over the fireplace. The grate, now that spring was here, was dark and empty. The chair where years before Howard Vincent's pet iguana had languished had all but collapsed under the appalling strain of its own chintz.

And behind the desk sat the Morose Major himself, E.F. Wodehouse KCB, KCVO. On his left, a portrait to remind him of *his* early days, a particularly drab corner of the Royal Albert Dock. On his right, a portrait of the other corner.

'I asked for you yesterday,' he moaned, his mouth like an inverted crescent under the moon of his nose. Years of tea-sipping had given him roseacea. Years of moaning had given him the elbow from the City Force. Now, for everybody else's sins, he was acting assistant commissioner with the Met.

'Really, sir? I had no idea.'

'Heads had better roll, then.'

'No, no, no,' Lestrade shook his head while it was still attached. 'No harm done.'

'In my experience,' Wodehouse droned, 'harm is *always* done. Otherwise, it isn't really harm, is it?'

'Er . . . no, sir,' Lestrade had never thought of it quite in those terms before. He doubted secretly whether he would again.

'Well, to the matter in hand,' Wodehouse unfolded a letter in front of him. Thanks to the angle of the watery April sun and a lifetime spent reading other people's mail, Lestrade could discern the watermark of the Devon Constabulary. 'You've doubtless heard of the affair at Peter Tavy.'

'Would that be Peter Tavy in Devon, sir?' Lestrade felt safe to enquire.

'Is there another?'

'Er . . .' Not for the first time in his long and distinguished career did Superintendent Lestrade feel let down by Mr Poulson's rather enfeebled grasp of geography.

'You're curiously vague this morning, Lestrade,' Woodhouse told the superintendent, 'I'm talking about the massacre. Four killed in a chaise crash.'

'A sort of . . . death trap?' Lestrade ventured and immediately regretted it.

'Let's leave levity to Mr Robey, shall we, Superintendent? A sense of humour has no place within these walls. How right Messrs. Gilbert and Sullivan were when they said "A policeman's lot is not a happy one". Nor should it be. The day I find something jocular in murder, fraud, larceny and sexual depravity, they can carry me out of here in a pine box.'

Lestrade checked the width of the door optimistically. Of course, the lift would be a problem . . . Perhaps if they tilted the Moribund Major upright a little?

'They've called in the Yard,' Wodehouse went on, 'I've a missive here from Sir Willoughby d'Eresby, Devon's chief constable.'

'But wasn't it an accident, sir?' Lestrade asked. The *Sun* wasn't usually wrong on these matters. All other matters, yes, but it was pretty good on horrific accidents, major catastrophes and so on.

'Not unless four traces can snap simultaneously on a hairpin bend on a clear day, no.'

'Ah,' Lestrade had to concede that Wodehouse had a point. 'Well, then I'm on my way, sir. May I take Walter Dew?'

'I have to think of expenses, Lestrade,' the acting assistant commissioner explained. 'Anyone over the rank of sergeant causes a pecuniary shortfall of some magnitude.'

'Dickens, then?'

'Dickens?'

'Sergeant, ex F Division, been at Headquarters now, ooh, man and boy . . .'

'Well, if you must. But I want everything signed for. Keep all your chits.'

'I'll try, sir,' Lestrade promised.

'And you mind how you go, Lestrade,' Wodehouse wagged a monitorial finger, 'April can be a treacherous month. And I wouldn't drink the Devon water if I were you.'

'You wouldn't, sir?'

'No. The *Lady Mostlikelyto* was washed up off Torbay in 1867. There's ballast slewing around those seas yet, I shouldn't wonder.'

'But don't the rivers flow into the sea, sir? Not vice versa?'

'Don't concern yourself with geophysics, Lestrade. Nor with vice. This is a murder inquiry.'

But Sergeant Dickens was not available. He'd been seconded by the London Polytechnic to answer questions in their Brian of Britain quiz. Yes, that *was* a misprint, but they'd had eight hundred posters printed and distributed and they had no intention of changing it. Anyway, it was only a Polytechnic. People would make allowances. So Adams it had to be.

He sat with his guv'nor in the second class of the London and South Western on that grey April morning. 'Do you know, Superintendent, I think spring is here. I was only saying to Mrs Adams the other day . . .'

'You've read the Chief Constable's report?' Lestrade cut him short. Sergeant Benjamin Harry Adams had the record in the Metropolitans for the longest deposition in their history. It ran to thirty-four sides of foolscap – and back again. And there possibly *was* some truth in the rumour that Mr Justice Swindlehurst had died of old age listening to him give evidence at the Bailey.

'I have, sir. Lovely hand, hasn't he, the Chief Constable?'

'Do you know Devon at all?' Lestrade couldn't see much of it out of the rain-lashed windows.

'Clotted cream is about the size of it,' Adams confessed, 'though I believe an uncle on Grandmother Adams's side once had a coracle on the Tamar.'

'Ah well,' Lestrade nodded between puffs at his Havana, 'it's astonishing what they let by in the old days. Here we are. Tavistock.'

It was raining in Tavistock, drifting in off the high moors to thump and bounce off the rhododendron bushes that ringed the church and to spatter on the thick ivy that crusted the walls of the guild-hall, crenellated in its Gothic attempt to match the abbey ruins. The Met men were shown up a creaking spiral staircase of wood to an oak-panelled upper room.

'Willoughby d'Eresby,' the bearded gent introduced himself. 'This is Inspector Tatum of the Tavistock police.'

'Superintendent Lestrade,' Lestrade said, 'Sergeant Adams.'
Hands were shaken in all directions.

'I've sent for some clotted cream, gentlemen,' d'Eresby said.
'We don't get many murders in Devon, Superintendent. I'd
be grateful if an early start could be made to clear this one
up.'

'I understood that four people had died,' Lestrade said.

'Indeed,' Tatum struck a match for the chief constable's pipe
with the lightning reflexes of a born crawler.

'Perhaps you'd care to begin at the beginning,' the superintendent suggested, 'the Sergeant here will take notes.'

'It's not pleasant, I'm afraid,' Tatum warned.

'Murder never is,' Lestrade nodded solemnly, 'it's likely to be
grisly, Adams.'

The sergeant nodded in turn, licking his pencil stub. 'Ready
when you are, sir,' he said.

'The driver of the gig was Captain Orange, a highly ex-
perienced man when it comes to a four-in-hand.'

'Captain?' Lestrade queried.

'Honorary title,' the chief constable explained, burrowing
deeper into his armchair. 'Plied a pleasure craft on the Tavy
for years.'

'He'd seen some service in the Merchant fleet,' Tatum added,
'Dartmouth man through and through. We found him lying a
few feet away from the overturned trap. He'd hit his head on
an elm tree. Cracked his skull from occipital to orbit. Died
instantly, I should think.'

'Who was in the trap with him?' Lestrade asked.

'His nieces, the Misses Caterham. Ellen was nearly thirty.
As on the shelf as a china spaniel – and not unlike facially,
either.'

'Steady on, Tatum,' the chief constable felt constrained to take
the briar out of his mouth, 'after all, the poor woman is dead,
you know.'

'Yes, sir, of course, but I'm Torquay born and bred. We speak
as we find. Her body was still in the trap or rather under it.
Broken neck.'

'And the others?'

'Victoria – she was seventeen, going on twenty-nine. A

worldly one, that. Had eyes for one of my constables. He's mortified, of course. Actually, it was him who noticed it.'

'Noticed what?'

'The traces. Well, he was born and raised on a farm, see, was Constable Meadowsweet. Been round horses all his life. And you'd know that on a wet evening in the station-house, I can tell you. Anyway, straight away, he pointed it out to me. Look for yourself.'

Tatum produced two lengths of harness leather from a black bag on the table around which the four men sat, the rain trickling like helpless tears the length of the leaded lancets.

'Hmm,' nodded Lestrade. 'What do you think, Adams?'

The sergeant perused them carefully. 'Harness straps,' he concluded, 'without a shadow of a doubt.'

There was an awkward silence all round.

'Made by Archer of Hatherleigh,' Tatum said. 'The Archers have been saddlers in these parts since Monmouth's rebellion. Those straps wouldn't have broken by themselves.'

'No matter what the strain on them?' Lestrade asked.

'Not that way. Look. Look here.' Lestrade did. There was a clean blade-made edge three quarters of the way across the leather's width. The rest was ripped away. 'Whoever wanted the Captain and his family dead cut almost through the traces, knowing they were weak. At any point on the journey, if the Captain braked, these traces would snap.'

'Where were the bodies found?'

'On the Marchioness's Ground, a bit below Abbott's Hill. There's a bad bend there.'

'I've never liked it,' the chief constable concurred.

'And they set off from . . .?'

'The Caterhams' house at Peter Tavy.'

'Where?'

'It's a village to the north-east,' Tatum said, 'across the moor from the prison.'

'That'd be Dartmoor, sir,' Adams said for the benefit of his superior.

'Thank you, Sergeant, I'd deduced that by a process of illumination. Whose was the fourth body?'

'The youngest of the Captain's nieces,' Tatum told Lestrade,

23

'Miss Daisy. She was sixteen last birthday. Hadn't even come out yet,' the inspector shook his head. 'Tragic, that's what it is. Tragic.'

Lestrade waited while a becapped floozie laid out the cream tea, scowled at the assembled company and left.

'Do we know', he asked, 'who hitched up the horses?'

'The Captain himself, according to Kenrick.'

'Kenrick?'

'The Captain's man. Plied the Tavy with him for years. The Dart before that. He's the Captain's factotum now.'

Lestrade and Adams exchanged glances. 'This Kenrick . . . *does* for the Captain, you mean?'

'In a manner of speaking,' Tatum said, 'but that's the sixty-four pound question, isn't it? Who did for the Captain?'

'You're assuming he was the target?' Lestrade's eyes narrowed.

'Had to be,' Tatum shrugged. 'Who'd have it in for three little fillies?'

'The report said the horses were all right,' Adams felt he ought to remind the company.

There was another odd silence.

'We'll need to see the murder scene,' Lestrade said.

'Of course,' Tatum passed round the scones. 'Will you be joining us, sir?'

'Thank you, no,' the chief constable rose and the others did likewise, 'it's the Bovey Hunt tomorrow. My nag needs some schooling.'

'Mine too, sir,' Adams grinned, 'shocking grasp of the English language, Mrs Adams. Still, I'd rather that than her being a suffragette. I said to her only the other day . . .'

'You'll keep me informed, Lestrade?' the chief constable ignored the idiot, 'Tatum?'

'Of course, sir,' superintendent and inspector chorused. Sir Willoughby d'Eresby saw himself out.

They were staying at the Queen's Head and between the bouts of torrential rain were able to agree with the gazetteer Adams had bought entitled *So You Think You Know All About Tavistock* that it was a very pretty little town. Fishing smacks bobbed

24

on the swollen grey waters of the Tavy and made a rather different view for Lestrade from the brick wall and lichen that held his gaze from his office at the Yard for most of the year.

'Noticed anything odd, Adams?' he asked, not quite used to having a saucer to put his cup into.

'The clock, sir,' the sergeant beamed, 'I wondered if you'd notice that. It's stopped at quarter to eleven. That's the time the Great Duke died.'

'Wellington?'

'No, sir. Bedford. Or Marquess of Tavistock, whichever and whomsoever you will. It says so here, in the gazetteer.'

'You did get *three* receipts for that, didn't you?' Lestrade checked. 'Only you know what the Miserly Major's like.'

'Oh, yessir. Everything in triplicate.'

'Good, because when I said "Noticed anything odd, Adams?" I didn't mean the clock.'

'What, then?'

'People. The good people of Tavistock. Funny lot.'

'Inspector Tatum was all right, sir. Lent me his pencil stub if you remember.'

'Oh yes, the local police have been co-operation itself. Even d'Eresby was civil – for a chief constable, I mean. No – you remember when you bought those chocolate eclairs at that restaurant?'

'The one near the river, with the rats?'

'Yes and that woman screamed.'

'And I dropped my wallet.'

Lestrade nodded. 'What fell out?'

'Ooh,' Adams frowned, 'now you've asked me. A bit of my wedding cake that I carry round for good luck. My Mavis's front tooth that that cabhorse kicked out . . .'

'No, no,' Lestrade sighed, 'think big. Nothing to do with family, Adams.'

'Er . . . my warrant card.'

'Exactly,' Lestrade clicked his fingers and the cup went flying. He pretended he hadn't noticed and wandered into the other wing of the visitors' lounge, 'and what happened then?'

Adams thought hard. 'Do you know, you're right. They all backed away, didn't they? As though . . . as though . . .'

'Yes?'

'Well, I don't want to be crude, sir, but as though you'd broken wind.'

'I?'

'No, no,' Adams was at pains to placate his commander, 'it was that kid with the red hair. He looked the sort.'

'And then downstairs, here at the hotel.'

'What? Somebody else farted?'

'No, Adams,' Lestrade moaned. It was going to be a long case. 'As soon as I announced our ranks, the clerk went decidedly cold.'

'So he did,' Adams stroked his heavy chin. 'Don't like coppers in Tavistock, then, eh?'

'Either that or they're hiding something,' Lestrade watched the rain bounce again on the window.

'What?' Adams asked.

Lestrade turned to him. 'What frightens a whole town? You tell me, Sergeant.'

'A conflagration, sir. An outbreak of bubonic plague, a reading of Miss Corelli's works? I wouldn't like to say, sir.'

'Well,' sighed the superintendent, 'you haven't done badly so far. I was actually speaking hydraulically, Adams – I didn't really expect an answer. No, I don't think somehow you've solved my problem for me.'

'Mr Lestrade?'

The policemen looked up. An elderly gent with a grey goatee stood framed by the awful flock wallpaper. Still sprightly despite the toll of the years, he crossed the hideous carpet and extended a hand, sweeping off his Homburg as he did so. 'My name is Charles Tenterden. I understand that you are conducting a murder inquiry.'

'You understand correctly, Mr Tenterden, but the local officer is Inspector Tatum. I'm afraid he isn't here at the moment.'

'All to the good. Who is this?'

'Sergeant Adams,' Lestrade said and then, by way of apology, 'he's with me.'

'May I?'

'Please,' Lestrade proffered the easiest of the chairs.

'Are we alone?' Tenterden's eyes flashed grey in the dim afternoon light.

'As a bowl of tartar emetic,' Adams assured him.

'I read in the *Tavistock Advertiser* of the sad deaths of Captain Orange and his nieces.'

'When was this?' Lestrade asked.

'The article or the deaths?'

'The article; I know when they died.'

'The day before yesterday. Have you spoken to the man Kenrick?'

'No. We only arrived this afternoon.'

'Do. He has some information for you.'

'Mr Tenterden,' Lestrade's steady gaze fixed the man, 'may I ask how you have come to be involved in this unfortunate affair?'

'Forgive me. It has all been rather a shock, I'm afraid. Could I have a glass of water?'

'Adams.'

'No, thanks, Superintendent. I'll stick with the coffee. Oh, I see. Yes, of course. On my way, Mr Tenterden. Won't be a jiffy.'

'Are you all right, sir?' Lestrade asked. Was it just the fading light or had Tenterden gone a shade greyer than he'd been when he came in?

'I'm sorry,' the old man gasped, his head lolling back in the chair, 'I'll be all right in a minute.'

Adams returned with a carafe and glass, but he'd had no success with finding any water so veered away again, ringing any bell in the vicinity. You couldn't get the staff any more. This was the unacceptable face of Campbell-Bannerman's England.

'Let me explain,' Tenterden said, some of the colour seeping back into his sallow cheeks, 'I have a house not far from here, on the banks of the Tavy. A country retreat, in fact. I live for most of the year in Bloomsbury.'

No accounting for taste, Lestrade thought to himself.

'I knew the late Captain Orange quite well. Before I retired I was a journalist, you see. Doubtless you've read my *Tales of the Riverbank*?'

'Well, I . . .'

27

'I know,' Tenterden smiled, 'doesn't hold a candle to the *Police Gazette*. Anyway, the Captain supplied me with tall stories of the sea and the river and I wrote them down. Oh, a modest enough little income, but it kept the bailiffs from the door,' he chuckled asthmatically. 'Imagine my horror, Mr Lestrade, when I read that the poor Captain was no more. And to die at the reins of a four-in-hand . . . Why, it would be like you breaking your neck by falling over your tipstaff.'

Lestrade wondered for a moment who'd been talking. He'd thought that surgical collar had been so discreet.

'So,' Tenterden went on, 'I went over to Captain Orange's house at Peter Tavy. I spoke to Kenrick. He told me . . . my God, I still can't believe it.'

Adams arrived at that moment with the water which the old man gulped down gratefully.

'What, Mr Tenterden?' Lestrade asked, 'what can't you believe?'

The retired journalist leaned forward, his eyes wild, his jaw set, 'Kenrick told me that on the morning of the "accident", the Captain had harnessed the trap himself.'

'Yes,' said Lestrade. 'Is that unusual?'

'No, but the visitor he had was.'

'Visitor?' Lestrade leaned back, 'Inspector Tatum didn't mention a visitor, did he, Sergeant?'

'No, sir,' Adams was adamant, 'he did not.'

'Kenrick did,' Tenterden assured them. 'He only caught a glimpse of him, apparently. When he turned to talk to him, he'd gone.'

'This was just before the family set out for the ride in the trap?'

'Yes. Just before.'

'Are you saying, sir,' Adams asked, 'that this visitor interfered with the Captain's trap?'

'I'm saying it's possible,' Tenterden nodded.

'Did Kenrick describe this man?' Lestrade asked.

'He only saw him briefly, Superintendent.'

'Even so.'

'Even so, he said . . . he said he was the tallest man he'd ever seen. Who is the tallest man you've ever seen, Mr Lestrade?'

'Er . . . well, if you exclude the stilt-walker at George Sanger's Circus, I suppose Captain Oswald Ames of the Life Guards.'

'Well,' a curious smile flickered over the old writer's face, 'there you have it. That gentleman, I gather from *The Times*, is due to retire from the Army.'

'Really?' Lestrade hadn't believed a word in *The Times* since they'd referred to the late Sherlock Holmes as a detective.

'The man I have in mind retired from the army a long time ago, Superintendent. Or perhaps he's never retired at all.'

'Er . . . I'm sorry, sir, I'm afraid I don't . . .'

Tenterden staggered to his feet, 'I've said enough,' he said. 'Talk to Kenrick. Ask him what he found in the Captain's breast pocket. As he lay sprawled with his head . . . battered. Ask him.'

'It would be easier to ask you, sir,' Lestrade suggested.

Tenterden held up his hand. 'Not now,' he said, 'you see, I'm not sure. No, I've said enough. I'm not sure. It was all a long, long time ago.'

2

They lay side by side in Mr Wilkinson's Emporium For The Recently Departed in Kelly Street, sunk in satin pillows with their hands clasped across their breasts and a single white lily gripped by their nerveless fingers. Captain William Orange was a large man, as his coffin reflected, with a nautical beard popular then in the Royal Family and much sported by its male members. He lay in his full dress Merchant Navy uniform, a ribbon of decorations sewn to his left breast pocket and a wealth of gold lace at his cuffs. Ellen Caterham did indeed resemble the glazed spaniels that adorned the majority of working-class mantelpieces throughout Campbell-Bannerman's England. Only the chain was missing, replaced instead by a froth of pink lace, of the sort they might have wrapped round her wedding cake and now never would. Her sister Victoria lay next to her, elbow to elbow, except for the pine that separated them, with the littlest, Daisy. All lay still, and that sickly-sweet scent of flowers that walks hand in hand with death hung heavy over the parlour.

Mr Wilkinson was aware of Lestrade's need to get to the bottom of the tragedy of Peter Tavy, but the embalmer had done his work and it would be such a pity to disarrange the deceased now. Couldn't the Superintendent just accept the cause of death as determined by the Coroner and relayed to him by Inspector Tatum? In the event, Lestrade could.

If the Yard men had found the people of Tavistock cagey, they found the people of Peter Tavy downright monosyllabic. The man Kenrick they found at the stables of the ostler Philips, known for reasons lost to time as Phil the Greek. He was the best four-in-hand man in the West Country it was said at the

Queen's Head and so Lestrade and Adams had caught two birds with one stone.

'This is Captain Orange's vehicle?' the superintendent asked.

'Ar,' the Greek was amazingly fluent in Devon noises, but his English left something to be desired.

Lestrade ran his eye and his hand over the spokes, the seats, the hames and only winced a little when the splinters caught him. 'Mr Kenrick, I gather you were first on the scene?'

'Ar,' the disease was clearly catching.

'Would you care to describe it to me?'

'Well, I told Mr Tatum,' Orange's man said, perpetually chewing on an ear of barley he'd saved specially since last harvest.

'Indeed; and now I'd like you to tell me.'

'Well,' I 'eard the crash, zee? Ol' Joris let out a fearful cry.'

'Joris?' Adams had stub to paper as all good sergeants of detectives do. 'Your wife, Mr Kenrick?'

The man looked oddly at him. 'The Cap'n's lead 'orse. Nothin' like the zound o' rippin' leather,' he went on, 'the smash of wood 'n' iron, the zcream o' brakes. I'z only glad I didn't get there in time to 'ear the thud o' zkulls on elm treez an' the znap o' pretty neckz.' He wiped his eyes on the sleeve of his smock. Both were equally rheumy.

'And you went to investigate?'

'I did, zir,' Kenrick said, 'I upped me gaiters an' ran. Lor', you never zee zuch a zight. Joris waz ztrugglin' to get up. Doris waz in a 'ell of a ztate.'

'The Captain's second horse?' Adams checked.

Kenrick's faintly quizzical look transfixed him again. 'My wife,' he said. 'She'd ran wi' me, y'zee. Only not zo fazt, on account o' 'er legz. I could zee they waz all dead, but I checked 'em. Cap'n, 'e were furthezt out, lyin' wi' 'iz 'ead all zmashed against a tree. Mizz Daizy were ztill in her zeat, but on 'er zide like, 'coz the cart 'ad tipped.'

'What did you do?' Lestrade asked.

'I unhitched the team an' calmed 'em down. I doubt Bessie'll be the zame again.'

Adams had learned his lesson. He wasn't even going to ask who Bessie was.

'Then I zent for old Doctor Trevelyan. 'E took one look at them 'ames with the leather cut through an' all an' 'e zent for Inspector Tatum.'

'Mr Philips,' Lestrade turned to the ostler, who appeared to have the rest of Kenrick's barley ear sticking out of his mouth, 'would you help us in a little experiment?'

'What?'

'An experiment,' the Superintendent repeated. Clearly the National Schools had not reached this far south-west.

'Well, I don't know.'

'I'd like you to drive us in your gig. They say you're the best four-in-hand man in the West Country.'

'Do they now?' Philips frowned. 'Well, whomever zays that'z lyin'. I'm the best four-in-hand man in England.'

'Tsk,' Lestrade beamed, 'misinformed again. Will you do it, Mr Philips?'

'Well, I dunno,' the ostler stroked his stubbled chin.

'Adams,' Lestrade raised an eyebrow.

The sergeant put his notebook away and his pencil and grabbed the ostler by his smock, 'Look, you little lump of . . .'

'No, no, Adams,' Lestrade cut in, grimacing in the direction of the sergeant's pocket.

'Oh, right, sir. Sorry,' he smoothed the smocking down on the ostler's chest and produced a crisp pound note from his wallet. 'Look, your little lump of experience is just what we need at the moment – *and* we're prepared to pay handsomely for it. You couldn't give me a receipt, could you?'

'The Greek' snatched the note, bit it carefully and stuffed it into the pocket of his moleskins. 'All right,' he said, 'where to, gentz?'

'To the Captain's house and then follow the route he took on his last journey. At the corner where he died, I want you to do what he would have done – short of actually dying, of course.'

'I waz goin' to zay,' Philips frowned, 'coz that'd cozt yer a bit more than a pound, that would. Comin', Zmudger?'

'Why?' Kenrick asked, 'why'd you need me?'

'Weight,' Lestrade explained. 'There were three passengers and a driver in the Captain's cart that Friday. The four of us make up the same conflagration.'

Philips hitched up his team, four splendid bays he hired out at a tidy profit to all the Lunnon ladies and gentlemen who came to the Tavy for the boating each summer. While he buckled and clicked, as for every trip, Lestrade passed a cigar to the late Captain's man.

'No thankee,' Kenrick said, 'I got my own,' and he held out the soggy straw.

'I had a visit the other day,' Lestrade said.

'Good for 'ee,' was Kenrick's comment.

'A Mr Tenterden. I gather he was a friend of the Captain's.'

'That'z right.'

'He said the Captain had a visitor on the morning of his death – that you'd seen him.'

'Did 'e now?' Kenrick wandered away across the straw-strewn stable yard to pat the glossy neck of one of the bays.

'Who was he?' Lestrade asked.

'Who waz who?' Kenrick busied himself with the dock of the bay.

'Mr Kenrick,' the superintendent leaned over and whispered in his ear, 'I've been patient in my inquiries so far, but I *am* investigating a murder. I would have thought you'd have wanted me to catch whoever killed the Captain?'

Kenrick straightened and looked his man squarely in the face, 'I only zeed 'im for a minute.'

'Where?'

'Out the corner o' my eye.'

'No, I mean where was he?'

'Behind the shrubbery. I zaid "Waroo, bucko".'

'I beg your pardon?'

'I zaid "Waroo, bucko".'

'Ah. And he said?'

'Nothin'. 'E'd be gone.'

'Gone where?'

'Just gone. 'T'were the damnedest thing. It waz az though 'e'd vanished into thin air. Mind you, up there you can.'

'Can what?'

'Vanish. Zee that?'

Lestrade tried to follow the man's pointing finger. It was a skill he'd never truly mastered. 'What?'

'Precisely,' Kenrick beamed triumphantly. 'You should be able to zee Mizter Tenterden's house from 'ere an' the Captain'z. An' on a clear day, the whole o' Cook'z 'ill an' the Great Miz Tor. Not today, though. Look at it. Comin' down like a great, grey curtain. No wonder they 'aven't found 'im.'

'Found who?'

Kenrick looked as though he'd seen a ghost. Then he recovered himself, 'the Cap'n'z vizitor,' he said, scowling.

'Had the Captain seen him, do you think?'

'I dunno,' Kenrick narrowed his eyes to help focus his memory. 'The Cap'n, 'e'd left 'iz crop in the 'ouse, zo 'e went back for it. The Mizzez, well, they wuz chattin', zitting on the gig. I zeed 'im, just for a zecond, min', lookin' from behind the rhododen'on bushes.'

'You saw his face?'

Kenrick screwed up his own. 'No. All I zeed wuz a tall man a'runnin".'

'Mr Tenterden said something else yesterday,' Lestrade said. 'He said you'd found something in the Captain's breast pocket. What was that?'

'You gentlemen ready?' Philips called. Adams was already on the seat behind him.

'Nothin',' Kenrick scowled. 'We'd best be a-goin' afore that mizt zettles in. I wouldn't want to be up on the Moor after that.'

But they were up on the Moor after that – all three hundred and sixty-five square miles of it. They began at the Captain's house and Lestrade took note of the rhododendron bushes where the tallest man Kenrick had ever seen had been skulking. Then they took the gravel drive that swept down the ridges with never a tree in sight until they reached the bend. Here the track swung sharply left and Phil the Greek did too. It was well he was the best four-in-hand man in England; if he hadn't been, Lestrade, riding beside him on the phaeton, might well have followed the late Captain to a disaster under the solitary stand of elms. As it was, his top lip collided with the footplate and only the elastic qualities of his moustache saved his two front teeth. As it was, too, his bowler bounced away under the hoofs of the prancing, snorting bays, as Mr Taylor, his old History teacher, had said Richard III's crown had gone. Or was it Richard II? Or was that the poker blokey? Anyway, schoolboy history was far from Lestrade's mind now. He'd never seen a hackney horse's bottom so close before. The experience left him a little unnerved.

Then Philips and Kenrick had insisted on returning to the village. Dusk was gathering with the grey-green swirling mist and this was no night to be out. Try as he might to work on the Captain's man as the phaeton rattled away, Lestrade could learn nothing more of what he had found in the Captain's breast pocket the previous Friday.

The Yard men crossed the road and followed the sheep trails that criss-crossed the bleak, open grasslands beyond the Tavy. Away in the distance lights danced eerily, pinpoints in the gathering gloom.

'Fireflies, guv'nor?' Adams had seen them too.

'Bloody big, aren't they, Sergeant?' Lestrade muttered, the sodden grass licking at his ankles. 'Unless fireflies in Devon *are* six foot tall.'

'Good God,' it was a possibility Adams had never considered before. 'What, then?'

'Shepherds,' Lestrade shrugged. 'Isn't it lambing time, or something? I expect they're rounding up their flocks. This fog probably isn't all that good for their little woolly chests. Ah, that must be it.'

The house of Charles Tenterden loomed out of the mist, its chimneys twisting in replica of a grander age, the ivy heavy around the door.

'There's no one in,' Adams said, 'no lights.'

'It isn't five o'clock yet,' Lestrade said. 'My God, it gets dark early up here.'

'You'd think, nearer the sky, it'd be lighter, wouldn't you?' Adams was good at pondering the imponderable. 'Shall I ring the bell, guv'nor?'

'Why not?' the superintendent let the sergeant be his guest. Far away the answering echo rang in some silent hall. The Yard men sheltered in the dripping porch; Lestrade was whistling.

'Catchy number that, sir, isn't it? Mrs Adams's favourite.'

'What?' Lestrade asked.

'That "Waiting at the Church". It's on the Glee Club's repertoire for the May Day concert.'

'Oh, good,' Lestrade smiled acidly, 'I must remember to have a pressing engagement.'

'It's no good, guv, there's no one in.

But Lestrade's shoulder had already leant against the glass-panelled door and it swung open. 'Funny he'd leave it on the latch, isolated like this place is.'

'Well, there you are,' Adams peered into the darkened hall, 'I suppose it's *so* isolated, there's no need to bother. Good God, what's that?'

Lestrade poked it tentatively with one finger. 'It's a stuffed bird,' he said, 'a caribou stork if my memory serves me right from the Zoological Gardens Case. It appears to be holding a tray. For the post, obviously.'

The door creaked closed on its hinges. 'Anyone there?' Lestrade called. 'Hello?'

Adams padded forward to the foot of the stairs, 'Mr Tenterden, it's the police.'

There was a flash and a report. For an instant the hall was bathed in light. Lestrade threw himself to the floor, his head against the oak panelling, his shoulders sprayed with the splinters of the bannister above him. There was silence.

'Adams?' he whispered.

'Yes, guv.'

'Are you all right?'

'Yes, guv.'

'What was that?'

'Dunno.'

Lestrade sniffed the air, 'what's that smell?'

'Sorry, guv. I think that's me.'

Lestrade rolled to his left, then crawled forward on his hands and knees to find his Number Two curled up in a tight ball at the bottom of the stairs. 'Are you all right?'

'A few pounds lighter, sir. I think I may have shat myself. Mrs Adams won't be pleased. She has problems with my combs as it is. "Abou" she keeps saying to me . . .'

'What?'

'"Abou", sir,' Adams risked uncurling his head, 'it's my nickname. From a poem apparently – Abou ben Adham. It's 'cos my name is Ben, see. Ben Adams. No other reason. Not that I'm a nigger or anything.'

'Shut up, Adams,' Lestrade hissed, 'and concentrate. I smell gunpowder.'

Adams sniffed. 'And me.'

'Yes, all right,' Lestrade had seen men crack before, 'I can smell you too.'

'No, I mean, I can smell gunpowder too.'

'What are you carrying?'

'About eight pounds more than I should be the Yard Gym Instructor says. But seeing as how he hasn't seen his tadger for the last ten years, I don't know how he has the brass neck. Frankly . . .'

'Weapons, man,' Lestrade snapped, kicking himself for the loudness of his voice, 'what weapons are you carrying?'

'Life preserver, sir. Leather thonged. Bit of the old ebony and ivory. You?'

'Knuckles and switchblade. Nothing long distance. And nothing fast enough to beat a shotgun either.'

'Is that what it was?'

'It wasn't a motor backfiring,' Lestrade assured him. As the owner of a four-year-old Lanchester, he knew whereof he spoke. 'All right, get back there, in the shadows. I'm going to talk him down. You stay out of sight and when you've a clear shot, throw your life preserver at him.'

'Where will you be?'

'Right here, on the stairs. But if you miss, you'll find me in this general direction – and there – and over there. Generally smeared over the walls, in fact.' He grabbed the man's neck firmly with his right hand, 'so the message of the moment, Adams, is "don't miss". Savvy?'

The sergeant swallowed. It wasn't every day a superintendent's life flashed before him.

'Mr Tenterden,' Lestrade called, his voice ringing in the silence, 'it's me' – he hoped the singularity might throw the man – 'Superintendent Lestrade, Scotland Yard. We spoke yesterday. Look, I'm sorry to intrude. I did ring the bell, but you may not have heard. Perhaps you could put that shotgun down, could you? And come downstairs?'

'Come and get me, copper!' a voice shrieked.

Adams's head popped around the panelling. 'He's disguised his voice. Why's he done that?'

'I'm going up,' Lestrade said. 'He'll be a sitting target against that window if he shows himself. That's your cue. Hit him with everything you've got. I'm coming up, Mr Tenterden. I'm sure we can talk about this, you and I. You know, man to man.' Lestrade straightened, his fist closed on the brass knuckles in his pocket, his heart thumping somewhere near his mouth. Tenterden had had some minutes to reload. Judging by the explosion earlier, he'd let fly with both barrels. Even so, there'd be another two cartridges in those barrels by now, each one capable of ripping a hole in a man you could put your fist through. Every stair creaked with his weight. Every nerve within him screamed. There was a click on the landing above. Adams whirled round out of his hiding-place and flung the ebony life preserver through the air. It caught Lestrade a nasty one on the back of the head and he went down, his nose bouncing on several risers as his unconscious body slid backwards and his feet hit the landing.

When he woke, it was to pitch blackness. A moustachioed face peered anxiously down at him.

'Mother?' he whispered.

'Guv, are you all right?'

'Just my idea of a little joke, Adams,' the superintendent hissed. 'What time is it?'

'I can't see in this light, guv. It must be nearly eight.'

'I'm not going to ask what happened, Adams, because I know. You hit me with your life preserver, didn't you?'

'Sorry, guv,' the sergeant was as sheepish as the creatures that cropped the grass on the silent, fog-bound Moor beyond the silent, fog-bound house. 'Caught you on the rebound, you might say. It's these lightning reflexes of mine. Mrs Adams is always saying . . .'

'What of chummy?'

'Tenterden? He hasn't moved.'

'Still up there, then?'

'Unless he can fly.'

Lestrade assessed the situation anew. He was where he'd begun. Or rather where Adams had begun four hours ago, crouching on the first of God-knew-how-many landings in a dark house with a shotgun-wielding madman. 'All right,' he whispered, 'we'll go again. Maybe he knows there are two of us, maybe he doesn't. But no chat this time. Softly, softly, catchee monkey. Last one in the morgue's a cissy.' And he hauled himself upright.

His head throbbed and his nose smarted. His balance wasn't over keen either, but he managed to turn the first corner. This was the most dangerous. If Tenterden appeared now, yes he'd be silhouetted by the night sky beyond the oriel window, but Lestrade would be fully lit by the same light and Adams had already proved he was no Little Miss Sureshot. He heard the sergeant climb behind him, riser by riser. Then, he'd reached the next landing, and the sheltering fronds of an aspidistra of heartening proportions. Here he crouched, getting his breath back.

He held out his left hand to signal Adams to wait, then began the final haul. The landing ahead of him was black as pitch and he couldn't focus. He stumbled upwards, his fingers sweating on the brass knuckles in his pocket. He was out of the direct light, but if Tenterden was crouching to the right, he'd still see Lestrade as a silhouette. The superintendent would have killed for a bull's-eye.

He sensed Adams on the stair behind him. The man was too close. At point blank range now, they'd both get it, blown to oblivion on the stairs. On the other hand, if Lestrade could drop to the carpet fast enough ... He pushed such ignoble thoughts out of his mind. Now his foot had reached the top stair. To his horror he realized there was a passageway to his left and to his right, each one blacker than the other. Terrified of a crossfire, he rolled forward, somersaulting over a cabinet and crashing into a door beyond it. Adams flung his life preserver again; again into the blackness. He heard it bounce on the wall and then he heard the grunt as it hit Lestrade on the recoil. There was a flash and a crash and a bedroom door creaked open.

Both policemen lay on the landing, panting. There was no second barrel. No feverish breaking of the gun and reloading. Only a quiet, steady drip as though a tap was not turned off. Lestrade clawed at the doorframe and held on to it. He was fifty-two and a superintendent of police. Time he left these heroics to younger men.

'Adams,' he said, peering into the bedroom, 'strike a light.'

'Ssh,' the sergeant flapped his hands in the darkness.

'It's all right,' Lestrade said, 'no need to be quiet now. He can't hear us.'

Adams joined him in the doorway, his hand wobbling around a lucifer. 'Good God,' he muttered, 'he missed.'

'No, he didn't,' Lestrade said. He held the sergeant's hand steady and took the match from him. Lowering it to the bed, he looked at the corpse that lay there, the head thrown back and shattered, the shirt soaked black in the gloom. From the ghastly face wound, the blood dripped steadily on to the bare floorboards.

'Why?' Adams appeared to have forgotten how to talk in his normal voice, 'why should Tenterden kill himself?'

'Because he killed Captain Orange and his nieces,' Lestrade said. 'We may never know why.'

'Who's up there?' a gruff voice called from below. The lights of bull's eyes darted up the stairs. 'Find a lamp, you men. Let's see what's going on.'

'I am Superintendent Lestrade of Scotland Yard,' he met them at the stairhead. 'Who are you?'

'Harriman, sir. Head gaoler at the prison. One o' my lads heard what he fancied was a shot.'

'He fancied right,' Lestrade said. 'He's in here.'

The grim-faced gaoler brushed past into the room, swinging his lantern to inspect the suicide on the eiderdown. 'Well, well, Barney. You've done it now, haven't you, good and proper.'

'You know Tenterden?' Lestrade asked.

'Who?'

'Tenterden,' Lestrade frowned, 'the dead man.'

Harriman stood up. 'Look, Mr Lestrade. I don't know why a Scotland Yard bloke should be here on the Moor at this time of year -- though I'd have that nose seen to, if I were you – but thisn's Barney Clough, sentenced to life at Kingston Assizes four years ago. He was out with a ditching party on the Moor five days ago and he got away from us. We've been combing the area ever since.'

'You're the fireflies,' Adams clicked his fingers.

'What?'

'Excuse my sergeant,' Lestrade said, 'it's been a long night.' He looked at the dead man. 'Hell of a thing,' he said. 'How old was he?'

'Twenty-four,' Harriman told him. 'Don't distress yourself, Superintendent; we have reason to believe he knifed a fellow prisoner for looking at him funny last month. He was one of those who'd gone, as we say, stir-crazy. Couldn't bear to be inside a moment longer. Well, I've got ten more years to go to retirement – I know how it feels. Be thankful it was him and not you. Unstable as a jelly, that one. Now, just for my records you understand, would you tell me what you're doing here, you and the sergeant?' Harriman didn't think that either man looked well.

Lestrade could see now the broad arrows on the dead man's trousers. 'We're conducting a murder inquiry,' he said. 'Perhaps you've read about it – Captain Orange and his nieces.'

'Oh, yes,' Harriman nodded, 'rum do. Ztill, over at Widdicombe we don't hear all that much. Like another world, is Widdicombe. Isn't this old Mr Tenterden's house?'

'It is. It was Tenterden we had come to see, which is why . . .'

'. . . Why you thought old Barney was him. Yes, I zee now. It's all fallin' into place, like. What's old Tenterden got to do with Captain Orange's death, then?' Harriman asked.

Lestrade shook his head – grateful, at least, that he could still do that, 'I'm not really sure any more, he said.

Inspector Tatum did not enjoy being summoned to the Queen's Head at that hour. But all in all, he'd prefer to take the drubbing that was due out of earshot of his lads. Anyway the cocoa at the Queen's Head was legendary.

'We were not informed, Mr Tatum,' Lestrade was more arch than Marble when he wanted to be, 'about the presence of a homicidal – and luckily for us, suicidal – maniac on the Moor.'

'Remiss of me, I know,' Tatum had the breadth of back to admit.

'Well, that's one way of putting it. Was that why the good people of this town and Peter Tavy have been so circumcized? They were afraid of this man?'

'Of the man himself, no. Of the image of a monster on the Moor, that's another matter. The combination of escaped convict and swirling mist is a fatal one, Mr Lestrade. I'm afraid Dr Conan Doyle has a great deal to answer for.'

'Indeed he does,' Lestrade agreed, 'but enough of fiction. What of fact? What sort of a man was Captain Orange?'

'Salt of the sea type, according to my inquiries,' Tatum said, coating his neat little 'tache with cocoa froth.

'No enemies?'

'The only one I found was old Harry Nurdin, the poacher. He and the Captain had a running feud on account of old Harry running amok on the Captain's land with his ferrets.'

'You've talked to this Nurdin?'

Tatum shook his head, 'I don't believe in all that spiritualism rubbish. Old Harry passed on this twelve year. They say one of his ferrets bit him and poisoned his bloodstream.'

'Ah, septuagesima,' Lestrade nodded sagely, 'nasty way to go.'

'Sirs,' Adams had been staring into the oil-lamp that lit the table beside them in the snug of the Queen's Head.

'Yes, Adams?' Lestrade said, 'you look like an ostrich about to lay. Out with it, man.'

'Well,' the sergeant's face betrayed that he was still wrestling with a half-born idea, 'call me silly if you like, destroy the fledgling confidence of a young man on the brink . . .'

'Get on with it!' Lestrade and Tatum roared.

'Well, so far – rightly, in my opinion – you've made the assumption that the target was Captain Orange.'

'So?' Lestrade shrugged, whisking the cocoa skin to one side.

'So what if it's not?'

'What?' Tatum frowned, 'one of the Caterham girls, you mean?'

'Why not?'

'Well, surely . . .' Tatum looked at Lestrade.

Lestrade looked back at Tatum. 'It's certainly food for thought,' he said. 'Anything known?'

'Not at the moment, no. But I'll get my lads on to it. Though how a sixteen year old could so annoy anyone . . .'

'It's not the sixteen year old,' Lestrade said softly, 'it's the person she annoyed. And anyway, you've forgotten that Ellen was twenty-eight. As a friend of mine has written, "The female of the species is more deadly than the male".'

'Well, you're right there,' Adams chuckled, 'Mrs Adams is a real Tartar.'

'What? Short fuse, you mean?' Tatum grinned.

'No, I mean her family came from Mongolia – oh, way back, of course. Came back with Marco Polo apparently.'

'Does this have any relevance, Adams?' Lestrade sighed, 'only it's . . .' He began to check his half-hunter.

'Telegram for Superintendent Lestrade,' a hotel lackey chirped, his buttons gleaming in the lamplight.

'Here, lad,' Lestrade clicked his fingers, 'Adams.'

The sergeant reached up and clouted the boy around the ear.

'No, no, Adams,' Lestrade nodded towards the man's pocket.

'Oh, right; good lad, good lad,' and he flicked the bewildered boy a sixpence.

Lestrade stood up, the telegram open in his hand, 'Adams, pack. Inspector, I'd appreciate a wagon to accompany us to the station. It's from my Number Two. We're needed back at the Yard.'

Walter Dew stood ashen-faced in the green-and-cream mortuary in Montague Street.

'My Susie's nearly her age,' he muttered. 'Horrible. Horrible.'

He met Lestrade's steady gaze across the body on the slab. 'I haven't got the sleep out of my eyes yet, Walter. What have we got?'

'Her name is Janet Calthrop – aged nineteen. Heir to the Spottiswoode estate.'

'Aren't they the tea people?' Dew's guv'nor asked.

'Coffee, guv,' Dew had the rank now to correct him. 'The Tetleys are the tea folk.'

'Well-heeled, then?' Lestrade glanced under the shroud.

'Not short of a bob or two, certainly.'

'Where was she found?'

'At the bottom of a staircase at King's College.'

'When was this?'

'Friday morning.'

'Friday?'

'Yesterday, sir. Why?'

'Oh, no reason,' Lestrade sucked his moustache. 'What does the police surgeon say?'

Dew riffled through papers on an empty slab nearby. '"Superficial bruising to the left temple. Fracture to occ . . . ock . . ." that bit of the skull,' he pointed to his own. '"Compound fracture of the third vertebra."'

'The hanging bone,' Lestrade observed.

Dew nodded. Both men knew the significance. When they placed men on the drop; when they pinioned wrists and ankles and hauled the white hoods over heads; when they slipped the noose and hit the lever; it was in that silence before the boots bounced on the floor that the third bone below the neck broke. It snapped the spine and tore the nerve – and brought no peace.

'Pretty kid,' Lestrade mumbled. He looked at the long, dark hair hanging lank across the shoulders. It had lost its sheen now and made the skin more pallid, grey. Someone, a thoughtful soul no doubt, had closed her eyes. Her pale lips still parted in a silent scream. The Superintendent peeled back the white cloth, feeling as he always did, like some sickening voyeur. Her body was perfect – firm small breasts and dark nipples, flat stomach and broad hips. He held her right hand, small and cold, in his own.

'What a waste,' Dew muttered. His Susie was nearly this girl's age. He had to turn away.

'All right, Chief Inspector,' Lestrade said softly. He let the hand go. 'So why the telegram? A waste, yes. Tragic, of course. But you don't need me . . .'

'Look down here,' Dew said. 'I didn't notice it at first; when the call came through. But in the Maria, I was sitting by her feet. What do you think?'

Lestrade peered closer, bringing the oil-lamp nearer for a better view. 'You're right, Walter,' he said, 'I must be getting old.'

There was a shallow indent across the dead girl's right shin, a foot or so above her ankle.

'What do you make of it?' Dew asked.

'Help me turn her over.'

The detectives rolled the corpse to one side. Dew held her as best he could while Lestrade brushed aside the long hair. 'Bruising,' he muttered. He checked the girl's right calf with the aid of a lamp. No dent. No groove. 'When you found her,' he said, thinking aloud, 'what was she wearing?'

'Over here,' they lowered the girl back to rest and rummaged on a sideboard top through her clothes. 'Bodice,' said Dew, mechanically listing the garments, 'blouse. Silk chemise. Er . . . I don't rightly know what this is, sir.'

'Tsk, tsk, Walter,' Lestrade shook his head, 'and you a married man. Isn't that what we used to call "Nether garments" in the old days? Where are her shoes? Her stockings?'

'Er . . .'

'Think back. You were in the Maria, sitting by her feet. You noticed that mark on her leg. Was she wearing shoes or stockings?'

'No, guv,' Dew was frowning with the effort of remembering. 'No, she wasn't.'

'Well, well,' Lestrade reached for a cigar and a lucifer. He offered neither to Chief Inspector Dew. 'A young lady, nineteen years of age, well dressed in day clothes, linked to a coffee-manufacturing family of not inconsiderable fortune and yet she's wearing neither shoes nor stockings.'

'That's why I sent for you, guv.'

'You did right, Walter,' Lestrade crossed back to the angel on the marble. 'So? Cause of death?'

'Did she fall or was she pushed, do you mean?'

Lestrade nodded.

'She was pushed.'

'How do we know that?'

'Call it . . . call it a gut reaction,' Dew said.

'I'm not sure they're very long on gut reactions at the Bailey,' Lestrade reminded him. 'Have the family been told?'

'Yessir,' Dew nodded, 'I went myself.'

'Good man,' Lestrade said. 'Never comes well, but always comes better from the senior man on the case. No doubt papa will want answers.'

'Wouldn't you?' Dew snapped.

Lestrade looked at him. 'Your Susie,' he said softly.

'I'm sorry, guv,' the chief inspector stuffed his hands into his pockets, 'I don't know why this case is winding me up. It's like a ligature round my . . .'

'I know,' Lestrade nodded. 'But you're not the only one with daughters.' He lit a Havana, as much to counteract the formaldehyde as to enjoy a smoke.

'God, yes, your Emma. She must be . . .'

'Going on thirteen,' Lestrade chuckled. 'Going on thirty-six according to Letitia. So,' he shook himself back from the laughing, golden girl in his mind to the dark one on the slab in front of him, the one who would never laugh again. 'What answers shall we give old man Calthrop then, before he leans on the Home Secretary at their club, I mean?'

'The mark on the leg . . .'

'Yes?'

Dew didn't like to say it in that ghastly place, where gas jets flared green on the walls and lost men slept for ever. 'A tripwire?'

He breathed a sigh of relief when his guv'nor's sallow face, made greener by the gaslight, broke into a smile. For all he was a chief inspector now, Walter Dew had all the instincts of a beat copper. There were times when he still felt the rim of that silly, pointed hat around his temples. The independence of command unnerved him. Oh, he went through the motions, gave orders, made decisions. But there was that terrible moment when all eyes were on him, waiting, watching. It was his shout, his call. But now and again, it was good to have the weight off your shoulders, your theories shared by somebody above. And good to know that *someone* up there, at least, liked him.

'So she was tripped?' Lestrade blew cigar smoke to the ceiling.

'That'd be my guess, sir.'

'Mine too,' Lestrade said. '*And* she was pushed.'

'Pushed too?' Dew frowned. 'Wasn't taking any chances, then, was he?'

'He?' Lestrade raised an eyebrow. 'Now, Walter, don't tell me you've got somebody in the frame.'

'No, guv,' Dew grinned, 'it's early days. How do we know she was pushed?'

'The bruise on her back,' the superintendent told him. 'Caused by a fist unless I'm very much mistaken. The lividity's about right. Nothing on the police surgeon's report about that of course?'

Dew shook his head.

'Remind me never to be found dead in suspicious circumstances, Walter. I'd only have to reincarnate and catch my own murderer. Where is King's College, exactly?'

King's College was exactly in the Strand, across a bit from the Wren church of St Martin. It jostled with the long, pale façade of Somerset House, crammed from floor to ceiling with shoe boxes full of facts about dead people. Come to think of it, very similar to Scotland Yard, really. The growler dropped them at the Fleet Street end, by those rampant griffon things that marked the boundary of the City, where two police forces eyed each other jealously and where once the heads of traitors had rotted on Temple Bar.

A liveried flunkey in a top hat led them up a twisting stair from the carpeted entrance hall. Marble busts stared down at them – Plato, Aristotle, other dead blokes with beards. The flunkey rapped on a large, studded door.

'Come,' a voice bellowed.

'The gentlemen of the police to see you, Dean,' the flunkey's forefinger tipped his hat-brim.

'Ah,' the Dean was a large man apparently nearing ninety, but years of scholasticism had not dimmed his eye nor lessened his larynx, 'you've found him, then?'

'Who, sir?'

'Reggie,' the Dean said, pausing in mid-thesis with his archaic quill-pen. 'I prefer these, you know,' he tapped the goose feather on his gilt inkwell. 'Not for me these Birds and Waverleys. A fountain is a display of water forced up by unnatural means. It is not a pen. All a cheap gimmick. They'll never catch on. Now, don't tell me,' he leaned back, beaming, the spring sunshine dazzling on his clerical collar, 'you found him in that Godless Institution in Gower Street; am I correct?'

'Who, sir?' Lestrade found himself repeating.

'Are you hard of hearing, young man?' the Dean thundered. 'Only, when I was your age I was shouting at coolies on the Yangtze. Been shouting at 'em ever since.'

'You have Chinese students at the college, Mr . . . er . . .

'Dean,' the Dean corrected him. 'No. One or two Indians of course. Brahmins and so on. I well remember that chappie Ghandi. Not at this college, but within the University. Had a ridiculous first name . . . Merchandise . . . that was it. Never forget a name. Bally nigger wanted to turn up to lectures in a loin cloth. Well, naturally the Law Faculty went ape. Told him to bugger off to South Africa, which I believe he duly did. Japes of course.'

'Er . . . I'm sorry?'

'It was student japes,' the Dean clearly wasn't making himself understood, 'Reggie, I mean.'

'Sir,' Lestrade could see the end of his tether in the not-too-distant distance, 'we are officers of Scotland Yard. We are here to investigate the suspicious death of one of your students, Miss Janet Calthrop.'

'Not here about Reggie? So you haven't found him, then? Well, the young gentlemen are going to be bitterly disappointed.'

'May we sit down, sir?' Lestrade sensed it was about to be a long morning.

'Please. Who did you say had died?'

Lestrade and Dew exchanged glances, 'Janet Calthrop, sir. What was she studying?'

'Reading, Sergeant,' the Dean fluttered his eyelids at the man's gross ignorance.

'That's superintendent, sir,' Lestrade said, 'Superintendent Lestrade. This is Chief Inspector Dew. He was here yesterday.'

'Really? I didn't think we had any mature students. Ah well, there it is. Sign of the times, I suppose.'

'So Miss Calthrop was studying reading,' Lestrade attempted to get back to the matter in hand.

'Reading?' the Dean frowned. 'We don't have a faculty of Reading. Unless it's that School of Irrelevant Studies old Latymer's always trying to set up. What was the name again?'

'Calthrop, sir,' Lestrade said carefully, 'Janet Calthrop.'

'Well, Superintendent Calthrop, I must say your parents had a rather bizarre sense of humour, didn't they? It might very well have blighted your entire life.'

'No, sir,' Dew saw Lestrade's knuckles changing colour on the rim of the Dean's desk, 'the dead girl's name was Janet Calthrop. Mine is . . . something else entirely.' He thought it best not to confuse the man still further.

'Oh, I see. Well. Well. This is the first I've heard of it. I'm sure there's some perfectly rational explanation. On the way out, have a word with that coolie . . . er . . . that flunkey chappie who showed you in. He knows just about everybody in the building. Has his finger on everyone's pulse, so to speak. He'll locate this dead person for you. Well, good luck . . . er . . . Janet, if I may be so bold. Oh,' he halted the Yard men's rapid egress to the door, 'you'll be sure and let me know the minute there's news of Reggie, won't you?'

The flunkey did indeed have his finger on the pulse and Lestrade and Dew wished they'd talked to him first and not wasted half an hour in the company of a man whose quill was clearly not dipped in his ink. As luck would have it, the History Faculty to which the late Janet Calthrop had been loosely attached, made the situation not a jot clearer.

'Professor Blasius?' Lestrade put his bowlered head around the study door.

'Not if my doctorate depended on it,' the wizened grey man beyond the desk bridled.

'I'm Blasius,' an even greyer man wheezed beside the fire, his dentures rising and falling as he spoke, 'Emeritus Professor.'

'Emeritus!' the first man snorted.

'This is Doctor Fellowes,' Blasius's upper set clacked on to his lower lip. 'He's absolutely green, consumed with jealousy. If you're from the *Literary Gazette*, take this down, "The unqualified success of my latest opus . . ."'

'No,' Lestrade interrupted him, 'I'm from Scotland Yard.'

'Ha!' Fellowes blurted, displaying a row of snaggled, brown teeth. 'They're on to you at last, you old plagiarist. Tell me, officer, what does lifting other people's scholarship carry these days? Ten years? Fifteen?'

'I am Superintendent Lestrade,' the Yard man said, plonking himself down uninvited. 'This is my associate, Chief Inspector Dew.' There was nowhere for the inspector to sit, so he perched gingerly on the arm of Lestrade's chair until a withering look from his guv'nor brought him to his feet again. 'We are here on a possible murder inquiry.'

'Aha, so you *have* read Blasius's rubbish? Not that I have, of course, but I am fully prepared to accept that he has effectively murdered the English language, not to mention Clio.'

'Cleo who, sir?' Dew had his notepad at the ready.

'The Muse of History, Inspector,' slurped Blasius. 'That was Fellowes at his wittiest. It doesn't get any better, I'm afraid.'

'Who's dead?' Fellowes lolled back in his chair, his pince-nez at an obtuse angle, 'apart from Blasius, of course.'

'A young lady named Janet Calthrop. One of your students, I believe.'

'One of ours?' Fellowes frowned. 'Do we have women, Blasius?'

'Women, Fellowes?'

'That's pretty damned unthinkable, isn't it? Women fellows – the very idea.'

'She was nineteen,' Lestrade said. 'She died in College yesterday.'

'Ah, Friday,' Blasius clicked, 'no, I'm never here on Fridays.

Come to think of it, it's quite remarkable I'm here today. Why am I here, exactly, Fellowes?'

'The Faculty meeting, Blasius. To discuss the Dean's senility.'

'Whose?'

'The Dean's.'

'Ah, yes, well, there you are. I've known him for thirty-eight years. Been gaga all that time, certainly.'

'We're still talking about the Dean, Blasius,' Fellowes grinned and slid a brass billiards scorer up one notch.

'We are talking about Janet Calthrop,' Lestrade reminded them, 'and my patience is wearing a little thin.'

The ancient historians turned to the outsider, their intellectual animosities forgotten against the common foe. 'Have you published, young man?'

'No,' said Lestrade, 'is that relevant?'

'Well, if you haven't published, I'm not really sure you ought to be here. This is a sanctuary of scholarship, you know. Professor Blasius here has just had his *Rise of the Lumpenproletariat* published by the OUP. It is his forty-second opus to date.'

'And Dr Fellowes is the progenitor of *The Rôle of the Missionary in Uttar Pradesh*. This is our life, young man. We have no interest in . . . police matters.'

'If I arrest you . . . gentlemen . . . for wasting police time, you'll certainly have an interest,' Lestrade growled. 'I don't think you'll find a very fascinating library in Wormwood Scrubs. Now, for the last time, do you or do you not know a female student called Janet Calthrop?'

There was a silence, during which Blasius's teeth snapped together. 'I suppose the boy might know,' he said.

'The boy?'

'Sparrow. He's our newest Reader. What is he, Fellowes? Forty-two? Three?'

'Can't be more,' Fellowes nodded ruefully. 'Only published six or seven, hasn't he?'

'Can't be more,' Blasius agreed. 'None of them made so much as a dent in the historico-literary world.'

'No, they wouldn't.'

'Where can I find this Dr Sparrow?' Lestrade asked.

'Mr,' Fellowes spat out the word with contempt, 'merely Mister. I suppose he'll be in his rooms – three doors down the corridor. Well. if that's all . . . er . . .'

'For now,' Lestrade was at his most cryptic. 'Please don't get up gentlemen, assuming that you can; we'll see ourselves out.'

3

But James Sparrow, the Reader in History, was not just down the corridor. The flunkey with his finger on everybody's pulse suggested to the Yard men that they try the library on the third floor. The combination of dust and dryness in the airless building brought that old familiar feeling to Dew's nose and he sneezed so that volumes rattled on the shelves.

'Pleath,' a librarian minced over to them, 'people are trying to thtudy here.'

Lestrade flashed his warrant card, 'I'm afraid I'll just have to disturb them.'

'What do you want?' the librarian rearranged a lock of hair that had become dislodged during some frantic indexing earlier in the morning.

'Mr Sparrow,' Lestrade told him.

'Impoththible,' the librarian lisped, 'Mr Thparrow gave exthplithit inthtructhionth. He hathn't been well, you know.'

Lestrade turned to his Number Two with a practised line: 'Those forbidden books, Chief Inspector – the ones we had a tip-off about.'

'Ah,' Dew knew the ploy of old, '*A Hundred and One Things To Do With a Boy.*'

'That was one,' Lestrade nodded solemnly, 'and the other was . . . ?'

'*Sweets – By A Stranger.*'

'That's right,' Lestrade stroked his chin, leaning on the librarian's counter, 'I was a *bit* surprised at Messrs Cadbury sponsoring that one.'

'I don't know what you're talking about,' the librarian stamped his little gadget in agitation.

'We had a little tip-off', Dew leaned beside his guv'nor, 'that this library was passing off imported pornography under the guise of incredibly boring old stuff about dead blokes,' he said, his clear eyes burning into the librarian's soul. The man flushed crimson.

'Perhaps you'd like to give us the Dewey number where you keep them,' Lestrade said.

'You'll find Mr Thparrow in the Annecthe,' the librarian said quickly. 'Can't mith him. Of a Thaturday, he'th likely to be the only one in the Abythinian thecthion.'

'Thank you,' beamed Lestrade and patted the librarian's hand. They made for the Annexe.

'Oh,' the librarian called and was immediately hushed by the various fossils dotted around the room reading. He grimaced and wiggled over to the policemen, 'about thothe bookth you mentioned . . .' His ringed hands fluttered in all directions.

'What books?' Lestrade said and spun on his heel, a chuckling Dew in his wake.

There was indeed only one man in the Abyssinian section. A large, bearded gent who looked positively boyish beside the other members of the Faculty. Odd to call it that really, when faculties were so obviously missing all round among those gentlemen.

'Mr Sparrow?' Lestrade and Dew loomed over the man, engrossed as he was in parchments and ancient, leather-bound volumes.

'Yes,' he said, 'who are you?'

'Superintendent Lestrade, Scotland Yard. This is Chief Inspector Dew. We are investigating the death of the late Janet Calthrop.'

'Ah yes,' the historian's face darkened, 'poor Janet.'

'Ah, so you knew her?' Lestrade reversed a chair and straddled it, wincing only slightly as he misjudged its width and excruciating pain shot up his.

'Of course. She was one of my students. Tragic. Tragic.'

'Neither the Dean nor Professor Blasius seemed to know anything of her, although the flunkey in the top hat assured us that you would.'

'Did he now?' Sparrow's eyes narrowed and wandered to the glass-panelled door.

'The Dean seemed more concerned with someone called Reggie,' Lestrade said. 'Is he quite the ticket?'

'Good Lord, no,' Sparrow chuckled brittlely. 'This college was due to be opened officially in 1831, Superintendent, but the ceremony was delayed because of the Reform Bill riots. Rumour has it that it was the Dean who persuaded the Leader of the Opposition, the Duke of Wellington, not to go.'

'And Reggie?'

'Is the mascot of the college – an iron lion guardant painted in a particularly vicious red. Every now and again, the students of University College nip over and pinch it. The Dean religiously calls in the police on each occasion. I'm surprised you fellows don't arrest him for wasting police time.'

'Why didn't Blasius and Fellowes know this dead girl?' Dew asked, 'I mean, if she was a history student . . .'

'Dodos, Chief Inspector,' Sparrow explained, 'London University has opened its doors to women now for some years. The likes of Blasius and Fellowes haven't realized that. Or if they have, they haven't accepted it. Do you know, I attended a lecture by Blasius last year in the Great Hall. As chance would have it, there were no men present from the student body, there being an inter-collegiate rugby match at Mitcham. There were no less than fourteen ladies in the auditorium, waiting patiently with pens poised. Blasius came in, took one look, said loudly "No one here today, Sparrow" and left. That's the sort of man he is. They both are – he and Fellowes.'

'How long have you known Miss Calthrop?' Lestrade asked.

'For nearly a year,' Sparrow said. 'She came to my tutorials.'

'Your . . . ?'

'Tutorials. A weekly meeting with me and a few students. We discuss their work.'

'Were these students always the same ones?'

'Yes. Janet . . . er . . . Miss Calthrop and three of the men.'

'We'll need their names,' Lestrade said.

'Of course,' Sparrow was keen to oblige, 'I have my list here.'

Dew copied the information into his notepad.

'Look, Superintendent, what is all this about? I mean, I know it's dashed awkward for the college – I mean, the girl dying on the premises. But it's happened before, you know.'

'It has?' Lestrade and Dew chorused.

'Oh, yes. Before my time, but it was still all the talk when I arrived. A student ate some cottage pie in the Refectory and died almost instantly. Apparently the post-mortem revealed a partly digested rat in his stomach. There was a hell of a stink.'

'I can well imagine,' Lestrade nodded. 'But we have reason to believe that Miss Calthrop was murdered.'

'Murdered?' Sparrow's face drained of colour. 'Oh my God.'

'Indeed,' Lestrade nodded. 'What sort of girl was she?'

'Er . . . bright, vivacious. Happy-go-lucky. I really hardly knew her, Superintendent.'

'But you met every week.'

'Who told you that?' Sparrow snapped.

'Er . . . you did,' Lestrade frowned, 'a moment ago. You said you had weekly tutorials.'

'Oh, yes,' Sparrow subsided, 'yes, of course.'

'Did she have any enemies, Mr Sparrow?' Lestrade asked. 'Anyone who disliked her enough to kill her. One of the men, perhaps?'

'No, no,' Sparrow dismissed it instantly, 'the men are delighted to have women here. After all, she was pretty, charming . . .'

'What are you researching, Mr Sparrow?' the Superintendent tried another tack.

Sparrow gathered his papers together. 'Oh, nothing,' he said and, sensing that his brusqueness was a trifle out of place, 'ha, we historians are very cagey about our research, Superintendent. Anyone could be a potential rival, you see. Even you.'

'Oh no, sir,' Lestrade chuckled, 'not me. I never got beyond the Medes and the Persians at school.'

'Well, another lifetime, perhaps,' Sparrow stood up. 'Now, gentlemen, you'll have to excuse me, but I have an urgent appointment . . .'

'Chief Inspector Dew here has a brain like a sieve,' Lestrade stood up with him.

'I have?' Dew was a little hurt. 'I have,' he didn't recognize this ploy but thought he'd better play along anyway.

'He came here yesterday to visit the scene of the crime and now he can't find it again. I wonder if you'd mind?'

'Well, I . . .' Sparrow hesitated, then agreed, 'but then I really must be away.'

He led them through a bewildering maze of darkened corridors, heavy with heating and water pipes, past the gym where the thuds and wheezes told the trio that the college boxing team were at home to the Metropolitan Police. Unbeknownst to any of them, PC Henry 'Steamhammer' Cooper had just taken a dive in the fourth. Yet another scandal to rock public confidence in the Force.

Down they went, the passageways narrower and murkier. Then they came to the top of a blackened stairwell. A solitary gaslight had lost its wick and gauze on the wall, half-way down. The only light came from a high window overhead, its panes misty with the grime of the city.

'Is this the place, Walter?' Lestrade asked.

'Yes, of course,' Dew beamed, 'I'd never have found it again without you, Mr Sparrow.' At last he'd followed the ploy.

'Indeed not,' Lestrade said, 'how did you know *exactly* where to bring us, sir?'

'Well, I . . .' Sparrow flustered, 'it's common knowledge.'

'One Dean and two lecturers in History didn't even know of the existence of the girl, let alone that she had died or where. You, however, seem singularly well informed.'

'Someone told me,' Sparrow said chirpily, 'F Corridor. Near the river.'

'F Corridor extends nearly the length of the building, sir,' Dew said, his topography having improved with lightning speed, 'not to mention the five twists to left and right, all of which are dubbed "F" on the college plan and three of which have staircases just like this one.'

'Well,' Sparrow bluffed, 'a lucky guess. Now, I'm afraid . . .'

'Yes,' Lestrade cut him short, 'I know you are. James Sparrow, go on down.'

The historian looked at the grim, moustachioed faces of the policemen, their set jaws, their cold eyes. He swallowed and shambled down the steps. He was nearly at the bottom, facing a brick wall, when Lestrade suddenly crouched above him, four steps from the top. He struck a match. 'Aha,' he muttered.

'What is it, guv?' Dew turned back to him.

Lestrade dabbed his fingers on the brickwork. It was damp. Sticky. He sniffed them, then drew a line in the air with his finger to the opposite wall. 'Putty,' he said, 'that's how it was done, Walter. A fine wire was stretched across here, anchored at each end with putty. The murderer must have been at the top,' he glanced back, 'around the corner in the shadows.' He reached up to the gas bracket. 'That's been out of order for some time,' he said. 'Can you see anything down there, Mr Sparrow?'

'Not a lot,' the historian's voice echoed in that dark space. 'My eyes are becoming a *little* accustomed to it, though.'

'I don't get it, guv,' Dew said, 'that's what I couldn't fathom yesterday. We didn't find a candle or a bull's eye or even a lucifer. Janet Calthrop was here in the dark. Now, I asked myself yesterday and I ask myself again today, "What sort of girl wanders about in such an isolated part of the college? In the dark, without a light?"'

'How far have we come', Lestrade asked, 'since we last saw anybody?'

'Couple of minutes, I'd say,' Dew answered. 'The last human contact was the noise in the gym – and that was on the floor above.'

'What is that, Mr Sparrow?' Lestrade asked, pointing to the bottom of the stairs and to the historian's left.

'It appears to be a door,' he said.

'And what's behind it?'

'A store, I suppose. I've really no idea.'

'Do you have a key?'

'No, of course not. I only have keys to my own study and the Faculty Library. Now, I've co-operated, gentlemen; I've brought you to where you say the girl died. Now I really must be going . . .'

But Dew blocked the man's exit. 'I'm afraid we'll have to detain you just a little longer, sir.'

Lestrade edged past them both, his boots clacking on the stone steps. 'Notice, Walter, how the studs on my soles make a devil of a racket.'

'Duly noticed, guv,' Dew hadn't taken his eyes off Sparrow.

'Given a somewhat lighter tread,' Lestrade grunted, as his

switchblade clicked into the door's lock, 'and a rather less manly boot which we can assume a young lady would wear,' he twisted sharply and the door creaked inward, 'and I think we can still assume that Janet Calthrop took off her shoes to minimize the noise she made.' He pushed the door back to its fullest extent, fumbling for his lucifers again. 'The noise she made when she visited her murderer, her lover, in this . . . storeroom, did you say, Mr Sparrow?'

Suddenly, the historian rammed his shoulder into Dew's stomach. The chief inspector went down on the angle of the stairs, but he still had the presence of mind to turn and grab Sparrow's ankle as he clambered upwards. A moment later and the man's wrists were locked behind his back, his nose trickling blood on the stonework.

'You're getting better at that, Walter,' Lestrade was impressed.

'This is outrageous!' Sparrow grunted.

'Yes,' Lestrade's voice called from the inner recesses of the storeroom, 'I think I'll have to agree with that. Walter, would you bring Mr Sparrow down here? I think he has some explaining to do.'

The chief inspector threw the historian forward so that he all but followed Janet Calthrop to bounce against the brick wall at the foot of the stairs. Then he kicked him sharp right so that all three of them stood in the little room. Lestrade had found an oil-lamp and lit it. The room was carpeted and the stark brick walls were hung with velvet curtains. On a large, brass-headed bed in the centre, lay a pair of stockings and a pair of black, lace-up boots. Lestrade hauled back a curtain that hung on rings and revealed rows of shelves, each of them lined with enough boots to fit a centipede.

'Well, well, well,' he said, 'I think our Mr Sparrow has a thing about feet, don't you, Walter?'

'You weird bastard,' Dew growled.

Sparrow stood sobbing in the middle of his love-nest. 'It was Nanny,' he blurted, 'whenever I was upset as a child, Nanny Dumplings used to stroke me with her feet. The very touch of silk, the smell of leather . . .' he shuddered.

Dew had to turn away.

'Walter,' Lestrade jerked his head.

The chief inspector turned back, 'James Sparrow, I am arresting you for the murder of Janet Calthrop of this college on or about the early morning of Friday 17 April 1906. You are not obliged to say anything, but anything you do say . . .'

'No!' Sparrow wailed, 'I didn't *kill* her. We were having a bit of a fling, that's all,' he turned quivering to Lestrade. 'Look, Superintendent, I may be a little odd. Sad, even. Although I defy any normal full-blooded man not to be touched a little by the rustle of silk stockings. If you roll up my trouser-leg, you'll find I'm wearing a pair this very day. Even the Dean . . .'

Lestrade clicked his fingers. Dew marched his man out.

'No,' Sparrow was still screaming, 'I didn't do it. I didn't do it.'

'Don't worry,' Lestrade heard Dew say, 'by the time this case comes to trial, they'll have set up this new Court of Appeal thing. Gives you total fairness and justice, you clearly-guilty, murdering bastard.'

'Has he coughed?' Lestrade peered through the smoky lamp-light that wreathed his office at the Yard.

'A few times,' Dew said, 'but I got Queux to go on hitting him anyway.'

'And?'

'Nothing.'

'Nothing?'

Dew was confused. 'Either he's as strong as a bloody ox, guv, or . . .'

'Or?'

'He didn't do it,' both men chorused.

'All right,' Lestrade said, 'talk me through it. What do we know? Oh Christ, who made this cocoa?'

'Me, guv,' Constable Bee buzzed through with a Remington under his arm.

'Put that cowboy painting down, Bee and give me a grovelling apology at once.'

'Sorry, guv,' Bee grinned.

'Yes, well, that'll do for now. Right, Walter.'

'James Camargue Sparrow . . .'

'Camargue?'

'French on his mother's side.'

'Hm,' Lestrade clasped his fingers across his waistcoat, 'nice to know there was somebody on his mother's side.'

'Do you want his antecedents, guv?' Dew riffled through the papers that Constable Queux had filed so assiduously with one hand while thumping the suspect with the other. No wonder it was called shorthand.

'No. We'll let the lab have a look at those later. Sparrow and the girl.'

'Were having what he calls a relationship.'

'And what you call?'

'Several one-night stands. She was a bit of a naughty little vixen, apparently. Quiet sort. Not averse to a bit with a man old enough to be her father.'

'Hmm,' Lestrade nodded. 'It's always the quiet sort. Where did these lianas take place?'

'Ah, well, that's the craftiness of it. They only ever did it in the college. He leased that little room from some porter or other. He had the only key. Then he'd inveigle young women students there and the rest you know.'

'Cunning little deviant, though, isn't he?'

'How so, guv?'

'Well if he's not guilty of murder, Walter, I'm not sure we can get him on anything. Ownership of several pairs of shoes and stockings is not, per say, an offence. Messrs Harrods must have hundreds. Unless he knocked them all off, of course.'

'I rather got the impression that they were souvenirs, as you might say, guv. Mementoes from a variety of lady-loves.'

'Is there a Mrs Sparrow?'

'There was, but she flew the nest some years ago. Found out about her husband's inclivities and left him, claiming she'd never liked it. Apparently, they'd had a flaming row and it all came to a head when she caught him in a shoe shop staring at the reflection in a pair of patents worn by a rather pretty assistant. At the angle she was at, he could see right up her frock.'

'Tsk, tsk,' Bee was sorting papers, 'the bastard. We should throw away the key.'

'I beg your pardon?' Dew rounded on him.

'Oh, sorry. "We should throw away the key", sir.'

Dew nodded.

'So what's his story for the night of the murder?'

'He was there. He found her.'

Lestrade's feet came off the desk and all four of his chair legs hit the floor. 'He admitted that?'

'Oh, yes, guv,' Dew said, 'which is what leads me to believe I may have been a trifle hasty in placing my hand on his collar in the first place.'

'Well, what's a little wrongful arrest between friends? Brush him down, give him his cab fare home and he'll be contributing to the Police Benevolent Fund by the end of the month. Tell me his version.'

'Well, they'd arranged to meet on Thursday night. Apparently, this was the regular drill. She'd go to his tutorial thingy with the others, they'd all have some tea and talk about . . . you know . . . dead blokes and things. Then she'd make a big fuss about going her own way. One of the men students would see her to the door and get her a cab. Then she'd whizz round the Aldwych and back down Surrey Street; in through the back door, so to speak. He'd meet her somewhere by the river and they'd sneak off to his little room of debauchery. Last Thursday was no different. They spent a night of – what's Queux written – "unbridled passion" (we haven't found the harness yet, by the way) – and about five in the morning he woke up and found her gone.'

'Gone?'

Dew nodded. 'He assumed to answer a call of nature. One of the shortcomings of that secret room of his is that it doesn't have a lavvy.'

'I noticed a guzunda,' Lestrade remembered having stubbed his toe on the thing. 'Had a picture of Mr Campbell-Bannerman at the bottom.'

'Singularly appropriate,' beamed Dew.

'Tsk, tsk, Chief Inspector,' Lestrade wagged an upbraiding finger, 'let us at all times remain politically correct, please. So she'd gone for a sh . . .'

'Sparrow supposed so, yes. It wasn't unusual. Then he heard the thud.'

'What time was this?'

'A little after five, he thought.'

'No scream?'

'No. Just the sound of her tumbling down the steps and then the smack as her head hit the wall.'

'What did he do?'

'Got up to investigate.'

'And?'

'Found her, outside the door.'

'So, if he's telling the truth . . .'

'*If*,' Dew was at pains to stress.

'If he's telling the truth, he was feet away from the murderer. The man had to be there,' Lestrade was thinking aloud again, 'he couldn't risk the tripwire not working. Where's the nearest privy?'

'Up the stairs, along the corridor, first on the left.'

'No, Walter,' Lestrade sighed, 'I've been in this building as many years as you have. I know where they are here. I'm talking about King's College.'

'Oh, yes, of course. Sorry, guv. Up the stairs, along the corridor, first on the left.'

'I see. So let's assume she was in there for, what? Five minutes?'

'Fair enough,' Dew agreed. 'Depending on what they'd had for supper. Apparently he used to nip out to the Wayzgoose in Fleet Street or the Strand Palace and order them a supper.'

'So our friend would have time between Miss Calthrop going up the steps and coming back to use his putty to fix the wire at ankle height.'

'He didn't realize she'd have no boots or stockings on. If she had, I'd . . . er . . . you'd never have found that mark on her shin. Funny she was fully clothed, though.'

'Yes. I suppose she was trying to make the best of a bad job. Wanted to appear respectable in case she bumped into a night porter, yet couldn't be bothered with all the fuss of tying laces. On the assumption she thought she was going back to bed, after all.'

'So it wasn't just to keep quiet, then? That she didn't wear her boots, I mean?'

'I don't know how sound carries in that building,' Lestrade said. 'Tell me; presumably Sparrow didn't hear anything else? Footsteps dying away afterwards? Kerfuffle on the stairs?'

'Not a thing. You didn't find any wire in his room, I suppose?'

'No,' Lestrade shook his head, 'nor putty either. All I found was this.'

'What is it, guv?'

Lestrade held it up. A primitive carving on wood, flat, about six inches long. 'I don't know,' he said. 'There was nothing else like it in the room. No knick-knacks at all that didn't belong to some woman, probably under twenty-eight and built like a wardrobe.'

Dew took it. 'Looks like . . . I don't know . . . a doll, doesn't it? Look, here's the face. Arms, legs. Ugly bloody thing. There's some glass on this top bit. Not a mirror, is it?'

'Sparrow didn't mention it?' Lestrade asked.

Dew flicked through Queux's notes. 'Not a dicky-bird,' he said.

'All right, Walter. We can hold him for another twenty-four hours. After that, if nothing breaks, you can let him go. Put a tail on him, though.'

'Right, guv. And look, I'm grateful for your help on this one.'

Lestrade rose and stretched. On the river, the lights of trailing barges twinkled at him in the early hours. 'Not at all, Walter, but it's past my bedtime. Give my regards to Mrs Dew and all the little Dews,' he leaned over his Number Two, 'and teach that lad how to make a decent cup of cocoa, there's a good Chief Inspector.'

That was the month and the year of the San Francisco earthquake. Its shock waves reached the Horse's Collar in William IV Street and even caused a tremor in the tankards at the Coal Hole in the Strand. Neither of these echoes of the Mercalli Scale caused Chief Superintendent Abberline to fall over. His enemies said it was drink. His friend said it wasn't. Anyway, he was seen by the police surgeon and told to take six weeks off. And other officers were asked to drop their trousers before the cold stethoscope of the good doctor as well. No one else, it was true, was sent home, but the loss of Abberline, albeit temporarily, meant there were open cases all over the shop.

'I doubt he'll last the year,' the Maudlin Major was saying, studying the doctor's report on the chief superintendent.

'Ah, you've met Ermintrude Abberline,' Lestrade beamed. 'Still, I wouldn't write old Frederick off just yet. I happen to know the Chief Superintendent is spending his convalescence in Penge.'

'So?' Major Woodhouse was too busy acting at being assistant commissioner to be aware of the remark's significance.

'So, he lives in Norwood,' Lestrade told his chief.

'Well, anyway,' the Morose Major scowled, 'he was working on a very delicate case, Lestrade. What are you on at the moment?'

'You got my report on the Peter Tavy murders, sir?'

'Oh yes. The convict did it.'

'Er . . . no, sir,' Lestrade explained. 'If you read page sixteen, para eight bee, you will discover that I have an open mind.'

'Yes,' growled Woodhouse, 'I didn't have to get that far to tell me that. Well, drop it. It'll keep. There are more pressing problems.'

Lestrade stood on the carpet where he had been countless times before – and no doubt would be again. 'Chief Inspector Dew is up to his unmentionables in the King's College affair, sir.'

'Yes, he's to lay off that one. I've told him. We've had complaints.'

'Really? Who from?'

'From whom, Lestrade,' the assistant commissioner corrected him.

'I was hoping *you*'d tell *me*, sir.'

'The Dean, for one. Two old duffers in the History Faculty for another. Anyway, I thought Dew had apprehended the miscreant.'

'So he did, sir. Sadly, it's not that straightforward.'

'No,' sighed Woodhouse, 'it never is. You know, Lestrade, I don't know why I became a policeman.'

Neither did Lestrade. He was vaguely astonished to see the Moribund Major cross to his door and lock it. 'I'll be honest with you, Lestrade,' he looked his man straight in the eye, 'I've never liked you.'

'Thank you, sir. What that does for morale, you'll never know.'

'I've never liked you, but with Abberline out with the falling sickness, you're the one man here at the Yard I'd trust with what's happened.'

'What's happened?'

'You'd better sit down. I am going to tell you a story so appalling, so terrifying, that if word of it reaches Fleet Street, there'd be a war.'

'War?' Lestrade's bum hit the leather. 'Who with?'

'Here,' Woodhouse hauled on a piece of string dangling by a filing cabinet and a map of Europe appeared on the other end of it. 'What is the one country we are all afraid of?'

'Er . . . Ireland?' Lestrade said, ever a man of current affairs; rather like Abberline really, although his affairs seemed curiously confined to Penge.

Woodhouse shook his head.

'Er . . . Germany?' Lestrade tried again.

'Spain!' Woodhouse's stubby fingers thumped into the plain of La Mancha.

'Spain?' Lestrade frowned. Clearly poring over the *Sun* on a daily basis had done him no good at all.

'Yes, yes, I know. Not exactly in the forefront at the moment. Not since the Armada and el Sieclo d'Oro, but in decline or not, Lestrade, if what I fear has happened, it will be war. France will join Spain. Russia will join France. The Algeciras Peace Conference will be blown out of the water.'

'Forgive me, sir,' Lestrade said, 'this is perhaps a rather presumptuous remark to make, not knowing, as yet, quite what it is you are asking of me, but isn't this sort of thing a job for . . .' and he sucked in his breath, 'Special Branch?'

'Special Branch?' Woodhouse repeated, 'are you mad? This is a case of the utmost gravity. The security of the nation itself is at stake. Do you think I'd leave it in the hands of seventeen bigoted idiots, half of whom are Irishmen and the other half paranoid?'

And at that moment, Major Woodhouse won the heart of Superintendent Lestrade, whatever paranoid meant.

'I've found him, guv.'

'I'm happy for you, Adams. Whom have you found? Oh, sorry,' Lestrade fumbled with his flies, 'I've just come from a meeting with the Miserable Major. You know what a stickleback he is for the English language.'

'Do I ever? Ooh, can I use your urinal when you've finished? Only mine's a bit high up.'

Lestrade shook his bits and pieces carefully the requisite three times and put himself away, rather like the artist Richard Dadd should have done a few years back. 'Yes, I don't care for these new Staffordshire things at all. Give me the old Deluge. You knew where you where with them.'

'They splashed your shoes, though,' Adams said, staring with relief at the green tiles and vaguely aware that his eyes were watering.

'So who have you found?' Lestrade wiped his toe-caps on his calves, one at a time, of course.

'Tenterden, sir. That old journalist-cum-writer blokey from Peter Tavy.'

'Ah, yes. Bloomsbury I think he said.'

'The square of the same name. Oh, bugger. I have wet my shoe after all. What a bugger.'

'Where is he now?'

'Tenterden? Outside. Or rather inside. Charge Room Six.'

'Charge Room?'

'Well, guv,' Adams joined Lestrade at the green-stained revolving washbasins, 'he did disappear in rapid order at the Queen's Head under rather mysterious circumstances. I thought the Devon police would find him under his own floor-boards when we discovered the runaway convict in his house. He of course has an altogether more rational explanation.' He caught the tilting washbasin a trifle too forcefully. 'Oh, bugger, I've wet my other shoe now. What a bugger indeed.'

'You've talked to him?'

Adams beamed. 'Couldn't resist it, sir. Mrs Adams is always saying to me "Push yourself forward, Abou", she says, "it's no good behaving like a virgin on her wedding night. You've got to get in there and . . ." You've never met the Missus, have you, sir?'

'No,' Lestrade finished drying his hands on the grubby towel, 'no, it's a pleasure I consistently deny myself. What did Tenterden say?'

'Nothing. Said he wanted to talk to you.' The sergeant followed his guv'nor up the back stairs, shaking the water out of his eyelets at every conceivable opportunity.

'Mr Tenterden,' they reached the grim, one-tabled cell where the single gas jet flickered.

'Ah, Superintendent. Am I glad to see you!'

'Are you, sir? How gratifying. You had us rather worried, you know.'

'I did?'

'Well,' Lestrade slumped into the other hard wooden chair. Adams lounged in a corner, nattering to the uniformed man who was there already. 'You *did* say some rather coptic things to us that night at the Queen's Head and the next day, when we called to continue our conversation, we nearly had our heads blown off by a maniac with a shotgun. Has Sergeant Adams given you a damage report?'

'Damage report?' Tenterden had gone as pale as the urinals the Yard men had just left.

'Oh, nothing vital. Some splinters in the bannisters and a few stains on the eiderdown. Superficial, really.'

'Well. I must apologize for the subterfuge, if that's what you thought it was. No, I'd always planned to come back to Bloomsbury on the twenty-fourth. That's why I saw you the night before. I had no idea about the convict, of course, until Sergeant Adams broke the news to me an hour ago – rather after he broke my door panel.'

'Tsk, tsk, Adams! For shame!' Lestrade rounded on him, 'send us a bill, Mr Tenterden. I cannot apologize enough.'

'No, I'd go along with that,' the journalist nodded, chuckling. 'But it wasn't strictly his fault. I *did* slam the door in his face.

It's funny, he *does* look like a Jehovah's Witness in this light. My apologies again, Sergeant.'

'That's all right, sir. The liniment's working wonders now.'

'We drew a blank with Kenrick', Lestrade told his man, 'as to what he found in the late Captain Orange's breast pocket. Wouldn't be drawn.'

Tenterden flickered, 'I see.'

'So, I was rather hoping, sir, that you . . . ?' Lestrade tilted back his bowler and gave Tenterden his most appealing look. The journalist closed to him so that their noses, one long and sharp, the other scarred and tipless, almost met across an uncrowded room.

'That's why I asked to see you. No disrespect to your Sergeant, of course. But it's too personal. Too incredible.'

'I'm all ears,' Lestrade clasped his fingers across his midriff, his legs stretched out before him. That much was evident.

'Ever been to Abyssinia, Mr Lestrade?'

'No,' the Superintendent said. 'Should I have?'

'I was there once. Oh, a long time ago now,' he smiled at the remembrance of it, 'when I was young and fancy free. I went out with Napier of Magdala as a war-correspondent, as they call them nowadays. I was there when he took the emperor's fortress.'

'Yes, yes, I'd be delighted to see your holiday snapshots,' Lestrade smiled, 'but what has this to do with . . . ?'

'Captain Orange?'

Lestrade nodded.

'I was coming to that,' a haunted look darkened the old man's face. 'You see . . . oh, I don't know . . . I'm wrong. I must be. May I go now?' He stood up. Lestrade was with him.

'You can't leave us dangling like that, Mr Tenterden,' he scolded. 'Please.'

'Very well,' Tenterden had made up his mind, 'but you'll think me mad. What old Kenrick found in the late Captain's breast pocket was a mirror.'

'A mirror?' Lestrade repeated.

'A small, circular mirror . . .'

'With a curiously carved handle? Rather in the shape of an ugly doll.'

69

'Why, yes,' Tenterden raised both eyebrows, 'so you *did* see it?'

'No, Mr Tenterden,' Lestrade shook his head, 'Not there. The mirror I saw was in altogether a different place.'

Whatever happened, Lestrade wondered, to Numbers One to Nine? Why did that rather dour little street start at Number Ten? Compulsory purchase orders, presumably. The anonymous black hansom rocked to a halt outside the polished door. Curious, they hadn't sent a motor car, but then, as Woodhouse had intimated, this whole thing was strictly hush-hush. A quiet cab, a driver with a collar turned up against the drizzle of a spring night and no heads would turn, no eyebrows rise.

The uniformed man on the door saluted him and a flunkey ushered him in. The wallpaper looked as though it hadn't been changed since Disraeli's time; the carpets since Melbourne's. And there were still the scuff marks on the skirting boards where Wellington's spurs had raked them.

He was shown into a drawing-room, heavy on the chintz. Fitting that, bearing in mind the new Prime Minister was a draper by trade and inclination. At a desk by the window, the lamplight glowing on his face, sat Sir Henry Campbell-Bannerman, Member of Parliament for the Stirling Burghs and His Britannic Majesty's Prime Minister.

'Y'know,' he looked at Lestrade over a pair of pince-nez, 'this is bloody awkward. Abberline going down like that. Breaks the rhythm, spoils the routine.'

'I'm sure Mr Abberline is mortified, sir,' Lestrade stood where he was, never at ease in the presence of greatness. And this was surely the greatest draper who ever lived.

'Aye, I had that distinct impression when I saw him last. Anyway, to cases. You're Defrayed, aren't you?' He waved him to a sofa.

'Lestrade, sir.'

'Eh? Oh, right. Well, I'll not beat aboot the bush, laddie. Something is afoot.'

Lestrade had not heard that phrase in a long time. He had actually hoped not to hear it again. It smacked of an odd couple

70

he once knew, one of them dead now as a result of visiting rather dangerous tourist attractions on a wet day.

'I haven't seen the file, sir,' Lestrade explained.

'What file?' Campbell-Bannerman asked.

'Mr Abberline's file,' Lestrade said.

'That's because there isn't one, laddie,' the Prime Minister told him. 'At least, I sincerely hope not. None of this that I'm about to confide goes on paper. It's too sensitive; too desperate.' He rummaged in a drawer and unlocked something inside that. He produced a second key and crossed furtively to a cabinet. 'Close your eyes, laddie' he said. 'You don't have sufficient clearance for this.'

Lestrade did and heard a heavy object being scraped back, two or three loud clicks and a grunt.

'Here,' he opened his eyes again to be shown a studio photograph of a rather haughty young man in uniform, 'what d'ye make of that?'

Lestrade summoned up all his deductive powers. Years of experience were brought to bear in the silence that followed.

'Not a lot, I see,' the Prime Minister poured himself a stiff malt, of the single variety. He did not tempt Lestrade by offering one to him.

'No, no, no, no,' Lestrade fluttered his fingers, 'it's a photograph of a rather haughty-looking man in uniform.'

'Regiment?'

'Er . . .' Lestrade squinted at it, 'Lancers.'

'Which one?'

'Er . . . It *is* a black-and-white photograph, sir.'

'Is there any other kind?' Campbell-Bannerman asked.

'I believe not,' Lestrade said.

'It's all a matter of lateral thinking, laddie,' the Prime Minister ran a hand through his silky white hair. 'Look at the tunic. Colour?'

'Sepia,' Lestrade did his best with the intelligence test.

'Colour of facings?'

'Er . . .'

'The collar, cuffs and front, man. Am I really to put the future of Great Britain in the hands of a man who doesn't know a plastron front from his left tit?'

71

'Darker,' Lestrade responded, 'darker sepia.'

'Precisely. There's the clue. Which Lancer regiment has darker facings than its tunic?'

'Er . . .'

'The Sixteenth, Lestrade!' Campbell-Bannerman was exasperated. 'The Scarlet Lancers. The tunic is scarlet, the facings blue. What else do you notice about this man?'

'Um . . . oh, how odd.'

'Yes?' the Prime Minister leaned forward, perched as he was now on the corner of his desk.

'He's got a patch over his left eye.'

'Tsk, man,' Campbell-Bannerman rolled on to the sofa beside the Superintendent, 'that's neither here nor there. Although it *might* explain, I suppose, how it happened.'

'What happened, sir?' Lestrade asked.

'I'll get to that. Look at his decorations.'

'Hm,' the Superintendent nodded, 'very nice.' That reminded him. His OM was lying around somewhere. He must fish it out.

'His Orders, man,' Abberline hadn't been as obtuse as this. What kind of idiot had Woodhouse sent him? 'Do you recognize them?'

'No, sir,' Lestrade confessed, 'I'm afraid not.'

'The Order of St James of Compostella,' Campbell-Bannerman pointed to the gong on the soldier's left breast, 'and', he pointed to his throat, 'the Golden Fleece.'

Lestrade had always remembered his Greek legends from school. He found himself wondering why Jason and his lads had gone to such lengths to get a bit of metal that looked like a dead sheep.

'Perhaps this will help,' the Prime Minister thrust a second photograph into the policeman's hand. It was of a young woman whose poppy eyes and expensive pearls could only denote one thing – she was rich and had thyroid trouble.

'Ah, now,' Lestrade tapped it, the name on the tip of his tongue, 'this is Marie Corelli, isn't it? The writer?'

Campbell-Bannerman's blubbery jaw dropped. 'No, Lestrade,' he said, his voice soft with incredulity, 'it is the Princess Victoria of Battenburg, known to the Royal Family, God Bless 'Em, as Ena. What about this one?'

Another photograph revealed another young man in the uniform of the Sixteenth Lancers, his swan's-plumed cap in hand, the light dazzling on his prickers. He had a centre parting, full lips, ears too low on his head and both his eyes.

'You can see it, can't you?' Campbell-Bannerman said, 'the jutting jaw, the huge proboscis. The old Habsburg strain is there still. Did you know that earlier members of that august Royal Family are credited with inventing the straw on account of being unable to eat properly because of the congenital juxtaposition of their chins and noses?'

'Good Lord,' Lestrade was astounded, 'fancy that.'

'It may well be that Mr Punch is based on them too.'

Lestrade looked again. From the angle of the photograph he couldn't tell whether the young man shared Mr Punch's appalling hump.

'His Majesty King Alfonso the Thirteenth of Spain,' Campbell-Bannerman announced, 'Colonel-in-Chief of the Sixteenth Lancers since last year. He is, as you know, the betrothed of Princess Ena.'

'How nice,' Lestrade smiled.

'Aye, well, the fairy-tale is turning out to be a wee bit grim,' Campbell-Bannerman downed his Scotch. 'Look at that first photo again.'

Lestrade turned back to the man with the patch.

'Juan Tomas de Jesus-Lopez,' the Prime Minister whispered, glancing around him. 'Supernumerary Major attached to the Sixteenth and ADC to His Majesty.'

'Juan Tomas?' Lestrade repeated. The rest of the man's name had vanished in a series of oral explosions as the Scotsman whose mother came from Manchester tried to wrestle with the peculiarities of Spanish pronunciation. The Superintendent wiped the spittle off his Donegal.

'John Thomas to you,' the Prime Minister translated. 'He's gone missing, Lestrade. Vanished.'

'I see.'

'No,' Campbell-Bannerman scrutinized the man through hooded eyes, 'I'm not sure you do. The King of Spain and Princess Ena are to marry in July. Jesus-Lopez is over here to work with the regiment and select an escort for the marriage in Madrid. Well, you see at once the delicacy of the situation, Lestrade. A top Dago nobleman disappears on English soil. If he turns up alive we're going to look bloody silly. If he turns up dead, it could cause an international incident. Not only no marriage, but Spain could turn nasty. There's a tangled web of international alliances out there, Lestrade,' the Prime Minister waved his hand to a map of Europe made out of chintz. 'If Edward Grey, my Foreign Secretary, were here now, he'd doubtless explain it to ye. As it is, he's off fly-fishing in Dumfries. Understandable, really. There's bugger all else to do in Dumfries. The point is, Lestrade, that we are sitting on a powder keg. We've got the biggest bloody Empire in the world and about the same number of friends as a leper. Och, the Fat Man at the palace does his bit, of course. But the Entente Cordiale is only as cordiale as the damned Frogs want it to be. I'm not sure young George has much of the diplomat in him – and I haven't been well mysen'. The Dagos have never forgiven us for the Armada, the Frogs for Waterloo and the Krauts for having more coastline than they've got. I tell you, Lestrade, we're on a knife edge. Whatever you're doing, stop it and find Jesus-Lopez.'

'I'm sorry,' Lestrade did as he was told, 'where do I start?'

'Beachy Head, of course,' Campbell-Bannerman told him. 'Must I do everything myself?'

The wind whipped something horrible around his Donegal. For all it was spring and the South Eastern had taken him through flocks of frisking lambs, up here on the lip of the Sussex wold, it was like standing on the edge of the world. He held his bowler to his head and surveyed the extraordinary scene. To the east lay the rocky outcrop of Dungeness where the Kentishmen had waited in their woad for the arrival of Julius Caesar. To the west lay the Wight and that haunted chine at Shanklin where Lestrade had held hands with a dead man in a cave an eternity ago. It was a time to remember, on this headland, in this spring, the wind whispering through the sea-lavender and the samphire.

'Any luck?' a voice made him whirl, his boots slipping on the chalk shale and his heart hitting his mouth, 'I say, steady. Didn't mean to make you jump.'

'Er ... that's all right,' Lestrade looked relatively well for a man whose life had just hurtled past his eyes.

'David Runton,' the bespectacled man in the plus-fours held out his hand, 'I'm a twitcher.'

'Oh, I'm sorry,' Lestrade said, 'does that run in your family? Or do you have a particularly stressful job?'

'Er ...' Runton frowned. 'Haha!' he thumped Lestrade in the shoulder so that the tears caused by the wind were joined by tears caused by the pain. 'Very good. Very good. Actually, I'm in haberdashery.'

Well, there you are, Lestrade thought to himself. Always somebody worse off than you.

'I was hoping for a rock pippit.'

'Yes,' Lestrade smiled, losing the battle with the wind and taking off his bowler, 'I suspect promotion in your line is as slow as it is in mine. Mustn't give up hope, though.'

'No, ... er ... no, indeed,' Runton unhooked a pair of expensive-looking binoculars and focused out to sea.

'Know this spot well?' Lestrade asked.

'Oh, yes,' the bird watcher told him, 'been coming here ever since I was a boy.'

'You weren't here on the twenty-second ult., I suppose?'

'Twenty-second?' Runton lowered his field glasses, 'what day was that?'

'Friday. Two weeks ago.'

'Yes, I was as a matter of fact. That was the day that chappie went over the edge.'

'Had a nervous breakdown, you mean?'

'No, no,' Runton began to write notes on a pad hooked under his arm. 'That's the third petrel I've seen this week. No, I mean, literally. He went over. I'm amazed the papers didn't print it.'

'You saw him jump?'

'Well, no. Not exactly.'

'Then how ... ?'

'Well, I saw him walking up here from the direction of Belle Tout ...'

'Bell Two?'

'Those ruins down there,' Runton pointed to the shell of a lighthouse far below on the edge of a shingle beach. 'I remember thinking how odd.'

'What?'

'Well, he was in uniform. Oh, nothing ordinary, mind you; walking-out dress or anything. No, it was full dress. Bright scarlet, plumed lance-cap, everything. Not exactly what your average twitcher or rambler wears, is it?'

Lestrade felt for this man, even in the course of his inquiries. The horrendous affliction which afflicted him had obviously so coloured his life, he assumed that everyone had the problem – or was deranged in some way because of it. 'Indeed not,' the Superintendent agreed. 'What did he do?'

'Well,' Runton sat cross-legged on the short-cropped, springy grass, 'I had some trouble focusing on a tern, so I didn't see him reach the dip.'

'The dip?'

'It's a depression in the chalk. Just over there. Popular with courting couples in the summer. Unfortunately,' he tapped his binoculars, then his nose, 'I'm not. You'd be amazed by the things I've picked up in this focal length.'

Probably, mused Lestrade. 'What happened then?'

'Well, the sun was in my eyes just then and I was desperate for a shag . . .'

'I beg your pardon?'

'It's a seabird,' Runton explained, 'not dissimilar, to the layman, to a cormorant. Look here, are you an ornithologist or not?'

'Not,' confessed Lestrade, 'I'm a policeman.'

'Oh dear. Oh, I see. How stupid of me,' the young man was covered in confusion. 'You must be from Eastbourne.'

Lestrade didn't see why he had to be, but he let it go for the moment. 'And after your sh . . . seabird?'

'No, I couldn't find one anywhere,' Runton sighed. 'Bit like a policeman, really. Never one around when you want one. Oh, no offence, of course.'

'None taken,' Lestrade assured him. 'What of the soldier?'

'Well, that was the damnedest thing. I dropped my luncheon

box at that point and when I'd picked up my bins and Eccles and so on, he'd gone.'

'Gone? What, you mean, left?'

'Left his clothes.'

'His uniform?'

'Yes. He must have stripped off just over there.'

'Show me.'

Runton took his man dangerously nearer the crumbling cliff face. The herring-gulls wheeled below them. Lestrade took one tentative glance over the edge. Some hidden force, a secret compulsion pulled his head forward and his shoulder followed. Go on, he swore he heard a voice whisper in his ear; go on, I dare you. Just for a laugh.

'Careful,' Runton checked his man again, 'it is five hundred and thirty-four feet down, you know. Not, I suppose, that you'd be counting.'

'No, indeed,' Lestrade thought it best to sit down. There was something in the loneliness of the wind, the solitary silence of the sea. It appealed to the suicidal in him. The suicidal in all of us. He'd once felt the same atop Clifton Suspension Bridge when he was under suspension from the Yard. The serenity of gliding, the peace of floating . . .

'The mess at the bottom,' it was as though Runton had read his mind.

'Mess?'

'Well, yes. It's pretty rocky down there, you know. Whether the tide's in or the tide's out, you'd be spattered all over the seaweed.'

'Well,' Lestrade tried to chuckle, 'my old dad used to say "When you're higher than the seagulls, it's either time to come down from the cliff or lay off the liquor". What did you do then?'

'Well, I looked about a bit. He wasn't east. He wasn't west. I concluded he could only be some other place.'

'Er . . . north?'

'No, that's where I'd come from, along the South Downs Way from Jevington. He'd gone south. Straight down.'

'You went down?'

'To the beach?' Runton asked, 'no fear. It takes hours and

anyway, I didn't really care for what I'd find. There was no chance of him surviving a fall like that. Of course they say it's the last four feet that kill you. Down to five hundred and thirty feet, he'd have been all right if a little dizzy. No, I just took his belongings to Eastbourne, to the police station there. Well, you know, your place.'

'Not quite *my* place,' Lestrade told him, 'I'm from Scotland Yard.'

'Ah, I see. Getting in the big guns, eh? Well, it's certainly a mystery.'

'What is?'

'The fact that they didn't find him. I've scanned the papers every day. There's been no sign. Even allowing for the fact that the tide was in and he'd been washed off the rocks by the force of the waves, you'd have thought the sea would have rolled him out somewhere. Spewed him out of its ravening maw, somewhere between Seaford and Pevensey. But that's why you're here, of course. Sleuthing.'

'Sort of,' Lestrade said. 'Tell me about his personal effects.'

'Well, I handed them in at the station.'

'Did you go through his pockets?'

'He didn't have any,' Runton remembered. 'No, I tell a lie. There was something in an inner pocket in the tunic. I thought it was a calling card at first. Then I realized it wasn't. It was a mirror.'

'A mirror?'

'Yes. Rather a fancy one as a matter of fact. Weird sort of carving. Does that mean anything? Important, I mean? I say, you look rather strange.'

'That's nature for you,' said Lestrade. 'Does a mirror mean anything?' The Superintendent wiped the guano off his shoulder. 'That's for a murderer to know and me to find out.'

4

The policemen tramped the shingle between the groynes; Superintendent Lestrade of the Metropolitan Police in his wind-swept Donegal and white-flaked bowler; Inspector Padstow in his black-braided patrols.

'Vain bugger, obviously,' was his conclusion.

'Hm?'

'The Lancer chappie who went off Beachy. Vain bugger, carrying a flashy mirror like that. Can't be regulation, surely?'

'I wouldn't have thought so,' Lestrade said. He stopped and turned back to look at the Wish Tower and the great white cliffs rising beyond. 'Tell me about the search again,' he said.

'Well, we did our best,' Padstow told him, watching the workmen polishing the rather hideous turquoise of the band-stand roof in readiness for the coming Season. ''Course, we can't really cope, can we? Against the rising tide of crime, I mean. How you blokes in London manage, I can't imagine. Bloody government underfunding again. Our Chief Constable, God rot him, *did* have the decency to ask the Home Sec. for extra-long truncheons the other day.'

'Oh! What did he say?'

'Herbert Gladstone? Hadn't read it. Didn't see the need. Usual rubbish.'

'Hm,' Lestrade sympathized, 'and the search?'

'Well, that bird-watching blokey came in babbling something about this soldier jumping off the top. Then it turned out he hadn't actually seen him go. Just found his clothes.'

'Which he brought to you?'

'Major's get-up. Sixteenth Lancers. At least, that's what the collar-badges said.'

79

'No sign of damage? A struggle? Nothing torn?'

'No.' Padstow turned to begin the long trudge back from the pier, 'nothing like that. Well, it *was* a bit odd, so I went out there with a sergeant and a couple of the lads. One of the lads went up top and when the tide permitted, the rest of us went along the bottom.'

'And nothing? You're sure?'

'Positive, sir,' Padstow assured him, 'and I've seen some remains in my time. One bloke drove a horse and cart over there once.'

'No!' Lestrade was appalled.

'Milkman down on his luck,' the Inspector said. 'You've never seen such a mess. My lads were picking glass out of themselves for weeks.'

Lestrade went back with his man to Eastbourne nick. There had been a telegram from a Chief Superintendent Abberline at Scotland Yard. On no account was the case to be followed up. Neither was it to appear in the *Eastbourne Gazette and Bugle*. The clothes of the man were to be carefully placed under lock and key and no one was to do anything until the said Mr Abberline arrived. That had been ten days ago. Since then, nothing.

Lestrade knew that the nothing had been occasioned by Abberline's collapse and in the interim, the Sussex police had kept a fairly firm lid on matters. Nothing it seemed had leaked to the press. As long as Mr Runton the bird watcher kept his mouth shut, all would be well.

Lestrade bought a pair of binoculars in the town and filled in the necessary triplicate sheets for the peace of mind of Major Woodhouse. He signed the register of Duntourin', a particularly seedy hotel, with vicious staircarpet, to the west of the Wish Tower, whose guns had once stood ready against the impending French invasion of Bonaparte and his grumblers. He spent the long spring night in the confines of his little attic room, listening to the rain drip on to the floorboards. He eased the skin off his cocoa, the one brought by the harridan with somebody else's teeth, and tried to tie together what he had. On the wall in front of him, where a particularly awful-looking farmhouse was nestling on a Sussex hillside and smelly-looking cattle were winding homeward o'er the lea, Lestrade had pinned a series of hastily scribbled notes to himself.

'Captain Orange', he began talking to himself in the lamplight, 'and his three nieces. Died as a result of a driving accident on Friday morning. A tall man seen near the house prior to the trap setting off. Hames cut nearly through. An African mirror found on the Captain's body.'

He slurped his cocoa.

'Janet Calthrop. History student. Found at the bottom of a staircase in King's College, her skull fractured, her neck broken. Apparently accidental, but signs of pushing and a tripwire across the stairs. Found dead on . . . Friday morning. A broken mirror in the little love-nest she and her lover used.'

He shot a glance at the third piece of paper, 'Major John Thomas Somebody-or-Other. Apparent suicide off Beachy Head. Friday morning. A mirror found in his tunic. So . . .' he got off the bed and hauled on his braces again, rubbing his eyes and his moustache to force himself to stay awake, 'what have we got, Lestrade?'

'Oh, for God's sake,' he scolded himself silently, 'I'm talking to myself, now. See; told you I was. What have we got, then?' He continued the conversation in silence. Five deaths and one supposed death, all on Fridays. A great deal of trouble gone to, to make five of the deaths look like accidents. And the sixth? Well, the sixth was a curiosity. A suicide from a spot where suicides were commonplace. Lestrade himself had felt the urge of gravity on that desolate headland. And yet the lack of a corpse, delicti or otherwise, unnerved him. It was curiously frustrating, like a sentence without an end or a tune somebody stops humming in the middle. It didn't suit his superiors at the Yard, with their bureaucratic love of dotting ayes and crossing tees. Yet Campbell-Bannerman and King Alfonso and even dim, unsuspecting, hypocritical old Abberline had provided Lestrade with a link. Was John Thomas his man? Had he, from some warped, Spanish motive, hacked the harness straps of Orange's cart? Had he fixed the putty-held tripwire across the stairs in King's and waited in the shadows to precip . . . pretic . . . bring about Janet Calthrop's fall from grace? And had the horror of his crimes so unhinged him that he had stripped himself of the British uniform he had so disgraced and plunged five hundred and thirty-four feet to a watery grave? Perhaps. There again, perhaps not. Lestrade caught sight of his reflection in a glass to his left, the sallow face, the haunted eyes.

'Mirror, mirror, on the wall,' he said, 'who's the guiltiest of them all?'

The surf roared at his feet and he heard the gulls scream as they wheeled above. There was a man below, they'd noticed with their keen, sea-scavenging eyes. A small man, in old-fashioned clothes. An off-duty undertaker, perhaps. Or a Board School Teacher unaware that they'd set up Education Authorities four years ago. Not a policeman, surely, struggling with the morass of murder? Anyway, perhaps he'd drop some crumbs. They swooped to investigate and spotted his bowler again as they flew.

He stepped aside from the crashing spume, shaking his suddenly damp right leg, and trained his binoculars on the white cliffs above. Yesterday he had looked down from that height and it seemed the sea had beckoned him. Now as he saw the clouds drift on a bed of blue and felt the May sunshine warm the earth, it seemed that Beachy Head itself would topple towards him, burying for ever a Superintendent of the Metropolitan Police.

Yes. There. There it was. What? Six, seven feet from the rim? A ledge where the terns nested. You couldn't see it from the top. He was sure of that. It looked narrow. What? Eight, nine inches wide? Difficult to gauge from here. But a mountain goat could do it. Or an ibex. Or a man, perhaps, who wanted to disappear. To disappear for just long enough to send a bird watcher off on a wild goose chase. Then haul himself back up in his combinations and away. But what if he'd been seen? Men didn't wander the Sussex Downs in broad daylight in their underwear. Not without somebody seeing them anyway. Or arresting them. No, he shook his head. It didn't make any sense. Perhaps the Spaniard had wings. He watched the herring-gulls wheel and glide. Then the ruins caught his eye and on a whim, he trudged towards them.

The sea was on his left now and the surf racing to the shore, stretching itself to curl and froth at his heels, hissing back on the shingle in its disappointment. Missed him again, it seemed to say. Next time. Next time. And the next wave launched its attack.

He left the beach. He left the sea, the dry pebbles crunching and rolling under his feet. At the hairpin bend on the coast road above him, he caught the rickety wooden rail of the steep steps, rising at crazy angles to the cliff tops, thirty feet up. Once, twice his boots slipped and his back jarred and his heart leapt. Then he was there, the grey shell of the old lighthouse called Belle Tout ahead of him, its tiny windows black holes, its once white-painted stones lying like broken teeth in the carpets of sea-lavender. He clambered over the parapet, careful to avoid the nettles that clung stubbornly to the mortar, unbent by wind, unmoved by rain.

A recently carved line in the stone informed him that Willie loves Fanny; but he knew that already. A less recent carving read 'Gladstone must go'. He knew that too – the Grand Old Man had gone in the full panoply of black eight years ago. Lestrade would not look on his like again. But it wasn't British graffiti that held his interest, nor the smell of urine in one dark corner. It was the hand that lay on the ground, the fingers curling to him in a mockery of life. Come on, they said. This way. This way to the peep show. Come and see who I was.

He knocked aside the rubble, flung aside the planks, hauled at the larger stones. What was left of a rather haughty young man lay in his grey combinations, a black velvet patch over his left eye. His mouth hung open, his good eye still staring at the ceiling above, the collapse of which seemed to account for his being here. Across his chest, a battered board with the barely legible legend, 'Danger. Keep Out'.

'Well, John Thomas,' Lestrade whispered, 'you should have watched your step.'

What was it Campbell-Bannerman had said? Perhaps it was his one eye that explained what had happened to him. Didn't he see the sign? Didn't he see the masonry and timber above him? Didn't he see the figure above it, perhaps a crowbar in his hand? The same figure who had stripped him of his uniform and gone walkabout to the top of Beachy Head? Who had waited until some wandering bird watcher had seen him and had pretended to jump? Why? Why? Why? And why, as Lestrade brushed the brickwork and dust from the dead man's leg, had the murderer left the dead man's boots behind? Campbell-Bannerman had been right twice in one day – the game *was* afoot.

'Well, I'll be buggered!' Padstow peered at the waxy features, 'Belle Tout. My lads and I never thought of looking there. Looks as if the sky fell on him. Shall I get a doctor?'

'He's dead, Inspector,' Lestrade was wringing out his right sock and thanking God it was his left one that had the hole.

'No, I mean, to do the post-mortem.'

'No,' Lestrade said quickly, 'I've got orders to keep things under my hat. So have you – now. Let's keep it to the few who were involved before that anonymous officer of Lancers took his own life off Beachy Head while the balance of his mind – and come to think of it, his body – was disturbed, shall we? Those two constables who helped us get him here?'

'"Biff" and "Boff"? Deaf mutes, both of 'em. Look, Superintendent, I'm not a naturally curious man. An unkind person might say that's why I never got higher than inspector in the East Sussex Constabulary, but I can't help wondering all the same – who *is* Dead Eye Dick here?'

Lestrade looked his man in both eyes. 'Believe me, Inspector, it's better you don't know. Just parcel him up and get him on the next train to London, will you? And mark it "Fragile. This Way Up". I'll do the rest.'

Lestrade had visited the Duke of York's Barracks before, an eternity ago when he went to arrest Colonel Valentine Baker for exposing himself on a train to Liphook. Lestrade had some sympathy for the man – he too had been to Liphook.

The smell was the same. Ammonia and pipe clay. The thud of the caracoling horses redolent of the tan he remembered from his days with George Sanger's circus when Disraeli had been Prime Minister and young Sergeant Lestrade didn't know a police speed trap from his elbow. He watched the four young men in their snug scarlet stable jackets, hooked in gold lace to the chin. They bounced past him in single file, their knees gripped to their chargers' barrels, their arms outstretched, like so many riding scarecrows through the morning sun.

'I was looking for Captain Fannin,' he called through a shaft of sunlight.

'You've found him,' an auburn-haired officer lowered his arms and wheeled his animal to amble up to Lestrade. What with the scarlet stable dress and the red hair, the man looked like a carrot. 'You must be the chappie from Fortnum's. Where's the hamper?'

'No, sir. I am the chappie from Scotland Yard.'

'Oh, really,' Fannin swung a pantalooned leg over his horse's glossy, arched neck, 'I didn't realize we'd changed caterers.'

'No, sir,' Lestrade instinctively backed away as the animal began to chew his Donegal flaps, 'I am a policeman, investigating the murder of Juan Tomas de . . . Thing.'

'What?' another horseman reined in and sprung down from the saddle, 'Tom? Murder, did you say?'

'I believe so, Lieutenant . . . er . . . ?'

'Harkness,' the newcomer handed his mount's reins to a groom, 'I say, you chaps; over here. Poor old Tom's bought it.'

The other two officers joined the group, 'Tom?' one of them repeated, 'bought it? Good God!'

'I suppose this means no hamper,' Captain Fannin muttered.

'Oh, shut up, Fanny, this is hardly the time,' Harkness said.

'Just remember these little beauties,' Fannin pointed to the three silver stars on his shoulder cord.

'In the Mess, old boy, we're all equals, you know that,' the third officer said, 'and I suspect we're *all* in rather a mess at the moment. You're Sholto Lestrade, aren't you?'

'I am,' Lestrade's suspicious old eyes narrowed. He took in the ox-like shoulders, the barrel chest, the tapering hips. 'Have we met?' There was something about the shifty eyes he didn't like.

'No, but I feel I've known you all my life. I'm Archie Bandicoot, Harry's smarter cousin.'

'Cousin Archie!' Lestrade shook the lad's hand warmly,

feeling his fingers sag in the grip, 'Harry's always talking about you.'

'Is he really?'

'Well . . . no, but he *has* mentioned you. You've got an estate in Norfolk, haven't you?'

'Suffolk. Stoke by Nayland.'

'Of course. You went to Eton, like Harry.'

'Harrow, unlike Harry.'

'Right,' Lestrade clicked his thumb and index finger, cursing his forgetfulness. 'Played scrum half for the First Eleven.'

'Wing three-quarter for the First Fifteen.'

'Well, never mind,' Lestrade patted the lad's shoulder, 'still a pretty exclusive number, Fifteen. You went to . . . Cambridge.'

'Oxford,' Bandicoot corrected him, 'Brasenose.'

For a moment, Lestrade wondered whether young Bandicoot was being offensive, then he dismissed it, especially as Captain Fannin was thwacking his thigh with his riding crop in some irritation. 'Have you come to interrogate us, then, Mr Lestrade?'

'No, sir,' the Superintendent said, 'merely to ask some questions.'

'Well, preternaturally saddened as I am by the news of poor old Tom, you'll have to talk to us while we shower.'

'Shower?'

''Fraid so, old boy,' the fourth horseman of the apocalypse had joined them now, '"Goughy"'s new orders.'

'"Goughy"?'

'Herbert Gough, VC. The Old Man. Nice enough old boy, but a stickler for steam baths. Believes that cleanliness is next to something-or-other. I'm George "Tippy" Hedron, by the way,' he glanced at Bandicoot, 'and I don't have a stupid cousin. Mind holding my towel once we're inside?'

Lestrade in fact held all four towels, each of them beautifully embroidered with the regimental device of the Sixteenth Lancers. He looked rather like an umpire at Lords, swathed in other people's jumpers. Batmen clashed hither and yon, carrying shaving tackle and sponging stains from jackets with a mixture of breadcrumbs and tartar sauce. The superintendent dutifully turned his back while four naked officers of the Lancers nipped gingerly through the hissing streams of hot water, angled above and from the sides. He noted with empathy the height at which the holes were drilled around the walls and was glad he was standing outside and still wearing his Donegal.

'Where's the soap?' a temporarily-blinded 'Tippy' Hedron called through the fog of steam.

'Yes, doesn't it,' the others chorused and proceeded to guffaw loudly, reminding Lestrade yet again why he hadn't joined the cavalry. That and the fact that he couldn't ride.

'Tell us about poor old Tom, then, Sholto,' Bandicoot said, soaping his chest and freeing his armpits to the steam.

'You first,' Lestrade called, 'what sort of man was he?'

'Sort of . . . foreign,' Fannin said. 'Supernumerary sort of chappie. Strictly ex-officio. Honorary type. Not a bad rider, though.'

'Why was he here?' the superintendent asked.

'Diplomatic mission,' Harkness spat water at Lestrade's back. 'He's a sort of go-between on behalf of King Alfonso and dear old Ena. Mind you . . .'

'Yes?' Lestrade asked.

'Oh . . . nothing. Look, Lestrade,' the lieutenant emerged from the steam, carrying his all before him, 'I really think we deserve to know what happened to old "Piercer", you know.'

'Piercer?' Lestrade turned, blushed and turned back again.

'One eye. Used to be referred to as a piercer in the old days. At least when my old pa was in the Sixteenth.'

'Do you know how he lost his eye, Mr Harkness?'

'Congenital, apparently.'

'Duel, he told me,' Hedron called, 'over a woman.'

'I got the wild stallion bit,' Bandicoot swept past and removed a towel from Lestrade. 'Of course, I didn't buy it for a moment. A stallion as wild as the one he described would have taken his head off, not merely poked his eye out.'

'Well, somebody had a damned good try to do that the other day,' Lestrade said.

'I thought he was just lying low somewhere,' Fannin took his towel and wrapped it around him, 'some woman, I understand. Kept, I think.'

'By Jesus de Zolep?' Lestrade asked.

'By anyone, was the impression I got. Tippy, you saw her, didn't you?'

'Oh, only once,' Hedron said, 'only from a distance. Nothing to write home about.'

'Do you know this lady's name, sir?' the superintendent had learned long ago that if a femme was involved, she needed cherching.

'No,' Hedron was combing his little moustache in a mirror, 'not a clue.'

'A roof fell on your friend,' Lestrade told them. 'Oh, a partially ruined roof, I'll grant you, but a roof, none the less.'

'Good God,' Fannin stopped brushing his hair, 'Marsh, where's my dressing-gown?' His batman appeared with a scarlet dressing-gown and gold-laced slippers. 'Where was this, Lestrade?'

'In a ruined lighthouse, sir, near Beachy Head.'

'Beachy Head?' Bandicoot repeated.

'Does that strike a chord with you, Archie?' Lestrade asked, handing Harkness his towel and admiring his pectorals.

'No . . . no, not really. Will you join us for breakfast, Sholto? My man Godfrey is a whizz at the devilled kidneys.'

'Thank you, no. I was hoping that one of you gentlemen might give me some kind of clue as to the kind of man he was. May I see his rooms?'

'Er . . . well . . . I don't see why not,' Fannin said, 'you being an officer of the law sort of chappie.'

'I'm not sure old Goughy would like it,' Hedron said.

'Since when did that bother you, Tippy?' Bandicoot thwacked the man with his dressing-gown belt. 'Hey, Sholto, just let me get my Walking Outs on and I'll take you across.'

'Breakfast, chaps?' Fannin asked the others, angling his gold-tasselled smoking cap above the auburn hair.

'Rather,' Harkness said, 'I could eat a horse – only don't tell Big Boy that.'

The others chuckled. 'Oh Lor',' Hedron said, 'I haven't sent that telegram to the old man – you know, the one acknowledging my undying gratitude for my allowance. I'd better do that. See you in the Refec. chaps. Goodbye, Mr

Lestrade,' he shook the Superintendent's hand, 'it's been . . . an experience.' And, like the late Juan Tomas de Jesus-Lopez, he vanished.

'Bally Hell!' an astonished lieutenant of the Lancers stood in his serge frock in the doorway of Juan Tomas de Jesus-Lopez's rooms, 'sloppy lot, the Dagos.'

'That's as may be,' Lestrade nodded grimly, 'but this place has been turned over.'

'Turned over?'

'Ransacked. And recently,' he pointed to the swinging light. 'The question is, why?'

Bandicoot shrugged. 'Someone was looking for something.'

Lestrade smiled knowingly. 'You're right, Archie. You *are* smarter than your cousin. You've been here before, of course.'

'Oh yes, on and off. Tom joined the regiment six months ago. Played a mean hand of vingt-et-un.'

'For money?' Lestrade asked.

'Is there any other reason to play vingt-et-un?'

'So you know the layout of this room fairly well, having sat in it playing cards?'

'Fairly well, yes.'

'Any idea where he kept his valuables?'

'Ah, as a matter of fact, I have.' He led the way through the wrecked study, kicking a few rattan chairs aside. The bedroom was as bad, the mattress ripped and feathers fluttering as they walked. 'They've given the guzunda a helluva licking,' Bandicoot said.

Lestrade glanced at the shattered porcelain at his feet and was glad that Bandicoot was speaking metaphysically.

'But . . . aha,' the Lieutenant hauled back a piece of regimental Wilton that graced the floor, 'our friend didn't find this.'

'Or didn't have time,' Lestrade mused as Bandicoot jerked up a floorboard.

'Look, officers and gentlemen and all that, Sholto. I can't rifle a chap's things without his express permission.'

'Well,' Lestrade knelt at the officer's feet, 'he's certainly not going to give you that,' and he thrust an arm into the dusty void. Out came a case, ornamentally chased. Then a small box, padlocked, 'I have to ask you, Archie, how you know about this.'

'Simple. There's a mirror next door – or there was before someone smashed it . . .'

'A mirror?' Lestrade raised an eyebrow.

'Yes, you know. A glass thing. For looking into. I noticed that one night, when Tom wasn't doing too well – luck not being a lady for him – he went to replenish his funds. When I looked in the mirror, I could see him digging down there. He'd forgotten to close the door.'

'Did anyone else see this?'

'I'm not sure, but we had a little laugh about it, so everyone knew.'

'Who was there?'

'The four of us, I think – we're usually together – Fanny Fannin, Harky Harkness, Tippy Hedron and I.'

'Bandy Bandicoot?' Lestrade smiled.

'How did you know?' the lieutenant brought his knees together sharply. 'Ah, of course. Harry. Wait 'til I see him next. I say, Sholto, is that quite cricket?'

'No,' Lestrade explained, a look of intense concentration on his face, 'it's a switchblade knife and it . . . usually . . . opens . . . uggh . . . locks!' This time was no exception. The ornamentally-chased lid flew up to reveal a pair of magnificent pistols, of Miquelet type, beautifully damascened in silver.

'Well,' Bandicoot sucked his teeth, 'I bet our untidy friend was sorry he didn't get his hands on those.'

'No,' Lestrade shook his head, 'I don't think that's what he had in mind at all.' He clicked the blade's point into the lock on the strongbox and jerked it quickly to one side. It flew off with a clatter to the floor.

'How do you do that?' Bandicoot asked.

'Trade secret,' Lestrade said, 'I once spent eighteen hours handcuffed to Jonah "The Pick" Wallace. We had to find something to talk about. Aha!' His eyes lit upon a small bundle of papers tied with a red ribbon. 'Archie,' he said, 'I suspect someone of your age, looks and intentions will know more about this than I do. Sniff that lot.'

Bandicoot took the bundle, 'Hmm,' he said, '"Be Gentle With Me".'

'I beg your pardon?'

'It's a perfume, Sholto. I believe it's made by A'bbatoir de Paris. Very expensive.'

'Is it?' Lestrade took the bundle back.

'So,' Bandicoot flopped on to the bed and a cloud of feathers burst skywards. 'We were right, then. An affair of the heart. Who was she, this Juliet of a night?'

'Oh, my God,' Lestrade's face fell. The letterhead aroused his suspicions. The signature confirmed them.

'Not Mrs Lestrade, surely?' Bandicoot grinned.

'My wife died thirteen years ago, Archie.'

'Oh, of course. Sorry, Sholto. So who are the letters from?'

Lestrade looked up at his man. 'From a young lady not a million miles away from the throne of England,' he said softly. 'Better not enquire further, Mr Bandicoot. I'm not sure you have the clearance.'

One top-hatted toff turned to the other. 'Who's that up there in the Landau with Kingy?'

The second toff consulted his hunter. 'Can't be his lunch, it's only ten thirty-eight.'

'Haw, haw. That's rather good. One of yours?'

'I fear not,' his friend told him. 'Actually I heard it, or at least a variant of it from a little chap in Teddington the other day. A seven year old called Coward. Not bad for a seven year old, is it? Ever heard of him?'

'No,' the first toff said, 'but then I haven't really heard of Teddington, either. Good morning, sir,' and they raised their toppers as His Majesty's carriage swept past.

'Afficionados of the Turf, Lestrade,' the king said, acknowledging them with a nod. 'My, but I enjoy being King-Emperor! You don't feel uncomfortable at all, do you?'

'Good Lord, no, sir,' Lestrade eased his jodhpurs aside.

'I mean, I know you're a trifle tall for a jockey, but since you're sitting down, nobody'll notice, will they?'

'Er . . . probably not, sir. No.'

'Anyway, you're in my colours, so no one will find it remotely suspicious. Just the foremost thoroughbred owner in the country chatting away with one of his jockeys on an Ascot afternoon. What could be more natural? By the way, could you adjust your cap? The peak should be at the front.'

'Ah, yes, of course.' He swivelled the silk accordingly. Edward VII was a stickler when it came to dress.

'Don't worry about the driver,' the king waved vaguely in the man's direction, 'deaf as a postillion. Goes with the job. Well, well, we've come a long way since the Ball of Lightning.'

'We have, sir. 1891.'

'Ah, a golden year. Still got your OM?'

'Of course, sir,' Lestrade frowned, 'it has pride of place on my mantelpiece.'

'Good. I just thought . . . what with times being hard, so they tell me, and the paucity of police pay and so on . . . Still, to business. Cigar?'

'Thank you, sir, but I don't expect jockeys do, do they?'

'No, probably not. Does something to their equilibrium.' He puffed at his own. 'Don't fret yourself, Lestrade, I'm not so rotund as not to be able to light my own Havana. I won't beat about the bush,' he tipped his hat to parasolled ladies as the open Landau swept past them. 'My God, look at the bustle on that.'

Lestrade winced.

'Little Ena,' the king said.

'Sir?'

'Beatrice's daughter,' the king explained. 'My niece. Pretty little filly. Headstrong, though. Needs a good snaffle.'

'If you say so, sir,' Lestrade shrugged. His tan-topped boots were killing him.

'And then there's George, the Prince of Wales,' His Majesty sighed. 'We've got one of those telephone thingies at the palace, of course.'

'Very useful, sir.'

'Yes, indeed, but do you know, I've never once caught him in deep, intimate conversation with anyone apart from his wife. Honestly, I do despair, sometimes . . .'

'I'm sorry, sir,' Lestrade leaned forward, his back to the horses, 'I don't think I follow this conversation.'

'Children,' the king said. 'Do you have any?'

'A daughter, sir.'

'Yes, well, there you are. Good girl?'

'The best, sir.' He remembered the last time he'd seen her. She'd caught him a nasty one on the ankle with a croquet mallet.

'No doubt, no doubt. But there you have it. George is straight as a die. As a rakish monarch, he'll make a bloody good chartered accountant. But Ena . . . well.'

'Well, sir?' Lestrade's eyes narrowed.

'Why did you want to see her?' the king blew smoke in his face.

'A delicate matter, Your Majesty.'

'"Matters" usually are, Lestrade, in my experience. But her papa's dead. I had this missive from Beatrice, saying that some police chappie had called to the house. I instinctively knew it was you.'

'I'm flattered, sir,' Lestrade smiled.

'Don't be,' the king scowled, 'I don't approve, Lestrade. I don't approve at all. This could be another Tranby Croft.'

'Perhaps you'd better tell me what you know, sir?' the superintendent suggested.

'You first, Lestrade. I'm the king.'

'Very well, sir. I found a bundle of letters on Buckingham Palace notepaper and signed by Princess Ena.'

'I see. And to whom were they addressed?'

'A cavalry captain in the Sixteenth Lancers.'

'A supernumerary dago, by any chance?'

Lestrade nodded. 'The same.'

'De Jesus-Lopez,' the king growled.

'Did you know him, sir?'

'Of course. I am paterfamilias, Lestrade, as well as the king. When I'm not at race meetings, I'm supervising the international marriage arrangements of my relatives. De Jesus-Lopez was over here as liaison officer with the regiment of which my future nephew-in-law is Colonel-in-Chief; if that isn't too Irish.'

93

Lestrade had assumed the man was Spanish, but he wasn't going to labour the point.

'Then he was daft enough to let a roof fall on him, I understand from my aides.'

'The question, Your Majesty, is . . . did it fall or was it pushed?'

'Oh dear,' the king frowned, 'this is worse than I thought.'

'I have reason to believe', Lestrade tried not to shout over the rattle of the wheels and the jingle of the harness, 'that Princess Ena had formed an attachment to this Spanish gentleman. They were, in the parlour of today's youth – and yesterday's, come to think of it – having an affair.'

Edward the king sighed again, drumming the side of the Landau with his stubby fingers and with frustration, 'I suspected as much,' he said, scanning the paddock lined with cheering crowds. 'It's all right in a Prince of Wales – expected even. Look at me for all those years. But in a young, beautiful, female member of the Royal Family, well, it's not done, Lestrade. It simply isn't done . . . I say, you don't . . . you don't think little Ena had a hand in it, do you? De Jesus-Lopez's death, I mean. You know – to shut him up.' The poppy eyes opened wide, the blubbery lips hung slack.

'No, no, sir,' Lestrade smiled, 'I don't think that. But Princess Ena might know a man who can help me with my inquiries. Unless I am allowed to speak to her privately, I'll never know. And a shadow will lie for ever over her forthcoming marriage.'

'Hmm,' the king chewed his lip. It was the sort of thing kings did when they worried. Richard III was always doing it, apparently. 'Very well, I'll allow it. But Beatrice must be there at all times. For all her diminutive stature, she knows a compromising question when she hears one. Driver, drop this chappie off, will you, before somebody asks him to get saddled up.'

Princess Beatrice, she of the Isle of Wight Rifles, sat beside the fire-dogs while a Superintendent of Police wound her wool for her. With his hands in that position, he might have been boasting again, but the mood was too sombre;

he topic too serious. After all, the royal wedding was only a month away.

'Well,' she raised her poppy eyes from the skein to the superintendent, 'if Bertie wishes it, then it must be so. He 's the King-Emperor, you know.' She said it as though trying to convince herself. 'You're about my age, Superintendent,' she narrowed her gaze at him, 'albeit the years have not been so kind. Even so, do you have children?'

'A daughter, Ma'am,' Lestrade told her. It seemed that the entire Royal Family had one topic of conversation.

'A good girl?'

'The best,' he assured her, feeling again the sickening pain shoot up his leg from the memory of the croquet mallet.

Princess Beatrice leaned forward, taking the wool from him. Just you be gentle with mine,' she whispered.

Perhaps the old Battenburg had the ears of a pipistrelle. Certainly, Lestrade hadn't heard the girl's approach. Yet here she was, what? eighteen? nineteen? Striking-looking filly for all she had her grandmother's eyes. Thank God she hadn't got her grandmother's girth.

'Superintendent Lestrade?' she smiled, 'I am Princess Victoria Eugenie, but you can call me Ena.'

'Ena!' her mother sucked in her breath and nearly swallowed a rope of pearls.

'Oh, Mama, this is 1906. We Royals must come off our pedestal at some point. Champagne, Mr Lestrade?' She tugged a bell-pull beside the huge, empty fireplace.

'It is a little early for me, Ma'am,' he told her.

'And for you, too, Ena. Now this nice gentleman wants to ask you some questions. I shall be just outside the door, should you need me.'

'Questions?' Ena frowned, 'what about? If it's that awful little statue at Sandringham, the frost cracked it.'

'No, Ma'am,' Lestrade said, 'it's not the statue . . .'

They stood in silence until it hurt so much that Princess Beatrice gathered up her voluminous skirts and left. 'Just outside the door, mind,' she said.

Ena threw herself back on to the *chaise-longue* and unpinned her golden hair so that it tumbled over her mutton-chop shoulders. 'Got a ciggie, Mr Lestrade? The equerries are getting frightfully stingy with them.'

'Er . . . no, Ma'am,' Lestrade was down to his last cheroot. And anyway, this woman was a niece of a king and would soon be a queen in her own right. She could afford her own, 'I have been trying to see you for several days,' he told her.

'Have you?' she grimaced. 'How exciting. But look, if it's about the personal detective job, I'm afraid that's been filled. Superintendent Quinn of the Special Branch . . .'

'. . . is an idiot and an incompetent. Yes, Ma'am, I know, but don't worry. I'm sure the man he has picked for you will be fine. No,' he had the brass neck to sit beside her, 'the matter I have to discuss with you is of the utmost delicacy.'

'Indeed?'

There was a knock on the door.

'Yes?' she frowned.

A poppy-eyed head popped around the door. 'That was Rigby with your champagne. I just popped my head around the door to tell you I've sent him away. Your father would be horrified.'

The door slammed again.

'My father died at sea, Superintendent,' Ena said wistfully, 'of a fever caught in the Ashanti War. We all loved him dearly, of course, but Mama . . . well, you know how this family wears its grief. Grandmama wore mourning for forty years after the death of Grandpapa.'

'And you, Ma'am,' Lestrade raised an inquisitorial eyebrow, 'for how long will you wear it?'

'What do you mean?' she sat bolt upright, blinking.

He reached inside his jacket and produced a bundle of letters bound in a red ribbon.

'Where did you get these?' She snatched them from him, then rose sharply and her teeth bit her lip to stop herself from crying. Then he was beside her. 'You knew Juan Tomas de Jesus-Lozep?'

'Yes,' she said, staring fixedly at the lawns beyond the maze where gardeners toiled in the spring sunshine, the sun glancing off their scythes, 'you might say that.'

'Might I also say that you were . . . friends?'

She turned to him, her face dark with anger, her grey eyes flashing. 'You've read the letters, of course.' It was a statement, not a question.

He nodded.

'Then you know – in the Biblical sense. Tell me,' she wanted to hurt someone, anyone. This battered, parchment-faced old policeman would do, 'do you detectives always ask questions to which you already know the answers?'

'You are to be married next month,' he said, 'to the King of Spain.'

'And I've been to bed with his aide-de-camp. Go on, say it!' She clenched her fists and stared him down.

'I don't have to,' he said, 'the letters said it all.'

She whirled away from him, then threw herself down and cried into the bolster of the *chaise-longue*. Lestrade crossed the room in three strides and locked the door, then knelt beside the sobbing princess.

'You don't understand,' she felt his hand on her shoulder. 'It wasn't like that. I *loved* him, Superintendent. I've only met King Alfonso once – and I wasn't very impressed, to tell you the truth. He's a crashing bore and seems to think the height of entertainment is to watch grown men sticking sharp things into defenceless bulls. I could see that in Smithfield every day of the week. But Tom . . . he was different.' She sat up, smiling through her tears. 'Kind and gentle. We . . . we didn't mean to. We only . . . slept together once. But,' her face crumpled again, 'I did love him, Superintendent. I still do. And through all my years as Queen of Spain, I always will.'

He nodded, drying her eyes with his handkerchief, 'I must ask you to look at these letters,' he said.

'Look at them?' she sniffed. 'Why?'

'Because they may have been the reason for Major de Zolep's death.'

She blinked back more tears, 'I couldn't bear that,' she said. 'To think that I should have been the cause . . .'

'Please, Madam,' he said, untying the ribbon for her, 'look at them for me . . . for him.'

She looked into the dark eyes of the Superintendent. There

97

was a sadness there, every bit as real as hers, and she did as he asked.

'I wrote them,' she said, 'but I thought . . .'

'Yes?'

'Mr Lestrade,' she looked into the eyes again, 'oh, Mr Lestrade, you must be the soul of discretion.'

'Of course,' he nodded solemnly.

'You see before you a silly slip of a thing, naïve, over-fond, headstrong perhaps . . .'

'Tsk, tsk,' he fluttered his hands and shook his head.

'But I am a Coburg too. And I know my duty. Not a word of this must come out. God, if Mama knew. And Uncle Bertie.'

She shuddered, her hands clasped tightly around the letters.

'I think you'll find they're more understanding than you know,' he smiled. 'Now, to the letters.'

'Why did you bring only a sample?'

'A sample?'

'There are only four letters. I wrote twenty-three to Tom.'

'Twenty-three?'

'One for each week that I'd known him. To write more often was too risky. I had to wait until there was an official despatch; then I sneaked one in.'

'Each one of them drenched in your perfume?'

'"Drenched" is a little strong, Mr Lestrade,' the princess said. '"Drizzled" would be better.'

'"Be Gentle With Me" by A'bbatoir of Paris?'

'Why, yes,' Ena was impressed. 'You detective chappies certainly know your job.'

'It's nothing, Madam,' Lestrade said. 'But I wonder why Major de Jesuz-Losep should have kept only these four?'

'He didn't. He kept all twenty-three.'

'But . . .'

'He was being blackmailed, Superintendent,' the Princess told him, calmer now and more herself. 'He told me about it.'

'He did?'

'The night we . . . the night I saw him last, here, at Buckingham Palace. He was obliged to buy the letters back, one by one, after some cad had stolen them. He was being bled dry, Superintendent, but what could he do? His sense of duty was as great as mine. We could no more report it than fly to the moon.'

'Did he say who it was? The blackmailer?'

She shook her head. 'Only that it was the last person he would have suspected. The situation was fraught with danger. All he could do was to pay the wretched man's squalid price . . . and I promised to write no more. Oh, Superintendent,' she held his lapels as he rose to go, 'I loved him. Loved him to distraction. Did I . . . did I kill him, too? I and those foolish, foolish letters?'

He held both her hands in his, 'No, Madam,' he smiled, 'you didn't. Sadly, as yet, I don't know the man who did. May I suggest that you dry your eyes and hide those letters once and for all? A fire, perhaps?'

There was a furious rattle at the double doors, then a violent tapping.

'Ena,' they heard a muffled voice call, 'open this door! What's going on?'

He patted her hand and broke the protocol of centuries by reaching down and kissing her forehead. Then he crossed the room in five or six strides and unlocked the door.

Princess Beatrice, never one to fail to mix it, had been squaring up, in the absence of a flunkey, to shoulder-barge the door. As it was, she hurtled past Lestrade, slid on the polished floors, somersaulted gracefully over the *chaise-longue* and caught herself a prostrating one on the brass fire-irons.

'Tsk, tsk,' muttered Lestrade, 'when you're better, Ma'am, I really think you should have this door catch seen to. Sticks like buggery. Good morning.'

Sir Daniel looked at himself in the mirror as he had each morning for the past thirty-four years. He turned to the left, then to the right. He took the metal object in his hand, checked the rheostat device and applied it to his skin. It smarted a little, but then, no pain, no gain. And a man singularly endowed with the Whiddon good looks couldn't afford to let blemishes grow. What had Muschik said? 'The removal of freckles and wrinkles guaranteed'? 'The restoration of the chemical tension of flabby and degenerate skin'? Well, nothing flabby or degenerate about

Sir Daniel. Not yet, anyway. But better to strike while the iron was hot. No sense in degenerating when Muschik's Appliance for Face Massage was on the market.

Suddenly, he switched it off. Otto Muschik had said nothing about his little contraption causing the headaches. Sir Daniel hooked the gadget back on its stand and reached instinctively for the other appliance lying on the dressing-table. He placed the iron frame around his head and sat down on the upright chair. He squeezed with his hand as the pneumatic pads began to press his temples. He moaned softly as the third nudged the back of his head. The pressure grew as the pads tightened, causing him to close his eyes. What a wonderful inventor Shanker Abaji Bhisey was. He could feel his head going as he sat there.

Then he stopped sitting there. Whiddon was upright again, Bhisey's contraption flung aside. He stared in the mirror in disbelief. It couldn't be. But it was. He was only thirty-four ... well, all right, forty-one. But that was nothing. Old Parr, it was said, had been one hundred and fifty-two when he died. And Gladstone couldn't have been far short of that. Yet there were distinct signs of it. An incipient double chin. The question was: should Sir Daniel avail himself of the appliance on his left, patented by Adelaide Turner née Claxton Ye Denne of Chiswick; or that on his right, by that well-known surgical appliance manufacturer, Mary Fava Pollock of Brockley? He was still deciding, when he felt his old trouble coming on. He glanced down at his naked body; then at the clock. It was only four thirty in the morning. The water closet was only yards away. But that wasn't the point. His body was a ravening beast to be tamed. His old nanny had taught him that. Accordingly, he reached for the little metal object he kept in the bottom left-hand drawer. He took a deep breath and applied it, shuddering as the cold metal met his skin. Then he screwed the threaded nut at the top and the clamp began to bite and the burning in his bladder ceased, his muscles relaxing. One last turn of the screw should do it.

He screamed as he felt the searing pain. He screamed again as his blood sprayed in an arc over the mirror. Then he slid to the floor. And the screaming stopped.

5

He guessed that the batman had put the late Major de Jesus-Lopez's rooms to rights. All was neatly stashed away, pillows and mattresses replaced. He pressed the key into the lock and put his weight against it. All right, so he'd missed them before; but he'd been in a hurry, thanks to that damned fool detective. He was pretty sure that de Jesus-Lopez still kept them – the letters he'd bought back. He prided himself on being a good judge of men. De Jesus-Lopez was vain and not a little sharp in the card school, but he was also incurably romantic and as silly in his own hidalgo way as the spoiled little vixen he was poking.

Well, he had plenty of time now, but he couldn't risk a light. These rooms had been sealed off and the regiment was polishing its metalware for tomorrow's funeral. He'd be there himself, pious, noble, grieving for a fellow officer. And he was grieving too, because somebody had stoved in the dago's head and that meant that there were still nineteen damaging letters unclaimed – and unpaid for. He was considerably out of pocket. That was cause for grief. Perhaps if he approached Princess Ena, though, all would still be well, financially-speaking . . .

Still, he had to cover his back. That Scotland Yard chappie might, if he found the letters, assume that blackmailer and murderer were one. If he found them, it wouldn't take him long to trace the authoress; questions would be asked in the Palace and before long, the long finger of the law would be pointing in his direction.

He was just unrolling the carpet when a bull's eye flashed on to his face. His heart stopped. 'Who's there?' he snapped, his mind and pulse racing.

'My name is Lestrade, Lieutenant Hedron,' the answer came. 'We met the other day.'

'Er . . . Lestrade,' Hedron got to his feet, 'I was looking for something.'

'Really?' Lestrade angled the lantern so that the beam was still on the lieutenant's face, 'what might that be?'

'Er . . . a book. I'd lent Tom a book. Too late to ask him for it now, so I thought I'd . . .'

'Regimental custom, is it, sir, to keep books under carpets? Most of us make do with bookcases.'

'Look,' Hedron tried the outraged approach, 'would you mind taking that thing out of my eyes and lighting the gas? I wonder what you're doing here, in the dark and all. This *is* private property, you know.'

'I might say the same of you,' Lestrade put a match to the gauze and the room was bathed in light. He switched off the bull's eye.

'I told you . . .' Hedron felt even more vulnerable by gaslight than he had in the lantern's beam.

'. . . You were looking for a book,' Lestrade sat down in a rattan chair. 'Yes, and I didn't believe you. Oh, you were looking for reading material, I'll grant you. And nothing you hadn't read before.'

'What do you mean?' Hedron stood on his dignity, what there was left of it.

'You are a sneak-thief and a blackmailer, Mr Hedron. The little conversation we're about to have will tell us if you are also a murderer.'

'How dare you!' the officer growled, 'I don't have to take this,' and he spun on his heel.

'You'll take it here or you'll take it at Scotland Yard!' Lestrade bellowed.

Hedron's hand rested on the doorknob for a moment, then he turned back. 'I haven't the faintest idea what you're talking about,' he said.

The superintendent sighed. 'All right,' he said, 'let's do it the hard way. The other morning when we met, I asked Lieutenant Bandicoot to show me the dead man's rooms. By the time we'd got here, the place had been ransacked. And recently – that gas mantle was still swinging where a tall man had bumped against it.'

'There are a lot of tall men in the Sixteenth,' Hedron countered.

'No doubt,' Lestrade said, although he had read somewhere that a Light Cavalryman should be no more than five foot four, 'but there are only four men in the Sixteenth who knew I was about to nose around these rooms. Bandicoot was only out of my sight for five minutes while he changed his clothes. That left Fannin, Harkness and you.'

'Well, there you are, then,' Hedron saw his loophole, 'it's one of them.'

'It might have been,' Lestrade nodded, crossing his legs, 'were it not for one thing.'

'What's that?' Hedron folded his arms with the air of a man outwitting his interrogator.

'These,' Lestrade produced his trump card – a bundle of nineteen letters tied with string.

Hedron's arms unfolded and he sat down, rather heavily for an innocent man. 'What are they?' He may not have been an innocent man, but he was a consistent one.

Lestrade sighed again. 'They are the nineteen letters you stole from these rooms some days ago. The other four – the ones you were looking for a moment ago are, I trust, by now a pile of ashes.'

'No,' Hedron's smile was that of a corpse, 'no, you've got me,' he feigned ignorance.

'I know I have,' he said. 'You see, these letters came from the strongbox in your rooms.'

'What?' the Lieutenant rose in anger, his jaw ridged, his fists clenched, 'you've searched my rooms?'

'Oh, don't worry,' Lestrade beamed, 'I didn't make any mess. I'm rather better at it than you are.'

'We've only your word,' the Lieutenant blustered.

'There's a chap at the Yard,' Lestrade told him, 'name of Stockley Collins. The things he can do with a brush would make your eyes water. When I hand these letters over to him, he's going to find under his microscope all sorts of interesting things.'

'Oh?' Hedron tried the uninterested air, 'such as?'

'Such as: my fingerprints, those of the late Major, those of Princess Ena of Battenburg, probably those of a Palace flunkey – and of course, yours.'

Hedron's air of casualness collapsed. 'How did you know it was me?' he growled.

'I didn't,' Lestrade said, 'I did over Fannin's and Harkness's rooms as well, but no luck.'

'You utter bastard,' the lieutenant hissed.

'Just doing a job, sir,' Lestrade shrugged.

'What happens now?' Hedron asked, 'the bracelets?'

Lestrade took the metal waste basket and fumbled for a lucifer. He struck one and watched as the flame crawled along the crease of the first letter. 'Well,' he said, 'in the good old days, I'd have gone to Old Goughy, spilled the beans as my Pinkerton colleagues say and you'd have been left alone in your rooms with a loaded revolver.' He looked his man in the eye. 'But they were the good old days, Lieutenant. I don't suppose you have the bottle, do you?'

Hedron's gaze flickered. 'More romantically, of course,' Lestrade consigned the first flaming paper to the bin, blew out the spent match and began on the second, 'you could fall on your sword.'

'If I'm put on trial, that's the end of my career,' Hedron told him. 'Why . . . why are you burning those? Aren't they evidence?'

'Indeed,' Lestrade said, 'but I'm not particularly interested in blackmail. Murder is my game. Besides,' he dropped the second letter to join the charred first, 'I've still got seventeen of these left. One would be enough to convince a jury.'

'All right. All right,' Hedron was a broken man, 'what do you want?'

'Answers,' Lestrade blew out his third match. He was glad really. This cat-and-mouse game was costing him a fortune in lucifers. 'First, how did you know about Ena?'

'I'd caught them together,' Hedron said, 'in a clinch. He whispering sweet nothings in her ear. It didn't look like the sort of rapport there ought to be between a Princess of the Blood Royal and a Major in the Dago Army – not even one attached to the Scarlet Lancers.'

'But you needed more?'

'Of course. I chaffed old Tom about it and he first offered to kill me in a duel, then begged me, for Ena's sake, to keep my mouth shut. For all his tall tales, he was an honourable old bugger – for a dago, I mean. What I needed was proof. A keepsake, memento, anything. The letters were a gift.'

'But what I don't understand is why you didn't know de Polez's hiding-place.'

'Hiding-place?'

'Under the floorboards next door,' Lestrade jerked his head in the direction of the bedroom.

'Shit!' hissed the Lieutenant. 'No doubt with all your vast experience, you found it.'

'Given time, I suppose I could have,' said Lestrade, 'if Archie Bandicoot hadn't beaten me to it.'

'Bandicoot?'

'He'd seen de Zelop going to the hiding-place to replenish his stocks during a card game. He said you were all there and laughed about it.'

'Damn,' growled Hedron, 'of all the nights to miss. I couldn't have been there, or it would have been the first place I'd look.'

'That's what I thought,' the Superintendent said. 'So he didn't hide them there in the first place?'

'No. I found them in an unlocked trunk along with his dago uniform. I suppose he didn't expect a visitor like me.'

'More to the point,' Lestrade produced another letter from his inside pocket, 'what about this?'

Hedron frowned. 'What is it?'

'It's a letter,' Lestrade said.

'May I?' Hedron asked.

'Uh-uh,' Lestrade shook his head, 'I may have seventeen of those, but I only have one of these.'

'I don't understand.'

'When I visited your rooms, I lifted *everything* in the strongbox.'

'What?' Hedron had turned a very funny colour.

'This letter is addressed to Major Jepez de Loses and invites him down to Beachy Head. It is signed "A wellwisher". It says,' and he cleared his throat, '"If you want all the letters back at once, that can be arranged. But you must come alone to the old lighthouse called Belle Tout at midnight on Friday." Not exactly deathless prose, is it, Mr Hedron, but it puts a noose firmly around your neck.'

'I didn't write it,' Hedron blurted. 'You must believe that. I'm not a murderer.'

'Then why was it in your possession?'

'I found it,' the Lieutenant said, 'when I ransacked these rooms the other morning. It was the first letter I found. I was in a hurry. I knew you were on the way and I just stuffed it in my pocket without thinking. It was only later that I read it and discovered its significance. It's from the murderer, isn't it? Inviting Tom to his death.'

Lestrade nodded. 'Careless of you to steal back your own letter.'

'But it's not my letter,' Hedron insisted. 'The handwriting. Check the handwriting. It's not mine.'

Lestrade leaned back in his chair, 'I know,' he said, 'I have. Even a disguised hand wouldn't look like that.' He stood up. 'Mr Hedron,' he looked down at his man, quaking in the chair, 'this letter I shall keep.' He put it away. 'These', he slipped the others into another pocket, 'shall be put under lock and key until such time as I read in the *Gazette* that you have resigned your commission in the Lancers. Hung up your spurs for good. I think that's the least you can do.'

'That's blackmail,' Hedron protested feebly.

'That's right,' Lestrade nodded. 'Sordid little game, isn't it? But I can live with myself. You can thank your lucky stars that I feel sorry for a rather sad little princess and, after my lights, that I care for my country. Otherwise, you and I would be inviting all kinds of gossip about now by walking out of here clasping hands around a pair of cuffs. Do you catch my drift?'

Hedron nodded. 'Goughy will have my letter of resignation on his desk by the morning.'

'Good,' said Lestrade. 'And one more thing, Mr Hedron – and I hope you won't take this personally,' and he smashed his fist into the blackmailer's nose, remarking as the man went down, 'just a little message from Princess Ena.'

* * *

It wasn't like Walter Dew not to be able to face his wife's tripe sandwiches. They'd been a favourite of his ever since he'd been a beat copper, tramping his way at that sedate two and a half miles an hour round the patch called H Division, where the Chosen People of Whitechapel rubbed shoulders, but rarely anything else, with the Gonophs of Shoreditch.

'You don't look well, Walter,' Lestrade threw his bowler at the hatstand. It missed, bounced off the wall and was caught expertly by a passing constable. 'Well done, Queux. A natural for the Commissioner's Eleven if ever I've seen one. Good God.'

Lestrade sat down in his old battered swivel rather faster than he intended. He glanced over Dew's shoulder and rather wished he hadn't. 'Anyone we know?' He twisted the photographs this way, then that.

'Sir Daniel Whiddon,' Dew told him, 'of the Buckinghamshire Whiddons.'

'Deceased, I take it?' Lestrade checked. The thought of the man living with injuries like that had his eyes watering.

'As a dildo,' Dew nodded. 'It'll be in all the papers tomorrow.'

'I've been . . . out of action for a while, Walter. You'd better fill me in. Bee, any risk of a cup of cocoa? May is a treacherous month and I thought I detected an East Wind blowing.'

'Coming up, guv,' the detective was glad to leave his depositions where they were for a while.

Lestrade crossed his legs on his desk and lolled back, cradling his head in his hands. Behind him the river barges twinkled and hooted at each other. Edward Henry was in his Heaven, yet all was not right with the world.

'Cause of death . . .' Dew began, but he had to clear his throat before he could continue. He'd never been the same since finding Mary Kelly in the butcher's shambles of Miller's Court that year of 1888 when the world was young and the Ripper stalked. 'Loss of blood.'

'From where?' Lestrade was almost afraid to have it confirmed.

'The tadger, guv.'

Lestrade raised an eyebrow. 'Is that what the police surgeon's report says?'

'No, guv. Old Doc. Glenlivet calls it a pego, but he *is* knocking on.'

'Anything in the margin?'

Dew squinted at it in the lamplight. 'Looks like Membrum Virile,' he said. 'Queux, you any good at Greek?'

'No, sir,' the constable was lost in thought, chewing his pencil-end.

Dew sighed to Lestrade. 'Of inestimable help, these young detectives, aren't they, guv?'

'Indeed,' Lestrade lit a cigar and watched the smoke snake around the light. 'Now, Queux,' he said, 'what does a wound in the tadger mean to you?'

'Sir?'

'The penis, man; the staff of life. I'd have saved your maidenly blushes, but the Chief Inspector has a corpse on his hands.'

'Well,' Queux cleared his throat, 'it means damned bad luck.'

'Bad luck?'

'Well, that must be one of the most embarrassing ways to go of all, really. I mean, I don't suppose it bothers the deceased either way, but my ol' mum always made me change my combinations when I was going out – just in case I was involved in an accident.'

'Quite right,' nodded Lestrade. 'And how old were you at the time?'

'I was twenty-six, sir,' Queux confessed.

'Ah, Bee,' Lestrade reached for the steaming mug, wincing in agony and tucking his scalded fingers under his armpit.

'Careful, sir, the cocoa's hot.'

'Is it my imagination, Detective Constable,' Lestrade hissed, 'or is there no handle on this mug?'

'It's the cuts, sir,' Bee told him.

'Well,' Lestrade blew on to his throbbing fingers, 'to cases, Walter.'

'Sir Daniel Whiddon,' Dew began, 'born 1865 in Kensington, the youngest child and only surviving son of the late Sir Algernon Whiddon, who apparently was something big in the Bank of England.'

'What, a vault, guv?' Bee was only half listening, wrestling as he was with a packet of Peek Freans.

The senior men ignored him. 'What did Daniel do?' Lestrade asked.

'Nothing,' Dew told him. 'He was so rich he didn't have to. Held a commission in the Bucks Yeomanry for a time, but apparently the bottle-green uniform didn't suit his complexion, so he resigned.'

'Just a bit precious?' Lestrade queried.

'Just a threat, I thought,' Dew nodded. 'His man said he had two passions – his appearance and his gadgets.'

'Gadgets?'

'Hundreds of 'em. I counted sixteen in the bedroom alone.'

'When did he die?'

'Doc. Glenlivet reckons about midday on Saturday.'

'Where was this?'

'In the bedroom of his town house – sixty-one Deluge Street, Chelsea.'

'Who found the body?'

'His man, Friday.'

'Friday?' Lestrade repeated. 'Black chap? Goes barefoot?'

'No, guv,' Dew frowned, 'white as a feather; comes from Congleton.'

'Just my idea of a little levity, Walter,' Lestrade sighed. 'What did he do?'

'Phoned the Yard at once.'

'Not the local blokes?'

'B Division, sir?' Dew frowned.

'Point taken,' Lestrade nodded. 'You were there?'

'Sergeant Adams was first. Inside the hour. I gave him a commendation.'

'Must be a first for him. And when you got there?'

'Whiddon was lying on the floor near his dressing-table. Stark naked he was. There was blood everywhere.'

'Signs of a struggle?'

'Nothing. It's my guess he was standing at the mirror . . .'

'The what?'

'Mirror, guv,' Dew said louder. Obviously, his old guv'nor was becoming a little mutt and jeff after all these years.

'Yes,' mused Lestrade, 'that's what I thought you said. Go on.'

'No furniture was disturbed. And the bedroom door was locked. Friday had to break it off its hinges.'

'What time was this?'

'Not until the Sunday night.'

'Sunday night?'

'Last night.'

'But you said Glenlivet fixed the time of death as midday on Saturday?'

'That's right, guv. Whiddon had given Friday and Mrs Friday the weekend off. Said he had a visitor coming and would do the entertaining himself.'

'Was that usual?' Lestrade frowned.

'Friday said he'd only known it twice before. On both occasions it was to do with an inventor.'

'Any inventor in particular?'

Dew shrugged. 'He didn't say. Might not've been the same bloke. Friday was of the opinion that at least one of these visitors was a woman.'

'A female inventor?' Lestrade was incredulous.

'This *is* 1906, guv,' Bee reminded them all. They withered him with their older-than-thou glances.

'Is there a Lady Whiddon?' Lestrade asked.

'No, sir. Friday seemed to remember a courtship. A betrothal even, but Sir Daniel broke it off.'

'Yes,' nodded Lestrade, looking again at the photographs, 'he almost did that again the other night. Who took these?'

'Constable Beaton, guv. P Division.'

'Hmm. What's your deduction then, Walter?'

'Well, it's obviously a sexual crime, sir.'

'Obviously,' Lestrade concurred. 'Are we assuming that the late Whiddon was not as other ex-officers of Yeomanry obsessed with gadgetry?'

'That would be my guess, sir, although . . .'

'Out with it, Dew,' Lestrade ordered, stirring his cocoa with Queux's pencil.

'Something doesn't sit right.'

'Go on.'

'Well, this sort of case . . . Remember Cleveland Street?'

Lestrade did.

'The Self Abuse Case?'

'God,' Lestrade chuckled, 'whatever happened to old Ebenezer Self? That takes me back.'

'Ralph Childers in the Hallowed House Affair.'

'The study in scarlet, yes indeed. I think I'm beginning to catch your scent. You'd expect . . .'

'Ropes or shackles or calipers. I'd expect ligatures and whips and thongs with intricate sailors' knots . . .'

'Tied by intricate sailors,' Lestrade was nodding expansively. 'And yet . . .'

'Nothing, guv. No marks on wrists or ankles. No other signs of torture, just a bloody great . . . well . . .'

'Naked, you say?'

'As a new-born babe. Mind you, Friday said he always slept that way. Had an aversion to wincyette. Didn't like the feel of it on his skin.'

'What about the locked door, Walter?'

'Simple. Whoever visited locked it on his way out and took the . . . oh no.'

'What?' Lestrade tried to read his chief inspector's notes upside down. It was difficult enough the right way up.

'No, I'd forgotten that. The key was still in the lock, on the inside. That's why Friday broke the door down. He couldn't get his spare key in and he couldn't get the deceased's out. Bugger!'

'Is that a clinical observation, Walter?' the superintendent asked.

'No, sir. It's just the sound of a theory exploding.'

Lestrade chuckled. 'Don't take on, Walter. We need to bounce a few ideas off the wall, that's all. The night is young. Constable Bee will brew us another of his nearly adequate cocoas and Constable Queux will knock up Messrs Peak and Frean for another packet of their delicious comestibles. You've been to Deluge Street. Where is the Whiddon country seat?'

'Marsh Gibbon, a few miles from Buckingham itself.'

'Excellent. Fancy a spin in one of the new despatch motors?'

'Er . . .' Dew's knuckles whitened on his pencil stub.

'It's all right, Walter,' Lestrade chuckled, 'don't worry. I'm driving.'

* * *

The village of Marsh Gibbon lies a little off the road between Aylesbury, famous for its duck and Bicester, not famous for anything at all, except perhaps gravy powder. It was the road that the Ministry of Transport, long years in the future, would christen, incomprehensibly, the A41. Driving as they were in one of those new despatch motors the Yard had been designated earlier in the year, Lestrade and Dew *ought* to have approached along the Roman Road to Wendover, by Tring and Lilley Hoo, as free men had done for centuries.

As it was, Lestrade was driving, de-doubling his clutch like a thing possessed, and they overshot a little. They were in the sleepy little townlet of Burford before darkness fell on a glorious spring evening and they checked in at The All And Sundry. Dew was paying.

The next day dawned bright and fair and they read in the dust of the despatch motor's rear window, the work of some wag's finger – 'Running In: Please Pass'. They took the road through Bladon where generations of the Churchills slept and out of Oxfordshire altogether into the right county. As Dew so tactlessly pointed out as they coughed and spluttered their way across the levels of the Great Western, the London and North Western and Metropolitan and G.G.J^T Railways, it might, after all, have been quicker by train.

The estate of the Whiddons was a magnificent Jacobean structure, its windows hand-mullioned by long-dead Cotswold craftsmen who had left their curious chisel marks all over the place. One that the sharp-eyed Dew noticed said, in sculpted copper-plate, '*The Duke of Buckingham is a . . .*' but weathering had saved the man's blushes. The steep roofs were layered with the local slate, dug up from the bowels of Stoneyfield and left to split on the frosty levels in the winters of the years.

The doorbell produced a distant answering echo and an ancient retainer, who looked as though he might have known the Duke of Buckingham personally, showed them into the Hall. Glass eyes stared down at them from wart-hog, wildebeest and eland and the ancient retainer hung their regulation driving capes and goggles on the outstretched paws of a particularly snide-looking Kodiak bear.

'Their ladyships are in the drawing-room,' he said and

ushered them in. 'Superintendent Dew and Chief Inspector Lestrade,' he said, 'from Scotland.'

Three equally ancient ladies rose as one. None of them reached Lestrade's tie-knot. 'From Scotland,' said one, 'how charming. It's many a muckle mak's a mickle, I ken.'

'I'm sure it is, Madam, but I'm afraid your butler was a teensy bit incorrect. We are actually from Scotland *Yard*. In London.'

'Oh, well, never mind. You'll have to forgive Oadby. Gaga as a troupe of monkeys, I'm afraid. Still, he does a rare morning coffee. Oadby!' the trill made the chandelier rattle, 'five coffees, please. Oh, and I've locked the tantalus.'

'Very good, m'lady,' Oadby scowled and managed to turn around in order to reach the door.

'Now, gentlemen, the honours are mine, I think. I am Elvira Whiddon – and before you ask, I'm eighty-six. Astonishing, isn't it? To think that when I was born, George IV was being crowned. Now, there *was* a monarch!'

'Nonsense, El,' another old lady chirped, 'he was a corpulent old lecher. Oh, I do beg your pardon.'

It was true there had been an inexplicable small explosion and there was a rather pungent odour wreathing the furniture.

'This is my sister, Matilda,' said Elvira. 'She is a mere eighty-three and as you are no doubt aware, had plum duff for supper last night.'

'I'm Henrietta,' the third old girl curtseyed, 'and I'm not telling you how old I am. Young man,' she squinted up at Walter Dew from behind spectacles that looked like goldfish bowls, 'how's your eyesight?'

'Very good, Madam, thank you,' he grinned.

'Well, while we're having a little chat – I expect your superior wants us to help him with his inquiries or something – could you look for a hatpin. I'm due at the vicar's later and I shall feel undressed without it.'

'Do sit down, gentlemen,' Elvira said. As tallest and probably oldest, she seemed to call the tune, 'I expect you've come about poor Daniel.'

'You know, then?' Lestrade said, feeling his back go as the springs of the sofa died beneath him.

'Why, of course. Friday made a telephone call to us directly he'd found him. Besides, it was all over yesterday's papers.'

'We *did* lose a day, sir,' Dew had the temerity to remind his guv'nor. He sat down smugly alongside the superintendent, but rose again immediately, 'Er . . . I think this must be your hatpin,' he said, smiling through tears as he wiped the blood off it.

Henrietta took the thing and held it so close to her eyes that it clinked against her glasses. 'No,' she shook her tousled old head, 'that's not it,' and she threw it over the back of her chair.

In the silence that followed there was another small explosion. All eyes turned to Matilda, but her eyes swivelled to a particularly moth-eaten ginger tom lying on the sideboard. A moment's glance confirmed Lestrade's and Dew's suspicions. The eyes of the tom were as glass as anything mounted in the hall. The animal was stuffed and whatever his guilt in the passing of wind while he was alive, he was beyond reproach now.

'There was a lovely obituary in *The Times*,' Henrietta said, surreptitiously digging about under her cushion for her lost hatpin.

'And that nice young man from *Gadgets Galore* telephoned us to say he'd be writing one next quarter,' Matilda informed them.

'Yes,' Elvira smiled, 'everyone's been so kind. At the moment I understand the coroner has poor Daniel. When might we have him back?'

'As soon as possible, Madam,' Lestrade said. 'We are deeply sorry that this should have happened. Please accept our condolences.'

'I cannot condole it, personally,' Matilda said, 'I told you his lifestyle would be his undoing.'

'Oh, whisht, Tillie,' Elvira chided her little sister, 'Superintendent . . . Dew, is it?'

'Lestrade, Madam,' Lestrade corrected her.

'Superintendent Lestrade, there *are* those . . .' and she glowered at Matilda who glowered back, jerking up and down every now and then as her wind got the better of her, 'who believe there was something odd in poor Daniel's mental make-up. But we've no proof he wore any.'

'Quite,' Henrietta sided with her biggest sister. 'He was after all engaged to be married once. What *was* that girl's name?'

'Euphemia Baggage,' Matilda remembered.

'Borage, dear,' Elvira corrected her.

'It *was*,' Matilda insisted. 'Anyway, Daniel broke it off. You have to ask yourself why.'

'Because she was a hideous old spinster, who had been on the shelf for so long she was covered in cobwebs,' Elvira explained.

A tap at the door heralded the re-entry of Oadby, his frock tails trailing on the carpet, his hands quivering around the rim of a silver salver.

'Ah, capital, Oadby,' Elvira was mother, though at eighty-six that was becoming increasingly unlikely, and she poured coffee for herself and her sisters. When it came to Lestrade's and Dew's however, she had to resort to a second jug and what came out looked curiously like hot water. Lestrade and Dew looked at each other.

'Not too strong, I hope?' Elvira smiled.

'Er . . . no, no,' Lestrade said quickly, 'just right.'

'Cream?'

'No,' said Lestrade, 'I'll take mine . . . black.'

'Lovely as it is,' beamed Dew.

'No, it's true that poor Daniel was a little odd, Superintendent, but Tillie's inference is very unkind. She never liked him.'

'That's not true,' Matilda flounced, releasing yet more wind, '*I* was always his favourite.'

'Simply because someone doesn't marry, doesn't make them . . . you know. Look at us. Three unmarried sisters. I've never had any inclination to . . . you know . . . with a girl of the same sort.'

'In fact the late Queen, God Bless Her, said that sort of thing didn't happen,' Henrietta said.

'Of course not,' Matilda agreed. 'It's a physical impossibility.'

Elvira had subtly reached across and pulled the bell rope. An increasingly exhausted Oadby shuffled back into the presence.

'You rang, m'lady?'

'Yes, Oadby. Could you open the French windows a notch? Miss Matilda is a trifle aerated this morning.'

'Very good, m'lady,' and he staggered across to wrestle with the catch.

'Were you in regular contact with your nephew, ladies?' Lestrade asked.

'Not exactly,' Elvira said. 'Although he insisted we have a telephone thingummy installed. I must admit, I hate answering it.'

'So do I,' Henrietta confided, 'you never know who's there, do you? In fact, that's the first thing I always say when I answer it. "Who's there?" I say. You can't be too careful, can you?'

'Indeed not, Madam,' Lestrade smiled, forcing down another sip of hot water. 'I understand Daniel was interested in gadgets,' he said.

'Obsessed,' Matilda corrected him. 'Always had been. When he lived here, an entire wing was given over to his bits and pieces. He'd spend hours fiddling about with things. They sent him down from Oxford for that, you know.'

'Really?' Lestrade asked.

'Well, for fiddling about with something. We've got the letter from the Dean somewhere.'

'Nonsense, Tillie,' Elvira said, 'Daniel was a genius. *And* a generous one. If he hadn't invented it himself, he bought from and patronized others.'

'Do you know', Lestrade asked, bracing himself for the big one, 'whether your nephew had any enemies? Anyone who would want to see him dead?'

There was a stunned silence. Not even Matilda farted.

'I understood that poor Daniel had taken his own life, Superintendent,' Elvira found the words first. 'That, at any rate, is what Friday told us on Sunday – on the telephone.'

'He may have believed that, Madam,' Lestrade said, 'or he may have been trying to spare your feelings. If it *was* suicide, it's the most bizarre one I've ever seen.'

'You're right, Superintendent,' Matilda said, 'we Whiddons are not, with hindsight, the self-destroying kind.'

'Ah, now, Tillie,' Elvira wagged her finger, 'you're forgetting Cousin Lyall.'

'Oh, lor', yes,' Matilda admitted.

'Cousin Lyall?' Dew had the daunting task, between sips of water, of writing all this down.

'Lyall Whiddon,' Elvira explained. 'He was gazetted briefly to the 4th Foot, but was never the same after Magdala.'

'Magdala?' Lestrade and Dew chorused.

'It's a place', Elvira said, 'in Abyssinia.'

'I wonder if *that*'s where I left my hatpin?' Henrietta muttered.

'Don't be a silly, Hen,' her biggest sister scolded, 'you've never been there, dear – Cousin Lyall went there and it turned him a little . . . Shot himself, didn't he Tillie?'

'I believe so, El,' Matilda said, fanning the air with her hand, 'but that was a long time ago.'

'I remember him saying', Elvira gazed into the middle distance, 'that what with the heat and the flies and the lack of white women, some men went mad.'

'His friend went mad,' Matilda remembered, 'that nice Captain Speedy.'

'Oh, I remember him,' Henrietta trilled. 'So dashing. And so *tall*. Why, he blotted out the sun that day on the picnic, when I was lying down . . .' and her voice trailed away.

'When was your cousin in Abyssinia, Miss Whiddon?' Lestrade asked.

'Now you've asked her,' Matilda chuckled, pointing at Elvira and lifting her left buttock as she did so.

'I remember perfectly.' Elvira rose to the occasion and opened the French windows wider. The spring flowers, nodding in the breeze beyond the house, fought back the increasingly unpleasant odour in the drawing-room. 'It was 1868 – the year that nice Mr Gladstone became Prime Minister for the first time.'

'Misses Whiddon,' Lestrade stood up, 'I wonder if I might impose and use your telephone?'

'Of course,' said Elvira. 'Do you understand how it works?'

'I think so,' Lestrade smiled.

'I'll come with you, guv,' Dew was beside him, 'in case it's tricky, I mean.'

'No, no, Walter,' Lestrade grinned, 'I can manage. You stay here with these nice ladies.'

'Yes, of course,' Matilda patted the cushion beside her and the dust rose in clouds. 'You come and sit by me, young man.'

'And while you're doing that,' Henrietta said, 'I shall pour you another cup of Oadby's delicious morning coffee.'

Lestrade was still grinning when he got to the hall and when he asked the operator for his number, 'Gerard Three Four Eight, please.'

There was a series of clicks and whirrs that stabbed his ear-drum, obliging him to hold the bakelite at arm's length. Then a monotonous female voice crackled, 'Hello. This is the Patent Office. Dierdre speaking. How may I help you?'

'This is Scotland Yard,' Lestrade shouted, 'I want to speak to someone about an invention.'

'Could you hold the line, please?' Dierdre picked up her violin and played a few hurried bars while connecting various wires and leads. No one had told her she needed the skills of a contortionist for this job. 'Putting you through.'

'Hello?' said Lestrade.

'Hello. This is the Patent Office. Marjorie speaking. How may I help you?'

'Yes,' Lestrade had been here before, 'this is Scotland Yard. need to talk to someone about an invention.'

There was a pause. 'An invention?'

'Yes. This *is* the Patent Office? The place where you register inventions?'

'Oh, *inventions*. I'm sorry, I thought you said "convention". Hold the line. Just putting you through.'

At least this time there was no violin music while he waited. Suddenly his ear-drum was assailed by the screech of wire on wire.

'What was the hell was that?' he hissed, his head ringing.

'Sorry,' Marjorie said, 'it's an Aeolian harp, only I just dropped it. Putting you through now.'

'Hello. Patent Office. Monica speaking. How may I help you?'

'Look!' Lestrade was pretty sure now he was ringing the Patent Office, 'I want to speak to someone – probably a man – about an invention.'

'Who's speaking?'

'This is Scotland Yard,' he was still bellowing.

There was a pause, a series of muffled clicks and scratches and what sounded like muffled conversation.

'Hello, this is the Patent Office. George speaking. How may I help you?'

'Ah,' Lestrade was getting testy by this time, 'you're a man.'

'Well,' George giggled, 'I was last time I looked.'

'This is Scotland Yard. I am making inquiries into a murder and I have reason to believe that the weapon involved may be registered with you.'

'Ooh, well I never. How exciting.'

'Yes,' hissed Lestrade. 'Can you help me?'

There was more ruffling and crackling during which Lestrade heard George say, 'there's some old geezer here wanting to know about murder weapons. That's peculiar, innit?' Then the voice came back more strongly. 'You want to talk to our Mr Hunter, the senior registrar.'

'Excellent. Put him on.'

'Oh, I can't. It's his day off.'

Lestrade toyed with throwing the phone through the nearest window. 'Will he be in tomorrow?'

'Oh, yes. Tomorrow. Yes.'

'Good. We'll be there.'

'You'll have to make an appointment.'

But Lestrade had already rung off. He rescued Dew from the three weird sisters, trying not to breathe in as he strode through the drawing-room and the Yard despatch motor roared off through the fresh air.

'Abyssinia, Walter,' Lestrade shouted above the throb of the engine.

'Going somewhere, guv?' Dew hoped not, considering that Lestrade was driving.

'No. Abyssinia,' his guv'nor repeated. 'The Whiddons' cousin went mad as a result of being there. Charles Tenterden knows Abyssinia. James Sparrow was working in the Abyssinian section of King's College where we found him first. And

119

Captain Orange, Janet Calthrop and John Thomas de Loops all had Abyssinian mirrors on or near their persons when they died. That's the heart of this case – Abyssinia.'

'But Janet Calthrop and Daniel Whiddon are my cases, sir,' Dew looked a little hurt.

'Now, now, Walter,' Lestrade tried to read the expression behind the goggles, 'no time for petty jealousies. We're all on the same team, you know. As the Spanish police say "Mi colla su colla".'

'Do they, sir?'

'Take my word for it, Walter,' Lestrade patted his oppo's leg as he changed gear and the wheels spun on the gravel. 'We must talk to Tenterden again. It's my guess he's holding something back. By the way, any idea where the Patent Office is?'

The Patent Office was in Southampton Buildings. Four years earlier they had built a magnificent library in the Art Nouveau style where interested parties could peruse the outpourings of other people's fertile imaginations. Sir Daniel Whiddon was often to be seen doing just that against a backdrop of lilies and peacock's feathers.

Lestrade and Dew, still bedraggled and dusty from their journey, waddled into the main lobby.

'Good morning,' the fetching young lady at the counter beamed, 'I'm Dierdre. How may I help?'

Dew saw Lestrade's jaw flex and his teeth grit. Perfectly civil question, he thought to himself. Perhaps his guv'nor was going through that funny time of life.

'By directing us quickly, without anyone else's involvement, to the office of Mr Hunter.'

'Our Mr Hunter?'

'I don't suppose he's anyone else's,' Lestrade observed.

'Do you have an appointment?'

'No.'

'Right. Unfortunately, I can't leave my desk, but if you turn right at the end here, at that model of Huish and Stevens's Device for Preventing Self Abuse in Horses, then go up three floors, you can't miss it. It's next to Hülsmyer's Hertzian-wave Projecting and Receiving Apparatus to Give Warning of the Presence of Metallic Bodies Machine.'

'Marvellous,' smiled Lestrade and tipped his goggles to the girl.

'I didn't know they did that,' Dew said as they walked past the first machine, 'horses.'

'Pit ponies do it all the time,' Lestrade said, 'that's why they're blind. You'd think they'd have a simple little gadget like a lift in the Patent Office, wouldn't you?'

On the third floor, next to something that looked like a huge compass – and indeed was – they found the office of their Mr Hunter. A small man with the face of a startled squirrel wearing pince-nez opened to them and gingerly crossed back to his well-padded seat.

'I should warn you gentlemen,' he said in a piping voice, broken now and then by an inrush of air, 'that we are up to our eyeballs in motoring devices just at the minute.'

'We are from Scotland Yard,' Lestrade explained. 'We are enquiring about one of these,' and he passed the metal murder weapon across the desk.

'I'm afraid you're too late,' Hunter said, scrutinizing it closely, 'Heinrich Peschken has beaten you to it by three years. Oh, no, wait a minute. This is different.'

'In what way?'

'Well, this . . . ooh, dear. This spike. The original has no spike – nor hole for it to pass through.' He looked up at them, tilting his pince-nez on his forehead. 'Gentlemen, I'm not sure His Majesty's Patent Office can entertain this idea.'

'I agree,' Lestrade said. 'It's not a very entertaining idea, is it? But we're not here to patent this, Mr Hunter. We're here to find out who made it.'

'I see,' Hunter crossed the room with difficulty to an enormous leather-bound ledger on a sloping shelf. 'Well, the prototype is, as I said, by Heinrich Peschken, pharmaceutical chemist of 168 Contrescarpe, Bremen, Germany. His agent in this country is . . . Henry O. Linck.'

'What is it for, Mr Hunter?' Lestrade had wondered this for days.

'For preventing the condition known as . . .' he sucked in his breath and sweat stood out on his upper lip, 'Enuresis Nocturna.'

'Er . . . En . . .' Dew was already struggling with his notepad and pencil.

'Night emissions,' Hunter explained, 'bedwetting. I've got one here somewhere.' He rummaged in what appeared to be a bottomless bottom drawer, bending and straightening with difficulty, 'here we are.'

The device he handed to the Yard men was the same, but different. The U-shaped bar had soft pads all round, but the pressing bar was flat and the thread nut had no sharpened end as the killer version had.

'It's easily done, I suppose,' Hunter said. 'All you need do is to drill a hole into the bar and substitute the sharp screw for the blunt one. Dear oh lor', it doesn't bear thinking about, does it?' His eyes began to water. 'All you need is one twist of the screw and that's it – punctured for life.'

'Or for death,' Lestrade nodded grimly.

'Did somebody actually use this, then?' Hunter asked.

'Tell me,' Lestrade said, holding the two versions side by side, 'in the dark, you wouldn't be able to tell these apart, would you?'

'Er . . . no,' Hunter admitted, gripping the rim with whitened knuckles.

'Are these things available on the open market?'

'Oh yes,' Hunter assured the Yard men, 'any surgical appliance shop will stock them.'

'Well, thank you, Mr Hunter,' Lestrade said. 'You've been of great help. Look,' he noted the man's distressed condition, 'I'm sorry if our visit has caused you upset. I can't pretend the victim didn't suffer.'

'No, no,' Hunter groaned, 'it's not that. We are all victims, aren't we, one way or another? I have the unpleasant task after luncheon of writing to Messrs Boddy and Bottomley of Leeds to tell them that their Medicinal Compound for the Treatment of Piles doesn't bloody well work!'

* * *

'Hello,' a rather hysterical voice called over the wires, 'who is it? Who's there?'

'It's Superintendent Lestrade, Miss Whiddon. We met yesterday. To which Miss Whiddon am I speaking?'

'Yes, that's right. This is Miss Whiddon. Oadby isn't here at the moment or he would have answered the telephone for me. Um . . . I mean, he is here. He and his three strapping sons.'

'Miss Henrietta?' Lestrade had a one in three chance of being right.

'Yes. Who is it? Who's there?'

'Lestrade. The man from the Yard. Scotland Yard. You gave us morning coffee . . . well, sort of. Yesterday.'

'Scotland? This telephone call must be costing you a lot of money.'

'About your nephew Daniel . . .' Lestrade said.

'Oh no. He doesn't live here,' the old girl said. 'He's dead, you know.'

'Yes, I know. Tell me, did he wet the bed?'

'Well, I don't know. I wasn't there. They say all your muscles relax of course, so it's possible. Look, are you trying in a convoluted way to sell me double glazing?'

'No, I mean, when he was a boy? Did he wet the bed; at night, I mean?'

'Oh yes, constantly. His father used to whip him black and blue – that was our brother. He was something big in the Bank of England. But if you print a word of this in the "Pink 'Un" I'll sue the bollocks off you. Ah, *there's* my hatpin,' and she hung up.

'Any luck, guv?' Dew asked, reaching for his bowler.

'Not really, Walter,' Lestrade sighed. 'But, on balance, I may have got the sanest of the three. We'll compare notes as we go.'

This time they caught a taxi – and Lestrade wasn't driving. In the half an hour it took them to reach Charles Tenterden's house, they thought they'd worked out how Daniel Whiddon died.

'He was visited on the weekend when he knew the servants would be away,' Lestrade said.

'By an inventor – one of two or three he invited to his house,' Dew added.

'Who swapped Peschken's harmless gadget for tying up your tadger for one that would pierce his penis and lead to, as things turned out, loss of blood.'

'Bit of a long shot, though, wasn't it?'

'What?'

'Well,' Dew steadied himself as the taxi took the curve at Marble Arch, 'a) that he'd use it at all and b) that he'd pass out or whatever before he could call for help.'

'You're right, Walter. It was someone who either knew Whiddon as a child and knew about his bedwetting habits, or someone who gained his trust more recently.'

'Not many men would come out with that sort of thing,' Dew reasoned. 'And anyway, why should it recur now, this weekend? Adults don't wet beds, do they?'

'Some do,' Lestrade said, 'depends how many they've had. For older blokes, of course, it's habitual,' and he didn't like the way Dew looked at him. 'I don't think our friend is in much of a hurry, Walter. He's relaxed. Casual. If that little gadget hadn't worked, he'd have rigged something else up later. Perhaps he just got lucky. You haven't told me what Bee and Queux turned up on the second search of Whiddon's Chelsea house.'

'Ah,' Dew beamed, 'I was saving the best until last.' He rifled through his pockets, 'look familiar?' He held up a broken mirror.

'Indeed it does,' Lestrade smiled, 'where was this?'

'Where the murderer left it, under the dead man's pillow.'

Lestrade took it in his hand. 'Abyssinian,' he said, 'and broken. Why is it always broken?'

'And that's not all,' Dew was beaming from ear to ear, wagging a little leather-bound book in his hand, 'the late Sir Daniel's diary.'

'Walter,' Lestrade smiled back, 'I think I'm about to offer you a cigar.'

'Steady, guv,' Dew chuckled and flicked to the relevant page. 'Friday evening, the fourteenth May. Eight o'clock. For dinner. Señor Alvarez.'

'Señor Alvarez,' Lestrade repeated, 'I must admit, Walter, I never expected the Spanish inquisition.'

6

Charles Tenterden was busy at his desk when the Yard men arrived. He looked older than ever by the light of his oil lamp and he broke off from writing with some annoyance.

'I thought you'd be back,' he said.

'Are we disturbing you, Mr Tenterden?' Lestrade asked.

'No, no. I was working on my magnum opus, Mr Lestrade – a book which will echo round the world. Possibly the most *important* work ever.'

'What is it about, sir?'

'An Odyssey, if you will. One man's journey home.'

'Ah, a travelogue.'

'Of a sort. It begins in Abyssinia.'

'That's funny,' Lestrade smiled, 'that, I suspect, is where my journey starts too.'

'Yours?' Tenterden waved them them into chairs. 'Oh, can I offer you something? Morning coffee perhaps?'

'Er . . . no, thank you, sir.' It was too soon for the Yard men. Given time, they would recover. Learn to trust their taste buds again. But for now, best to decline.

'Mr Dew and I are investigating a series of murders, sir.'

'A series? You mean, not merely Captain Orange and his family?'

'They were the first, yes. But they were followed by a young student of history at King's College, London University; then an attached officer of the Sixteenth Lancers; now a gentleman whose hobby was inventions.'

'Can all these people have died by the same hand?'

'It's more than possible,' Lestrade nodded. 'And in cases such as these, sir – mercifully rare in England – we look for a central theme, a common denomination.'

'Which is?'

Lestrade leaned forward to his man. 'Which is mirrors, Mr Tenterden.'

The retired journalist looked at Lestrade, then at Dew, then at Lestrade again. 'Mirrors?' he repeated.

'The object found in Captain Orange's breast pocket was a hand mirror you described as probably Abyssinian in design. Walter.'

Dew flipped open his notepad. 'A similar mirror, broken, was found near the body of Miss Janet Calthrop, the student whom the Superintendent mentioned a moment ago.'

'An exactly identical mirror was found near the corpse of Major Juan Tomas de Jesus Slope, the officer attached to the Lancers.'

'And in the case of the late Sir Daniel Whiddon . . . what, guv?' Dew was suddenly lost.

'We believe he died in front of a mirror – or at least it is likely that he was gazing into one shortly before he died. But an Abyssinian one was found under the dead man's pillow.'

'I see,' Tenterden stroked his grey chin. 'But why are you telling me all this, Superintendent?'

'Because, Mr Tenterden, we have reason to believe that you are not being wholly truthful with us. Walter.'

Dew flipped to another page. 'We believe you're holding something back.'

'I told you about the mirror.' Tenterden's mouth felt bricky-dry, 'in a round-about sort of way.'

'Indeed,' said Lestrade, 'and for that we're for ever in your debt. But there's more, isn't there?'

Tenterden's eyes flickered. Lestrade could read that like a book. So could Dew. They'd seen it before – the tongue flicking over the lips, the muscle tensing in the jaw, the shaking knee, left or right. Charles Tenterden was hiding something.

Lestrade helped him. 'Does the name Alvarez mean anything to you?'

Tenterden frowned. Whatever he'd been thinking, this wasn't

t. It was a different tack and he seemed grateful for it. 'Not a hing,' he said firmly. 'Should it?'

Then Lestrade was back on line again, going for the jugular with the speed and accuracy of a trained hunter. 'Who was the all man?' he asked, 'the one Captain Orange's man Kenrick saw hovering near the house just before the trap overturned? You know, don't you?'

'No.' Tenterden stood up sharply, his movement too sudden, his denial too emphatic. He crossed to the window, to where the blossom smothered the acacias and children scrambled in the park. He turned back to them. Regulation men in their regulation serge, regulation bowlers upturned on their laps. Impressive moustaches beneath solid, dependable noses, even if one of them did appear to have its tip missing. Bright, watchful eyes that gave nothing away. Tenterden sat down.

'After Abyssinia,' he said, 'I was sent by the *Graphic* to Perak, in the Malay States north of Singapore. Oh, it was the merest skirmish in comparison with Magdala, but during it, I spent some time with the officers of Colonel Badcock's regiment and of an evening, with the dragonflies skimming the waters of the wadis, we'd play cards. Well,' Tenterden gazed through the window again, as if the spring sunshine gave him courage. 'It became obvious over a few days that one of our number was cheating. I don't know what you know, Superintendent, of the honour of a regiment, but cheating at cards in the Mess is the equivalent of murder, or worse, in civilian life. It just isn't done. I faced the cheat. Had it out with him, man to man. He denied it. But I was so sure – and so furious at the boundah's insolence – that I took my suspicions to the Colonel. Alexander Badcock was not a man to trifle with – I can see him now, in his Engineer's patrol jacket, huge dundrearies, hard eyes. He was appalled, first with me as a mere scribbler, then, when he saw I had a point, with the cheat. He said he'd confront him, officer to officer.'

Tenterden's voice trailed away. Then he cleared his throat and found it again. 'The next night we heard that the cheat had shot himself with his own pistol. Badcock said that was the end of the affair. But it wasn't.'

'Not?' Lestrade asked.

Tenterden shook his head. 'The cheating went on. I'd been wrong, you see, Superintendent, wrong all the time. Another man was guilty. He didn't give a damn. When Badcock faced him, he just laughed. "Where's your proof?" he said, "where's your proof?" And there wasn't any. I was *so sure* I was right. And an innocent man had gone to his grave because of it.' His tear-filled eyes met Lestrade's. 'So you see, Superintendent, in a way, I am a murderer. As surely as the man you're looking for now.'

Lestrade looked at Dew, 'I don't follow, sir,' he said. 'What has all this to do with Captain Orange and the mirrors?'

Tenterden turned to the window again, resting his hands on the sash. 'Tall man,' he said. 'Mirrors from Abyssinia. It must be . . . but it can't be.'

'Who?' Lestrade was at his elbow. 'Who is the tall man?'

Tenterden looked at him. 'What if I'm wrong? As I was wrong in Perak?'

'Lightning doesn't strike twice,' Lestrade told him, 'and anyway, we aren't going to hang a man on your word alone, Mr Tenterden. British justice demands proof – and that's our responsibility. You give us the tools and we'll do the rest.'

'Speedy,' Tenterden whispered.

'I'm sorry,' Lestrade said, cocking his head.

'Speedy,' his man repeated, louder this time. 'Captain Charles Speedy.'

'We've heard that name, sir,' Dew was on his feet by now.

Lestrade nodded.

'He was Napier's Chief Intelligence Officer in the Abyssinian Campaign. Fought for the Emperor Theodore in 1860 and been made a full General in the Abyssinian army. He'd seen service in New Zealand too, against the Maori. Napier asked for him specially, recognizing his experience as being invaluable.'

'He was tall?' Lestrade asked.

'Six foot five,' Tenterden said.

'Why couldn't it be him?' the Superintendent wanted to know.

'Hmm?' Tenterden was miles away, his mind racing over the moon-like deserts of Abyssinia where fierce warriors with painted Egyptian faces chased him through the windy corridors of night.

'You said a moment ago: "It must be, but it can't be". Why can't it be Speedy?'

'He disappeared on the night before Napier stormed Magdala, the mountain fortress of the emperor. I may have been the last white man to see him alive.'

'He was killed?' Lestrade asked.

'Missing. Presumed killed,' said Tenterden.

Lestrade shook his head, a strange prickling of the hairs on his neck. 'Presumption doesn't rule out murder,' he said. 'How well did you know him?'

'How well does any man know another?' Tenterden asked. 'He was ... strange. Convinced he'd discovered a mighty secret, somewhere in the desert.'

'What secret?'

'I don't know,' Tenterden said, returning to his chair, 'except that it had to do with a mirror that was magic. That's the exact phrase he used, "the mirror that is magic" and something about a glass church.'

'A glass church?' Lestrade frowned. He'd heard of – and indeed often visited – the Crystal Palace, but this was a new one on him.

'And he was always whistling the same wretched tune.'

'Oh? What was that?'

Tenterden laughed. 'That's just it. I can't remember. I was blessed with a totally unmusical ear, Superintendent. Just occasionally, I fancy I hear it, or snatches of it on the wind. Or in the Underground while I'm waiting for a train. Never any words. Just a tune – a note here, a chord there. But he'd be ancient by now ... what? Well over seventy.'

'It fits,' said Lestrade.

'It does?' Tenterden asked.

'Whoever our murderer is, he uses clever methods, not brute force. All the murders so far have been rigged to look like accidents. The most energetic thing he had to do was to loosen rubble on a lighthouse roof. And bearing in mind that roof was in a state of decay, it probably didn't need much persuasion.'

'But why, Superintendent? If I'm right. If you're right. Why?'

Lestrade smiled and picked up his bowler. 'If you're right,' he said, 'if I'm right, when we find him, we'll ask him.'

They sent out a reward notice that afternoon; the reward in question coming from the Yard Missing Persons Fund. Inspector Lovell of that Department was less than hopeful. After all, a grown – at six feet five, *very* grown – adult, arguably in possession of all his faculties had disappeared thirty-eight years ago in a country thousands of miles away. The trail had, to say the least, gone a *little* cold by this time. In the days ahead, however, no less than eighty-three helpful members of the public in the Metropolitan area reported a tall man acting suspiciously. One of them proved to be a stilt walker from Hengler's circus, whose height was actually five foot one and thirteen of the others were women. On the bright side, it did lead to one arrest, of a very tall man caught interfering with a tortoise while delivering it to a friend. Whether all this could be said to constitute helping the police with their inquiries, was however debatable.

It was then, as Lestrade was combing fruitlessly through Kelly's directories in search of any likely Charles Speedys or Señor Alvarezes, that news came through from Madrid of a bomb outrage at the wedding of King Alfonso and Queen Ena. Four officers of the Sixteenth Lancers, forming the guard of honour, had behaved splendidly, as befitted the British in Spain and one Archie Bandicoot had been particularly magnificent, not even flinching as a piece of shrapnel caught him in the czapska. The same paper carried the glad news of the resignation from the same regiment of Lieutenant George Hedron, who had left to make a new career for himself in Papua, New Guinea.

The telegram that came later that morning was of more interest however. It came from David Runton, the twitcher whom Lestrade had met at Beachy Head. It was marked 'urgent' and 'personal' and asked Lestrade to come at once. His reports on the Princess Ena scandal typed up in triplicate and left with the morose Major Woodhouse for his seal of approval before passing upstairs to the King-Emperor, the superintendent packed an overnight Gladstone, went down to the station and caught him a train.

W.H.Smith's wasn't what it was. He'd read *The Last of the Barons* before and anyway, historical romance didn't do much for him. He'd guessed who dunnit – Bulwer Lytton in fact – by page five. A new book of medieval adventure was on all the bookstands, called *Sir Nigel* but when he saw it was Conan Doyle's latest, he put it back. Since he didn't fancy playing with himself at the games of chess provided these days for train journeys, he bought a copy of *The Times*, spread it over his face and went to sleep.

David Runton had promised to meet him at Eastbourne station, but instead a uniformed sergeant was there, his face crimson with the exertion of cycling uphill in what promised to be the hottest flaming June on record.

'This is rather a coincidence,' Lestrade said, 'but that cardboard sign you are holding over your head seems to bear my name. Are we related?'

'I don't think so, sir,' the sergeant wheezed, 'on account of my name being Gerald. Inspector Padstow's compliments, sir. Could you join him at haitch queue.'

'You've got transport?'

'Only my ol' bike, sir. You're welcome to use the cross bar, of course.'

'Nice of you,' Lestrade winced, 'but if I'd wanted to sing soprano I'd have joined the Glee Club. How did Inspector Padstow know I was coming?'

'Runton told him, sir.'

'David Runton? Yes, he was supposed to be meeting me here.'

'Ah well,' the sergeant grinned, 'he's a bit indisposed at the moment is Mr Runton, if you get my drift.'

'You mean he's ill?'

'Not 'arf as ill as he's goin' to be,' the sergeant felt it reasonable to put his arms down now and the card with Lestrade's name on it clanged into a bin.

'Meaning?'

'He's in custody, sir. 'Elping us with our inquiries, so to speak.'

'On what charge?'

The sergeant stopped, looking hard at Lestrade. 'Unspeakable charges, sir. Unnameable crimes. I cannot divulge, of course, you understand, but let's just say that they involve . . . women's clothing.'

'Women's clothing? Runton?' Lestrade was amazed. He'd struck him as a thoroughly tweedie sort of bloke.

'Oh, we've had our eye on him for some time,' the sergeant flashed a wink to the blind horse drinking from the trough, then hailed a cab. 'He's known as "Camp David" down the nick.'

'I see.'

'May I ask, sir, in order to enhance my chances of promotion, what is your business with this Runton?'

Lestrade turned to his man. 'No, you may not ask, Sergeant,' he said, 'but I assure you it has nothing whatever to do with womens' clothing. Cabbie, Sussex Constabulary Headquarters, please. They'll pick up the tab. Well, off you go, Sergeant; on your bike.'

Inspector Padstow was barely visible behind a pile of ladies corsetry that would have turned Messrs Harrods green with envy.

'None of your rubbish,' the local man said, his eyes watering behind the cigar smoke. 'Most of this is imported direct from Paris.'

'Where did it come from?' Lestrade asked.

'I told you,' Padstow frowned, 'Paris.'

'No, I mean, more recently.'

'Ah, well,' the inspector beamed, removing the cigar, 'there's the beauty of it. From bed – and other – rooms belonging to one David Laurence Runton of Thirty-four Magnolia Villas.'

'The bird watcher? I mean, we are talking about the same man?'

'This isn't London, Superintendent,' Padstow reminded him. 'There *is* only one David Runton in Eastbourne. And the bird watching was just a cover.'

'For what?'

'Procurement.'

'I see.'

'I know, I know. He didn't strike me as the type either. Stout, lace-up brogues, plus-fours, pair of calves on him like exhibits at the County Show. That rich, baritone voice. But they're always the worst, you see. Scotch?' he rattled his decanter.

'I think I'd better,' Lestrade said, 'I must be getting old. I can usually tell a Maryanne a mile off.'

'Ah, take my word for it. This is a whole new class of deviant. Blame the war.'

'Runton was in South Africa?'

'No. But we've got him bang to rights this time.'

'On procurement?'

'Look at this.'

'What is it?' The photograph appeared to be of a privet hedge.

'Clever, isn't it? Behind that hide is Constable Waters, my undercover man. Then, there's this.'

The second photograph was even more indistinct. 'Er . . .'

'That's Constable Waters.'

Lestrade turned the picture around. 'Really?'

'And this . . .' Padstow beamed with pride as he produced a rather fetching photograph of a young lady naked except for an asp, coiling round her . . . self.

'Runton?' Lestrade asked, astonished at the anatomical verisimilitude.

Padstow snatched it back. 'Sorry, that's . . . something else entirely.'

'Handsome woman, Mr Padstow,' Lestrade smiled.

'Is she? Er . . . oh yes, of course. Of course. No, this is the one.'

The third photograph was of a rather rough young lady lounging against a door frame.

'Should I know her?'

'I shouldn't think so. That's Michael Appleby. He's the local postmaster.'

'Good Lord.'

'And this,' Padstow was more careful with his photographic selections now, Lestrade noticed, 'the one on the left with the ample bosom is George Carson, local builder.'

'And the one on the right?'

'Don't know him,' Padstow took it back to recheck, 'but *thi* one', he threw it on to Lestrade's lap, 'is my piece of resistance John Moulscombe, curate of the aptly named St Botolph's. The vicar's going to be livid.'

'Where were these taken?

'In the back garden of Runton's house, the aforesaid Magnoli: Villas.'

'Is this all the proof you have?'

'Oh, no,' Padstow assured him, 'I led a raid, once we'c developed Waters's snaps. Dawn affair. Timing was perfect. had snipers on the Methodist Chapel roof.'

'Snipers?' Lestrade repeated. 'Bit heavy to catch some cross dressers, wasn't it?'

'Yes, I suppose so, but most of my blokes wouldn't know a cross-dresser from a Welsh dresser. Anyway, why should you blokes in the Met get all the fun? Went like a dream. Operation You Weird Bastard. I thought of the name myself.'

'Inspired,' said Lestrade. 'But I have stumbled into all thi: unawares, Inspector. I received a telegram from Runton . . .'

'I know. He's coughed everything from smoking behind the outbuildings at school to peeking up his Nanny's frock as a kid I wouldn't be at all surprised if he doesn't own up to causing the San Francisco earthquake by lunchtime.'

'Can I see him?'

'Be my guest,' Padstow threw Lestrade the keys, 'but I'd keep my back to the wall, if I were you.'

David Runton had lost some of the hearty bonhomie he'd displayed when Lestrade had spoken to him last. He now looked rather crestfallen, sitting on the hard iron bedstead in his cell, his breakfast crust untouched, his morning water unsipped.

Lestrade sat down quietly and waved the attendant constable away.

'You asked to see me, Mr Runton?' he said.

The twitcher-transvestite could not look him in the eye. 'That was before all this,' he whispered, afraid of his own voice in he stillness, 'I had hoped to talk to you in more convivial surroundings.'

'Indeed,' Lestrade nodded. 'To talk about what?'

'The man I saw on the cliff tops,' Runton said, 'I may have a name for you.'

'May?'

Runton looked his man in the face for the first time. Eastbourne is a sleepy little place, Mr Lestrade. You wouldn't think that behind those lace curtains and those endless coffee mornings and those meetings of the Primrose League, there would be a ring of vice, would you?'

'I've been a policeman for . . . well, never you mind how long . . Mr Runton. Very little surprises me any more.'

'Mr Lestrade, I won't mince words with you.'

Lestrade was glad there was *something* Runton wouldn't mince.

'On the one hand, this is 1906. We are all men of the world. When I visited Turkey three years ago in search of the Lesser Ibis, I saw a lot of this sort of thing. A boy's bottom was cheaper than goat's milk.'

'And on the other hand?' Lestrade asked.

'I haven't finished with the one hand yet,' Runton insisted. The point is that our circle – we called ourselves "Glad to be Gartered" – is composed of a number of like-minded individuals, all consenting, all adult and we only ever wear frocks in the confines of our own homes.'

'I see. And what else goes on in these homes?'

'I beg your pardon?' Runton's mouth gaped.

'Come, come, Mr Runton. It has been necessary in my time to traverse the area around Charing Cross – the Maryanne's Mile – on several occasions. I am not unaware of . . . certain practices, shall we say? On one occasion, and strictly in the line of duty, I assure you, two colleagues and I posed as women in order to catch a murderer on the Underground.'

'Really?' Runton's throat tightened. 'What . . . er . . . what did you wear?'

'You offered me a name,' Lestrade brought his man back sharply to the present.

'On the other hand,' Runton responded to the jolt, 'although

135

nothing else "goes on", as you delicately put it, at our full dress parades, I suppose I cannot expect moronic policemen, intolerant old judges and blind justice to understand our peccadilloes. So I need a deal.'

Lestrade rose. 'It's not within my power,' he said.

'Drop the charges and I'll tell you the man's name. The Sixteenth Lancer officer I saw on top of Beachy.'

Lestrade turned. 'Why didn't you tell me before?' he asked. 'Did you not suspect you were being watched by the local police?'

'Not a dicky-bird,' Runton shrugged, 'but that isn't the point. I didn't know it until a friend joined our circle last week.'

'A friend?'

'Someone I'd met in London.'

'Who?'

'Uh-uh,' Runton wagged the finger of a cross-dresser at Lestrade, 'first, the deal.'

'This isn't my patch,' Lestrade explained.

'But you're working on the disappearance of the Lancer. Or should I say the murder of that Spaniard. It *was* all over the papers in the end. The *Eastbourne Bugle* is a clarion call when it's roused. Rather a good likeness of you, I thought.'

'That's different,' Lestrade said. 'For that I was invited in by the chief constable of the county – that's how it works.'

'Well, get him to invite you to give me a deal,' Runton shouted. Then, calmer, 'Lestrade, I *can't* go to prison. Those awful, awful clothes. Those rough men. Contrary to what you believe I am perfectly heterosexual, I believe is the word. Except that I like my women in cravats and plus-fours. And the birds, Lestrade. There are no birds in prison.'

Lestrade looked at his man, the fear in his eyes, the terror in his heart. It had a strange ring to it – the Bird Man of Wormwood Scrubs.

'I'll see what I can do,' he said. 'But . . .' and he held up his hand to prevent Runton from collapsing at his feet, 'I can't promise.'

'That's all right. That's all right,' the man gabbled. 'I understand. Really. I do.'

'Very well,' Lestrade sat down again. 'Now. Your part of the bargain.'

'This friend,' Runton sat beside him, animated now and happy; his old self, in fact – very like the man with the binoculars Lestrade had met on the springy grasslands high above the coast, 'the one I met in London. I told him all about the incident at Beachy. He was fascinated. Well, most people are by murder, aren't they? He was particularly keen to know what the man looked like. Well, as you know, I didn't get a very good look at his face, but it seemed enough for . . . my friend. He has one of those photographic memories for faces. One glance and it's fixed for ever. He's not so good on names. The only thing was, the height was wrong.'

'The height?' Lestrade frowned.

'Yes, the man I saw was too tall. He must have been well over six feet. Well over. Didn't I mention that?'

'No, Mr Runton, you did not.'

'Is it important?'

'It might be,' Lestrade said. 'So, let's get this straight. Your friend recognized your description of the man wearing Lancer uniform at Beachy Head, except that he was too tall for the man he thought it was.'

'Precisely.'

'So he was wrong about who it was.'

'Not necessarily. I told you. He has this thing about faces. Never wrong, apparently.'

'But he's not so good on names,' Lestrade sighed, expecting the inevitable.

'No, he's not,' Runton confirmed, 'but he remembered this one.'

'He did?' Runton interested Lestrade strangely. Bearing in mind the contents of his wardrobe, that was hardly surprising.

'Another Spaniard, although he didn't have much of an accent, it seems. Name of Alvarez.'

'Alvarez?'

Runton nodded. 'Pedro Alvarez.'

Lestrade was on his feet again. 'This friend of yours. What's *his* name?'

'Oh, no,' Runton frowned, 'I couldn't do that.'

'Goodbye, Mr Runton. I'm afraid all deals are off.'

'Wait a minute. You promised!' Runton was on his feet.

'No,' Lestrade corrected him, 'on contrary, I said I *couldn't* make any promises. I think you'll find those prison clothes aren't so bad, you know. Those arrows are quite fetching, really.'

'Russell,' Runton shouted.

Was this a command, Lestrade wondered. 'What?'

'My friend's name. It is George Russell. He's a brewer.'

'Russell's and Mordecai's?'

'That's the one.'

'Headquarters in Chiswick. Suppliers to the Police Ball.'

'You know him, then.'

'No. We deal with old man Mordecai. Or did before he died. It'll have passed to his son now, I suppose.'

'The deal, Mr Lestrade,' Runton blurted, 'I've played fair with you.'

Lestrade looked at his man. 'I'll see myself out,' he said.

Superintendent Sholto Lestrade was a man of his word. He paid a visit to the chief constable of Sussex, put Runton's deal before him and was refused. On his way out, however, Lestrade paused at the door and called back across the chief constable's hall, 'Clarissa La Belle and half a pint of whipped cream.' It was enough. The chief constable reached for his telephone and by evening David Runton was a free man, stuffing fol-de-rols into a travelling trunk and making for Ostend, watching the cormorants wheel and dive. So did the wheels of justice grind in Campbell-Bannerman's England.

Russell's and Mordecai's had been brewers to the gentry and lots of other people since the reign of George III. They handled imports in those early days and the young Mr Pitt himself had drunk their fine port wines. They – and stress – had conspired to kill him. More recently, Prince Albert, no less, had made them his own when he stopped off for a pint on his way between Dover and London on the occasion of his marriage to Queen Victoria.

'*Mein Gott*,' he had exclaimed on his first introduction to English ale, '*Was ist dass*?'

'Russell's and Mordecai's,' they had told him and even so, it got the royal patronage so vital in those days.

Lestrade had no appointment, royal or otherwise, to see George Russell. He simply turned up the next morning at their Chiswick premises, where huge drayhorses placed large deposits on the cobbles. The roses twining around the main entrance looked destined, on that hot June morning, to be the finest for many a long year.

'Mr Russell is in the tasting cellar,' a cobwebbed retainer told him, 'would you care to walk this way?'

Not in the slightest, Lestrade thought, although jokes of that kind would have to wait another seventy years before becoming popular. Besides, he didn't want to be offensive to the old retainer.

'You'll have to mind your . . .' There was a sickening crunch as Lestrade's head hit the brickwork, 'head,' the retainer told him. 'It's ever so low down here.'

His ears ringing with the collision with the vaulted roof, the stench of yeast enough to make your gorge rise, Lestrade groped his way through corridors where musty barrels stood sentinel.

'Will!' the old retainer called, a bunch of keys jingling at his arthritic hip, 'Will. Is Mr Russell down here?'

'Old Mr Russell or young Mr Russell?'

'Young Mr Russell.'

'I dunno. Who wants him?'

A leather-capped head appeared around a brick wall. His eyes were large and poppy and his rather archaic sidewhiskers black and bushy. There was a gap in his teeth.

'This is Superintendent Lestrade, Will, from Scotland Yard. Will is our Head Vat Man, Superintendent.'

Lestrade shook the man's hand. 'Been with the firm long?' he asked.

'Nigh on fourteen year,' Will told him, 'man and boy. I dunno,' he looked at the barrels stacked behind him, 'you load sixteen tuns and what d'you get? Another day older and deeper in debt.'

'I was hoping to talk to Mr Russell.'

'Yes,' Will wiped his hands on his leather apron, 'well, I 'aven't seen 'im today.'

'He came down to the tasting room,' the retainer said, 'I'm sure that's where he said he was going. This way, Mr Lestrade.'

He led the Yard man over puddles of beer, past huge vats where something sticky and noxious bubbled at the surface.

'Hops,' the retainer explained as though he'd read Lestrade's mind. 'Oh, my giddy aunt!' And he stood stock still, so that Lestrade had to nudge him aside, reflecting for a moment on the likelihood of such an old man having any relatives at all, never mind unbalanced ones.

In the corner ahead of them lay an untidy heap of barrels, as though two or three of the higher ones had fallen, spilling their fermenting contents on to the cobbled surface of the floor. But it wasn't the spillage that had caused the ancient retainer to react in the way he did. It was what was floating in one of the still upright barrels. An adult male, of indeterminate age, was suspended in beer, his face down below the frothy surface, his hands hooked like grappling irons round the rim. He looked for all the world like a pickled something in the museum at St Bartholomew's Hospital. And not at all like George Grendell Russell, brewer to the gentry and lots of other people.

Will and Lestrade fished out the corpse and laid him on a low table nearby. The superintendent ordered lights and action. A message was to be sent to Scotland Yard. He wanted Chief Inspector Dew, Inspector Collins of the Fingerprint section, Constable Beaton and his camera, two other constables and on no account was *any* leak of what had happened to reach either the workforce in the brewery or the Russell family. While the retainer and Will scuttled away to do the man's bidding, only telling the odd passing brewer and vat man what had occurred, Lestrade went to work before the police surgeon had a chance to muck things up.

George Grendell Russell was fully clothed. He had not been in the liquid for long enough for the usual signs of drowning to be obvious. In fact he looked so well that Lestrade wondered if he hadn't got out three or four times to go for a pee. It was when he saw the face that his heart jumped. It was the man in the photograph, the one Padstow's man had taken from the hedge outside Magnolia Villas. Russell certainly looked different now, his hair plastered to his head, his face sticky with yeast and hops. And there was no hint of his splendid elegance in the satin day dress with the sequins. Lestrade placed his bowler on the bench beside him and putting both hands to the shoulders, rolled Russell on to his front. The body was quite cold, the suit clammy in its wrinkles, but it was still pliable. No signs of lividity yet, no stiffening of the sinews. There was a large area of matted blood across the back of the head, which tended to give the whole barrel he'd been in a reddish tinge.

Lestrade crossed to the scene of the crime, returning to it as policemen did more often than murderers. He lit a lucifer in the dark corner and could see at a glance in that flickering light what had happened. The shelf at eye level had slipped at one end, causing three or four barrels to slide off and to crash on to others below. It seemed reasonable that George Russell had been tasting a barrel, with the lid removed, when he had been struck from behind with such force that it had knocked him into the very liquid he had been trying out. So it was an accident. They happened all the time in this business. Lestrade lit a second match and peered closer at the wall where the shelf had been. The screws had been loosened – they were still protruding from the end of the timber, though in the half light, Russell would not have seen that. And anyway, Lestrade lit himself a cigar as he pondered it, his friend specialized in accidents. Mr Alvarez knew enough about his victims to know their movements, their ways and what dangerous gadgetry came to hand in the course of their daily lives.

He sat on a barrel and waited for his lads to arrive.

While Bee and Queux roped off the cellars with a blue cordon and Beaton's tripod sploshed down in various puddles of beer, Lestrade and Dew began interrogating the staff on the floors above – dray men, vat men, typewriters, accountants, clerks – the whole clutter of a busy brewery. Stockley Collins, with his jars and accoutrements, fussed and ferreted about, flicking things with his brushes and powders. Lestrade knew it would be of no use. Mr Alvarez was far too clever to leave his dabs anywhere. There had been none in the Chelsea house of Daniel Whiddon. There'd probably been none in the ruins of the lighthouse Belle Tout, although as the Sussex Constabulary didn't have a fingerprint department, he'd never know for sure. And there were so many in the corridors of King's College that Collins had given up and gone for a saveloy in the Strand.

Together the Yard men pieced together the last hours of a man's life. And it was two tired detectives who crawled into Lestrade's office that night, at that kink in the passageway where the latrine used to stand.

'Right, Walter,' Lestrade drove his knuckles into his burning eye sockets, 'next time I suggest a pint, remind me of today, will you?' He sniffed his armpits. 'Clings, doesn't it?' He had thrown his jacket over a chair and his bowler to the winds. It was nearly midnight, 13 June 1906. He flicked the calendar over. With a certain inexorability, it clicked over to 14 June.

'Tell me about wee Georgie Russell.'

'George Grendell Russell. Aged fifty-two.'

'A terrible age,' Lestrade shook his head in a heartfelt sort of way.

'A good businessman, by all accounts. But mean.'

'That's what makes him a good businessman.'

'Not all that popular either,' Dew yawned, trying to focus on his notepad.

'I got that impression,' Lestrade nodded. 'A Mr Bristow in Accounts had a target on the back of his door. He plays darts in his spare time.'

'So, guv?' Dew was too tired for the niceties and to make corrections.

'I flipped the board over to reveal a quite convincing sketch of Mr Russell. There were more holes around his tadger than I've had hot dinners.'

'Which leads me to wonder about disgruntled employees,' Dew mused, lolling back in his chair.

'Hm,' Lestrade nodded, 'fickle lot, your employees, disgruntled or still gruntled. 'Course, we called them servants when I was a lad.'

'Does that have a bearing, sir?' Dew was tired indeed. Not for all the world would he have offended his old guv'nor.

'Who knows,' Lestrade sighed, 'everybody keeps reminding me it's 1906. Perhaps there's a new breed of criminal at large. Go on with your disgruntled employee.'

'Well,' Dew chewed his moustache, 'the whole thing is made to look like an accident. Right?'

'As ninepence,' Lestrade said.

'So it's in keeping with the others. You're happy that it's all by the same hand?'

'Reasonably,' Lestrade said, 'although I have to admit there's no mirror this time.'

'Very well,' Dew's mind was trotting by now. At that hour, after the day he'd had, 'racing' was out of the question. 'What if the others have been a smokescreen? What if *this* is the real one? The killer's been playing us for fools all along?'

'That's possible,' Lestrade said, 'but why this one? Why not one of the others?'

'Well, surely once he's hit his real target, he wouldn't go on killing, would he? Unless he's a lunatic, of course.'

'No, Walter,' Lestrade said softly, gazing at the green baize wall ahead of him, cluttered with clues, festooned with photographs, 'he is very, very clever, but he isn't a lunatic. There's method in his method. And besides, we don't know that George Russell is his last one, do we? Do we, Walter?'

A soft snore came for answer. Dew had fallen asleep, still resting on one arm at Lestrade's desk. The superintendent stood up, hauled a rug around Dew's shoulders and tilted his bowler over his eyes. 'I'll get a message to Mrs Dew,' he whispered, 'tell her you couldn't make it back tonight. Good-night, Walter.'

'Hhhmhhh,' Dew murmured and Lestrade blew out the light.

The Granary, Ossington Street, Bayswater was an opulent villa of the 1880s, that heady decade when young men's fancies turned to the cycling craze and when the Ripper struck. This was a far cry from the damp and fermentation and horse shit of Russell's and Mordecai's Brewery. Here were aspidistrae of elephantine proportions, objay dar from all over the world and framed advertisements from years of brewing – 'Pure Genius', 'Probably the Finest Beer in the World', 'A Russell's and Mordecai's Works Wonders – So Drink One Today' and so on. At least in this black-and-beige hall, it was blissfully cool after the fierce heat of the June day.

Old Mr Russell was in the summer house and Lestrade was taken through to where a rustic table was set for luncheon under the cedars. There was still countryside in Bayswater in those days and Lestrade tipped his bowler to the ancient man with his sleeves rolled up, his Panama tilted against the sun.

'Superintendent Lestrade, sir, Scotland Yard,' he said, 'I've come about your boy.'

For a moment, he thought he saw the chin go, the lower lip hang loose, but it may have been a trick of the light, the dappling of the sun through the leaves.

'We had the news last night,' old Russell said, his voice brittle with the years, 'from old Droop, my Head Brewer.'

'Yes,' Lestrade remembered, 'I spoke to him.'

'I'm glad young Georgie's mother isn't alive to see this. It would break her heart. Ellen!' his voice cracked when he tried to lift it and he shielded his eyes against the sun's glare, 'Ellen, come here. This involves you.'

A respectable-looking lady emerged from the summer house, her hair piled high in the Edwardian style, her frothy blouse failing to conceal what the years had done to her waist. She was one of those unfortunates for whom the brassiere was to come too late.

'Superintendent Lestrade, Madam,' said Lestrade, risking sunstroke by doffing his hat entirely.

'I am Ellen Russell,' she said, 'widow of the late George Russell.'

'Please accept my condolences, both of you,' Lestrade said. 'It must have come as quite a shock.'

'It did,' his widow said. She was not wearing black, but then that was probably because this was 1906 and the deadly tentacles of the Women's Social and Political Union may already have reached Bayswater. 'Droop was quite overcome.' She glanced sideways at her father-in-law, 'we all were.'

'Not me,' the old boy was quick to correct her, 'I haven't shed a tear since old Crusher Horsnell tried to squeeze me through a mangle. I was six at the time. Haven't wasted 'em since. No point. It's God's will, this sort of thing. It's all up to Him, you know, that great Landlord in the sky. When he calls "Time!", that's it; there's nothing you can do. But listen, old Droop said you fellows were treating it as a case of murder. That can't be right, surely?'

'I believe it is, sir,' said Lestrade, 'I believe that your son's death was one of five that we are currently investigating.'

'What?' Ellen Russell sat down heavily.

Lestrade nodded. 'There is only one difference,' he said. 'I don't suppose either of you have seen a hand mirror, about six inches long with a rather crudely carved handle?'

Ellen's frown against the sun vanished and she stood up. 'One moment,' she said, 'if you'll excuse me,' and she swept indoors.

'Your son's staff tell me that on Fridays he always got to the brewery early.'

'That's right,' the old boy winked, settling himself in an armchair, 'as I did when I ran the business and my father before me. The Mordecais run the business end, the distribution and so on. We Russells are more about creative beer making. We're at the froth face, so to speak.'

'And this was common knowledge?'

'Among the staff, yes.'

'What time did he leave yesterday?'

'You'd have to ask Ellen. I was asleep.'

As if on cue, the lady of the house reappeared on the verandah. As she did so, Lestrade caught a movement out of the corner of his eye – a net curtain shivered aside. The second floor, west wing, if the sun was running true to course.

'Is this what you were looking for, Mr Lestrade?' Ellen Russell held up a small hand mirror, its handle carved with primitive squiggles, ugly, like a doll.

'It is,' Lestrade told her. 'Where did you get it?'

'It came in this morning's post. I thought you'd appreciate the packaging, but I'm very cross that the glass is broken.'

Lestrade smiled. 'That's very good, Mrs Russell,' he said 'You'd have made a good detective. But I'm not sure the Post Office is responsible.'

'As you see,' her face remained stony, 'it's addressed to my husband.'

'Posted late yesterday,' Lestrade read the evidence of the postmark, 'at Beckenham. I noticed as I came in, Mrs Russell various native auntifacts in the hall. Could this be another for your husband's collection?'

'It's my collection,' old Russell corrected him. 'Besides, all those came from Borneo and Sarawak. That's not from there.'

'No, sir, you're right,' Lestrade said, 'it's from Abyssinia.'

'Abyssinia?' Mrs Russell frowned, 'that's somewhere in Africa, isn't it?'

Lestrade nodded.

'Well, I can tell you, Superintendent, that my late husband had no connection whatever with Africa.' Her face hardened a little, 'neither was he exactly in a position to be a missionary.'

'What time did he leave the house yesterday, Mrs Russell?'

'His usual for a Friday. Five thirty.'

'So he would have arrived at the brewery . . . ?'

'Before six. He drives himself in the motor.'

Lestrade knew that. He'd already had Stockley Collins go over the car with a fine-tooth comb. Lestrade had been a *bit* surprised that Collins hadn't used his usual brush but it couldn't be denied that the fingerprint man knew his business. Nothing. The lad who slops out at Russell's and Mordecai's had polished the vehicle on the Thursday. The only dabs on it were his and the dead man's. That at least ruled out a casual hitchhiker who may have thumbed a lift and for whatever nefarious purpose have followed Russell into the cellars.

'From there', Lestrade was thinking aloud, 'he parked the car in the forecourt, turned left into the alleyway and up the fire escape. He let himself in with his key, went to his office as usual and then down to the cellars, past Sanderson the night watchman.'

'Did Sanderson see anyone else?' old Russell wanted to know. 'On the premises, I mean?'

'No, but he did say it was possible to get in at the back if the latch had not been fastened. Faulty door, I gather.'

'That's right,' Mrs Russell said quickly, 'we'd intended to have it fixed.'

'Tell me, Mr Russell,' Lestrade twirled the mirror in his hands, so that the light from it dazzled on the old man's cherry face, 'can you think of anyone who would want to see your son dead?'

'Anyone from Squeers,' he scowled.

'Squeers?' Lestrade repeated.

'Squeers' Beers, "The Biggest" and I quote "West of Watford". The biggest what, they aren't saying. Georgie and Henry were about to buy them out. It would have meant the loss of jobs for hundreds. Squeers is a proud old firm, Superintendent, like Russell's and Mordecai's. Family. We have a saying in this business – "blood is thicker than beer". I think you may already have found that that's true.'

Lestrade had, but this probably wasn't the time or the place to say so. 'Where is Mr Mordecai?' he asked.

'Brussels.'

'Where?'

'Brussells. It's a place in Belgium. They have all kinds of beer festivals there. Henry Mordecai is probably winning a gold medal as we speak, just like his father Abednego before him. Georgie would have gone, but he's been too busy. I would have gone, but for this flaring vegetoid arthritis,' and the old man sat down gratefully.

'Is there anyone else in the house?' Lestrade asked.

'Only Maitland,' Mrs Russell said. 'He showed you in. The rest of the staff have the day off every fourth Saturday. We are enlightened employers, Mr Lestrade.'

'Of course,' beamed the inspector.

'By the way,' Ellen Russell held up a box of chocolates lying on the luncheon table, 'would you like a creme passionelle?'

'Thank you, no,' Lestrade said, 'I must be going. If I might take this, Mrs Russell? Evidence, you see.'

'The mirror? Oh, yes. Yes of course. But what does it mean?'

'I wish I knew,' Lestrade admitted. 'You're sure that neither of you have seen it before.'

'No,' they chorused.

'Well. No, no, please,' he waved Ellen Russell back to her chair, 'I'll see myself out. Enjoy your lunch.'

It was a little surprising that he hadn't been asked to stay. It would have been courtesy to have been *asked* at least, especially as there was no one else in the house and there were settings for three people. But then, he reasoned, as he climbed the steps on to the terrace and barked his shin on a Dog of Foo, perhaps that was for Maitland. After all, the Russells *were* enlightened employers.

It was as he was crossing the hall that he heard it. A sharp hiss as though those little bastards were sticking nails into the tires of his Lanchester again. He walked on. Obviously Maitland was doing something culinary in the kitchen. There it was again. He stopped, half turned and felt his wrist click as a hand lunged from nowhere, caught his and pulled him bodily into the billiards room.

He looked into the red-rimmed eyes of a woman. What was she, thirty-five or so? She'd never been attractive, but her pinched face was pale and her nose red with crying. She had bare feet and wild hair.

'Are you looking for a murderer?' she asked in a sweet, melodic voice.

'I . . . er . . .' Lestrade looked frantically around for signs of help.

'Because you've just been talking to one. If you let me sit on your lap, I'll tell you how I know.'

7

It wasn't the usual interrogation procedure at the Yard. Not in 1906, anyway. And certainly it featured nowhere in Lestrade's official report. In fact, with the appearance that month of the returnable carriage on typewriters, it would be some weeks before *any* reports appeared and many were the handleless cups that would spill their steaming contents over the Yard floor, smashed into oblivion by a runaway carriage, returning a little too fast for anyone's liking.

It was a fact however that in the dark recesses of a small ante-room at Ossington Street, the demure, red-eyed young lady did sit on Lestrade's lap. Further than that he was not prepared to go and mercifully, it seemed, neither was she.

'Are you sitting comfortably?' she asked him.

'Reasonably,' he said, shifting the brass knuckles in his pocket for the sake of them both.

'Then I'll begin,' she said. 'You're Superintendent Lestrade, aren't you?'

'Yes, Madam; and you are?'

'Certified, but I'm quite observant. I am Jane Russell,' she sat upright so that her breasts were as protruberant as possible. All in all, not very impressive. 'Billy was my brother.'

'Billy?' Lestrade repeated.

'George Grendell,' she explained. 'As children we had nicknames for each other. He was Billy and I was Nanny – on account of father being such an old goat.'

'Of course,' Lestrade's fixed grin was beginning to hurt. 'Miss Russell, I . . .'

She held her finger to his lips. 'We don't cry in this family, Mr Lestrade. Something to do with not crying into beer, I think, way back. But we mourn. Father in his stiff-upper-lip way. in mine.'

'And your sister-in-law?'

'Well, there you are,' Jane smiled wistfully, 'not a trace of black anywhere, was there? Except around her heart. And you can't see her heart.'

'What are you trying to tell me, Miss Russell?'

'Are you married, Superintendent?' she asked.

'No,' he said slowly, 'not at the moment.'

She gazed into his eyes. 'You should be,' she said. 'We all need someone,' and she held his hand. 'I am trying to tell you that my sister-in-law murdered Billy.'

'Really? How?'

She stood up suddenly, 'I may be under house arrest,' she said. 'I may not be allowed sharp things, and I suppose I am a little ... unwell, sometimes, but I know things. I know this house, for instance – all its little crooks and nannies. Ellen doesn't. She doesn't know about the passageway that connects the library to her bedroom.' She moved closer to him, 'I've heard things, Superintendent. At dead of night when the dead walk. There are ghosts here, Mr Lestrade,' her wild eyes rolled around the room. 'Can't you feel them, reaching out for you with their fingers? Sshh!' she froze, putting her own fingers to her lips, 'can't you hear them whispering to you? Do you know what they say?'

Her eyes closed, her voice altered. It was harsh, masculine, strange. All the stranger because it came from her lips.

'I've found someone, Nell. It won't be cheap. But he's good.'

'Who is it?' her voice was that of her sister-in-law, cold, calculated.

'Better you don't know.' It was the man's voice again. 'But it will be a week Friday. Where are you?'

'Here. As always.'

'Not good,' she swayed, her eyes still tight shut. 'Make sure you're elsewhere. You must have an alibi.'

'Can we trust him, this man?'

'As far as we can trust anyone. You're sure he'll be at the brewery?'

'You know he never misses. I hate him, with his hypocrisy.

His indifference. And why does he look better in a bustle than I do?'

'That's settled, then.'

She shuddered. Her eyes flicked open.

'Fascinating, Miss Russell,' Lestrade said. 'Your sister-in-law I recognized, but who was the man?'

She whirled three times. '"She left the web, she left the loom, she took three paces through the room."'

'I'm sorry?' Lestrade was lost now.

'Henry Mordecai,' she said.

'As in Russell and Mordecai?'

She nodded.

'So,' he stood up too, 'let me see if I've got this straight. You claim that your sister-in-law and your late brother's partner are . . . what?'

'Having an affair, Mr Lestrade. That's not all I've heard,' she giggled. 'The bedsprings . . .'

'That is not an indictable offence, Miss Russell,' Lestrade smiled, 'though doubtless there are those who say it should be.'

'But murder, Mr Lestrade . . .'

'You overheard a plot', the Superintendent said, 'between Mrs Russell and Mr Mordecai to employ someone to kill your late brother?'

She smiled, 'I am of course only mad "Nor" by Nor'-West".' Her smile vanished. 'You don't believe me, do you?'

'Miss Russell . . .'

'Don't patronize me, Mr Lestrade,' she suddenly hissed. He was glad she wasn't allowed sharp objects. 'They'll be desperate now. Unable to see each other except for the funeral. No letters. No telephone calls. They'll be afraid they're being watched. *That*'s when they're vulnerable, when they'll snap.'

Lestrade smiled. 'You know, Miss Russell,' he said, 'you'd have made a pretty good detective, too.'

'So would you,' she said.

A bell rang on the wall.

'Ah,' she beamed, 'it's time for my luncheon. Every Saturday, I'm allowed to eat with them.' She ferreted in her underwear, hauling up layers of petticoat, 'and I think it's time to add this to Nell's salad.'

And she held up the dangling body of a dead rat.

'Raving, then, guv,' Sergeant Adams stirred his tea with his pencil.

'As a hatter,' Lestrade confirmed. 'And yet . . .'

'Yet?'

'You found Henry Mordecai's home address?'

'Thirty-one Ravenswood Road, Balham.'

'Married?'

'Divorced.'

'Expensive business.'

'He can afford it. Bought a pint of Russell's and Mordecai's recently?'

'I don't know,' Lestrade said. 'It must be my age. I always seem to forget my wallet when I'm in a pub these days.' Adams noticed Constables Bee and Queux nodding behind Lestrade in a heartfelt way. 'How long ago?'

'The divorce? Four, five years.'

'How did he seem?'

'Oily bastard,' the sergeant said. 'Bit of a smell under his nose.'

'How did he react to the questions?'

'Question One,' Adams quoted from his notepad, '"What was your relationship with the late Mr Russell?" Answer, "He was my partner." Question Two – "When did you last see your partner?" Answer, "Wednesday afternoon, at the Board Meeting." Question Three – "Can you think of anyone who would want to see him dead?" Answer, "No."'

'Forthcoming, then?' Lestrade mused, watching the sun dance on the river and the flies chase each other over the hot bricks of the wall that blocked most of that view.

'As a mute,' Adams confirmed.

'And what of his mien?' Lestrade asked.

'His mean what, guv?'

'His behaviour, Sergeant,' the superintendent was patience itself. 'How he inducted himself?'

'Don't know,' Adams sucked the tea off his pencil, his eyes narrowing, 'I wouldn't like to go into the witness box on it, but

152

I'd say he was shitting himself. In a controlled sort of way, of course.'

'You rattled him, then?'

'Like a cage. Like you suggested, guv, long meaningful looks. Stagnant pauses. He was smoking like a chimney when I left.'

'And the telegram?'

'Sent at . . . Bee?'

'Ten thirty-seven, Sarge.'

'Ten thirty-seven, sir.'

'Who's on surveillance?'

'Royal.'

'"The Shadow"?' Lestrade checked.

'The same.'

'No one better. What about our man at the telephone exchange?'

'"Ears" McMullen? Sitting by the switchboard as we speak.'

'Right,' Lestrade lolled back in his swivel, 'so we've got it covered, whichever way he jumps. Fancy a game of "I Spy", Sergeant?'

Henry Mordecai was clearly over six feet tall. Standing fully erect – as he often was in the presence of Mrs Ellen Russell – he could pass for a little short of six feet five. He was one of a family of the Chosen People who had found it expedient in years gone by to drop that dubious claim and cross to the Gentile camp. Only the dark features and slightly hooked nose betrayed him now. The married eyebrows were carefully shaved and a fortune spent on elocution lessons had lessened his lisp.

He stood perusing the goodies on display on the first floor of Harrods, waiting for his paramour. He had caught a closed cab to Hyde Park, then doubled back by motor taxi, circling the cavalry barracks and Tattersall's until he felt safe. Damn that silly woman. He didn't think she'd crack. But she had. One brief, frantic telephone call. 'Harrods,' she had said, 'four o'clock.' Constable McMullen had put her through.

He found himself riveted by the glittering array of silverware before him, repulsive dessert stands, jardinieres and cutlery sets. Everything in fact for the gentleman whose income topped ten thousand a year. He wandered along the rows of claret jugs, the presentation cups, the salvers. One particularly caught his eye, but he couldn't afford to make a fuss and draw attention to himself, so he just patted the bruise with his handkerchief.

In the Pen Hall, a particularly ornate pencil case drew his attention. It was in the form of a naval cannon and only three and six. Must be wrongly priced, he thought. Some old crone was fiddling with it too, sucking her empty gums as she tottered on the arm of her grandson, so he turned away. Then, there she was. Was it the light? The cut of her choker? Was she less attractive than when he saw her last? Less alluring? Still, she always looked best just before he ripped the chemise from her shoulders. She started as she saw him, but he frowned and jerked his head as he caught sight of a young man to his left, eyeing the coffee sets and the cruets. She crossed to the central aisle, then studied the nautilus spoon warmers with an intensity rarely found in the most ardent shopper. She saw his reflection swivel into view in the silver mirrors of the soup tureens and he stood with his back to her.

'You're late,' he hissed.

'I couldn't get away,' she moved as close as she dared. 'Father was having one of his turns.' She ran her hand up his thigh under the jacket.

'Please,' he almost shouted, pulling away, 'not here. This is stupid, Nell. We agreed. No contact, apart from the funeral. Not yet. It's too soon.'

'But I want you, Henry,' she whispered, feeling her composure slipping.

The old crone had hobbled round the corner, announcing her presence by catching her toe a nasty one on a dinner gong.

'Steady, Granny,' her young man said, 'you know what the doctor told you.'

'I'm having my day out,' the crone shook herself free of him. 'Doctors! What do they know?'

The young man looked acutely embarrassed and wandered away, leaving the old girl to peer through her pebble-dash glasses at the tantali.

'Why did you ring?' Mordecai waited until the hubbub had died down and everyone seemed engrossed in their mooching.

154

'You said there was a hitch,' she whispered. 'On the telephone on Thursday night, you said the man had gone down with the 'flu.'

'So he had,' Mordecai examined the asparagus tongs as though his life depended on them.

'But . . .'

'Look, Nell,' he was almost tempted to turn, but checked himself, 'I don't know what happened. All I know is that my man said he was ill. He sent me a note which I burned, of course. I was making plans for next week. Then our ancient retainer telephoned me on Friday to say that George was dead.'

'So what happened?'

'I haven't had a chance to find out. Presumably, our man recovered and decided to go through with it.'

'We've got to *know*,' Ellen Russell was quietly hysterical.

'All right. I'll see to it.'

'Now!'

The old crone was pulling away from her grandson again, catching him a nasty one on the shin with her surprisingly large lace-up boot, 'I *will* look at the fish forks,' she insisted.

'Now?' Mordecai turned away from the old trout. He checked his watch. 'It's not exactly convenient.'

'Do you want me?' she faced him for the first time. He spun back, finding the egg cups irresistible.

'Of course.'

'And the money,' her whisper hardened. '*All* of Russell's and Mordecai's.'

'Very well,' he nodded abruptly, 'but no more calls. No letters. And no more meetings like this.'

'I promise,' she shuddered.

'One more thing. That mad old sister-in-law of yours hasn't said anything else, has she?'

'Leave Jane to me,' Ellen whispered, 'I've increased her dosage.'

'Good. Have the police been to see you?'

'An idiot called Lestrade. A superintendent. He suspected nothing.'

'A superintendent?' Mordecai bridled, 'I only got a sergeant. Sub-human.'

155

'Aren't they all? *A bientôt*, dearest.'

They moved apart. 'Wait,' she sprang back to his side. Mordecai looked frantically around, but no one seemed to have noticed. The old girl was fingering the nutcrackers in a way that would have made Tchaikovsky wince.

'What *is* it?' the brewer was beside himself.

'This man,' she muttered, 'you know. *The* man. Is he trustworthy?'

'Calm yourself. We've been over all this. He doesn't know my name. He's never seen my face. All he knows is that I paid him to do a job. That's all. Or rather I've half paid him. The rest is to come when I'm sure it's safe. Now, please, Nell. Act naturally,' and he broke curtly away.

'You two!' a voice boomed through the silver hall. For a moment, time stopped. Mordecai steadied himself, his hand on the stair rail. Ellen backed into the snuff boxes, praying that the ground would swallow her up. In an instant the stupidity of this rendezvous hit them both. Not *too* unusual for a man and his dead partner's wife to meet at one of their houses – better still, the brewery. But this supposedly chance meeting at one of the better stores in Knightsbridge strained credulity.

'I've been watching you,' but the man with the booming voice swept past them both, gently sidestepping Ellen Russell with a polite, 'Excuse me, madam,' and made for the old crone and her grandson. Their hearts back in position, Mordecai and his illicit love went their separate ways.

'I am the store detective,' the man bellowed with no hint of that decorum one would expect in a shop like Harrods, 'and you've been behaving rather oddly. It's an old ploy y'know and I've seen 'em all in my time. The old girl behaves peculiar while her accomplice', he laid hands on the young man's collar, 'swipes the silver.'

'Take your hand off my shawl, sonny, or you'll spend the rest of the day looking for your teeth.' The old girl had rather a mannish voice suddenly and she'd straightened up to be a foot taller.

'Now, look here . . .' the detective refused to be nonplussed.

'Show him your warrant card, Queux,' the old trout ordered and the young man did.

'Scotland Yard?'

'Correct,' snapped the old girl. 'One more word out of you and I'll arrest you for interfering with a police inquiry.'

'Blimey.'

'Oh, and another thing,' the crone turned back to him, 'if you really think anybody would want to swipe any of this old tat, you need your head read. Queux!' And they dashed for the stairs.

'Christ, guv, you didn't half catch me a nasty one on the shin back there.'

'Sorry,' muttered Lestrade, hauling off his wig and bonnet, 'but having agreed to shave off my moustache, I had to go the whole hog. There. There he is. Getting into that cab. Taxi!'

They ran the length of Knightsbridge before a cab swerved in for them. "Ere!' the driver got a closer look at Lestrade, 'you're wearin' a frock.'

'Very astute,' the Superintendent replied. 'It was half price in Harrods and I just couldn't pass it up. Follow that cab. Double the fare if you don't lose it. Queux, dig my suit out of your Gladstone, will you?'

The detectives piled into the motor and the driver swung out into the traffic. 'Wot abaht speed traps?' he called back to them.

'Not much fear of that,' Lestrade ripped at his bodice – he hadn't done *that* for some little time – 'not at the speed you're going.' They turned right along Park Lane, then left past Cumberland Gate and back around Marble Arch.

'Whenever I pass here, guv,' Queux said, handing Lestrade his socks, 'I think of Tyburn Tree. You know, where they used to hang folks.'

'Ah, the good old days,' Lestrade wrestled with his tie.

'Do you know, guv,' Queux was staring at his guv'nor, 'you ought to keep that 'tache off. Takes years off you.'

'Thank you, Constable,' Lestrade rummaged in the bottom of Queux's Gladstone to find his tiepin, the one given to him by a grateful firm in the Case of the Tiepin Pool, 'but when you haven't bared your upper lip for thirty-one years – not even to play Sarah Bernhardt in the Police Revue – June can be a treacherous month.'

'He's pullin' over, gents,' the cabbie shouted.

'Pull over there,' Lestrade ordered. 'The other side. Where are we, Queux?'

'Manchester Street, guv. He's going into Number Twenty-eight.'

'Right. Pay the man.' And Lestrade was gone, ramming the bowler on to his head and checking the brass knuckles in his jacket pocket. Behind him, an impoverished constable sat open-mouthed.

'That'll be three and six,' the cabbie beamed.

Mordecai had taken the stairs to the left, iron treads that went to the basement. He waited in the shadows, a place where the summer sun never shone and then he saw Lestrade coming for him.

'Who the devil are you?' he wanted to know.

'The devil indeed,' said Lestrade. 'Henry Mordecai, I am arresting you on a charge of conspiracy to murder. You are not obliged to say anything, but anything you do say will be taken down and may be given in evidence.'

'Bastard!' growled the brewer, bracing himself.

'Yes, that will endear you to the judge.' Lestrade's switchblade was faster than Mordecai's fists. The tip glinted dully below the brewer's chin as Queux arrived at the top of the steps. 'Now you go into custody with this nice policeman, there's a good felon. The grown-ups want to talk.'

All in all, Mordecai didn't have a great deal of choice from this point onwards. Queux, who had after all been voted the Biggest Lad in Accounts, Metropolitan Division, hooked the brewer's arm behind his back and cuffed him to the railings, carefully out of sight of the door that led to the basement. When the coast was clear, Lestrade knocked again.

This time there was a rattle of bolts and a sliding of furniture and a rather small, unprepossessing figure appeared in the doorway. 'Yes?' he said. He was a man the wrong side of forty, with a bald head and a nervous tic. Not quite what Lestrade was expecting. 'I'm Henry Mordecai,' the superintendent lied, aware that above and behind him, increasingly irate residents noted a young detective clapping a massive hand over the mouth of a criminal chained to their front railings.

'Congratulations,' the little man said, displaying a slight northern twang. 'You're not a Jehovah's witness, are you?'

'No,' Lestrade assured him, 'but we do have business, you and I.'

'Oh?'

'May I come in?'

'If it's Life Insurance,' the little man said, 'I will willingly call on you, but at the moment, I'm not well. I've had the influenza.'

'I know,' Lestrade pushed past him into a murky passageway, 'that was the business which I colluded to. George Russell.'

'Ah,' realization dawned, 'you're the gentleman who left the money in the usual place.'

Lestrade nodded.

'Come in,' the little man said. 'Would you care for a cup of tea?'

'Thank you, no,' Lestrade tried to keep his aloof brewer impression going for as long as possible. 'I'd like some answers.'

'So would I,' the little man said, waving him into an excrutiatingly uncomfortable armchair, 'I feel I've been short-changed, Mr Mordecai.'

'How so?'

The little man produced a copy of *The Times*. 'Page fourteen,' he said. 'The Obits. column. "Brewer Found Drowned".'

'Yes,' Lestrade said, 'that was very good. I've come to pay you what I owe you.'

'No, no, no,' the little man's tic was more persistent than a grandfather clock, 'you miss my point. I didn't do that.'

'You didn't?'

The little man swept off his glasses and wiped them on a handkerchief. 'Surely you got my note – in the usual place – to the effect that I was under the weather? You see, mine is a precision art, Mr Mordecai. Any stiffness of the joints, any fuzziness of the head, and all can go wrong.'

'You mean . . . you didn't kill George Russell?'

'Of course not. It has none of my hallmarks. Without giving

159

too much away, had it been me, there would have been no marks on the body whatsoever. Which brings me to my point. Your contract-breaking.'

'My . . . ?'

'Well, clearly you got somebody else in,' the little man said. 'A decided amateur at that.'

'But it looked like an accident.'

'Oh, superficially, no doubt,' the contract-killer said. 'That's what *The Times* says certainly. But to anyone who has an awareness of these things, it's really quite puerile. I suppose there's a certain poetry, though, in Russell ending up in one of his own vats. Rather like the Duke of Clarence, isn't it?'

Lestrade knew that the Duke of Clarence had died of 'flu back in 1892. The connection was lost on him, but the little man was in full flight, '"I, that was wash'd to death with fulsome wine" – only in this case, beer. Still, Mr Mordecai,' the tic had suddenly gone and the little man's eyes looked cold behind the glasses, 'you employed someone else and thereby broke your contract. Now, clearly, I cannot sue you in a court of law, but I want you to know that the PMA takes a pretty dim view of this sort of thing. And I'll have the rest of my fee, regardless.'

'The PMA?'

'The Professional Murderers' Association,' the little man smiled. 'Oh, you won't find us in the telephone directory, but, although under another name, we are a registered charity.'

'I see, Mr . . . er . . .'

The little man shook his head. 'You know the rules,' he said, 'no names. My little card in the window of the Post Office says "Instant Removals. Departure Guaranteed". I promise to deliver – anytime, anywhere – well, almost, if it weren't for this damned 'flu. But as to names, I prefer anonymity.'

'So be it – for now,' Lestrade said, shrugging, 'Mr Anonymity, I am Superintendent Lestrade of Scotland Yard and I am arresting you for . . .'

'Oh, bugger,' the little man said softly, and the next thing Lestrade knew he was flat on his back, his legs in the air, pinned to the floor with the little man's boot on his neck and his right arm extended, his fingers bent backwards in the little man's grip. 'As soon as I saw you had recently shaved off your moey, I

160

should have been suspicious,' he said, twisting Lestrade's hand for good measure. There was a horrible cracking sound and it induced the Superintendent not to move, 'Men only remove their moeys for two reasons – because they're being chased. Or they're chasing. Either way, it's a dead giveaway. And I missed it. Well, it's the 'flu. I really haven't been well. I see, from the way you fell for that move, that you are unacquainted with the ancient Japanese art of ju-jitsu, Mr Lestrade. I'm telling you all this because I like a subject to know what's going to happen to him. It means the gentle way, quite literally. Now you're . . . what . . . about five years my senior, I suppose, but you must be four inches taller and a good two stone heavier. Even so, I'm going to kill you without breaking into a sweat. It's a bit awkward, really. I do so hate doing it at home. It's the old disposal of the body bit that's the problem. Still, I'll wrap you in the carpet and take you to the canal after dark, I think. That'd be best.'

Lestrade lashed out with his right boot, but the little man was faster and he caught it and flipped the superintendent over like a coley at Billingsgate, so that his nose bounced on the mat.

'There, now,' the little man said. 'You'll have terrible carpet burns, now. Better just to lie still. I've trained under the great Raku Uyenishi himself. If things were different, I'd introduce you to his school in Golden Square. Still, there it is. Funny how things work out in life, isn't it?'

Lestrade lifted himself up on his hands, but his leg was still held firm behind him, like a rather geriatric ballerina who needed some help with her *pas de deux*.

'I don't really know what you're trying to achieve, Mr Lestrade,' the little man said, 'you see, ju-jitsu is all about leverage and balance. It really wouldn't matter if you weighed twenty stone. You wouldn't lay a finger on me.'

Lestrade threw his body weight to the left, expecting the little man to roll with him. He didn't. He simply stepped aside, hooked Lestrade's legs under him and hauled him upright by the hair. He now sat cross-legged in the middle of the floor. 'That's very good,' the little man said. 'That's what they call the lotus position in Eastern philosophy.'

'Lotus' to Lestrade was a firm of shoemakers. How he could try on a pair of shoes with his feet where they were, was beyond him. The little man looked at his watch. 'Tsk, is that the time? Well, I'd love to continue the lesson, Mr Lestrade, but I *do* have a pressing engagement. You know, this'll be my first day out since Tuesday. I'm quite looking forward to it. In ju-jitsu,' he caught Lestrade's left arm by the wrist, 'the joints are dislocated by the laceration of ligaments and the muscles are torn from their origins by over-extension and twisting, like so,' he twirled round, taking the arm with him.

Lestrade shrieked.

'Now, normally, of course, at this point, were this a bout, you'd submit. But in this case, I'm going to break both your arms. Why? Well, because I enjoy it really and besides, you'll fit better into the carpet later.' He braced himself to turn again, a move which must rip Lestrade's upper arm from his shoulder socket.

There was a thump at the door. For a fraction of a second, the little man's concentration wandered; his eyes flicked to the passageway. In that instant, Lestrade's right arm thumped forward, the brass knuckles pounding into his assailant's ribs, the switchblade ripping in under his diaphragm so that the blood trickled out over the brass.

'Oh, bugger,' the little man said, 'I told you I hadn't been well,' and he slumped on to his knees before collapsing beside Lestrade.

There was another thundering at the door, followed by a crashing of timbers and a hatless Queux stood there, panting, looking at the curious sight of his guv'nor, pinned to the ground with his legs in a knot and to an inoffensive-looking little man who was probably a Life Insurance salesman.

'Everything all right, guv?' he asked.

'What was his name?' Chief Inspector Dew was constantly adding bits of paper to the wall in Lestrade's office. In the corridor outside, uniformed constables took bets on how often his head appeared above the glass partition.

'The flat was listed in the name of Cotterell,' Lestrade said. 'The landlord thought he was an insurance salesman.'

'Some insurance salesman,' Dew looked at his guv'nor, his left arm outstretched in plaster, his neck in a surgical collar. 'Did they say when the swelling would go down?'

'Nineteen fourteen,' Lestrade winced, grateful at least that his right hand was still vaguely in working order and could hold a teacup.

'We visited that Japanese bloke, guv,' Bee said, 'the one who runs the ju-jitsu school in Golden Square. He knew Cotterell and was pretty appalled that the little shit – his words, not mine – should be actually killing people with a technique designed for self-defence only.'

'How's Cotterell himself?' Lestrade asked.

'Punctured lung,' Queux said. 'He'll be fit enough to stand trial for attempted murder.'

'Good,' Lestrade said without malice. 'But I'll be happier to get him on other counts. Bee, you're good at the long words. Have a shufty through unsolved murders of the last, say, three years. Anything with the victim unmarked except for broken necks, that sort of thing. If we can tie friend Cotterell into one of those, I'd breathe easier in my splint.'

'Where does this leave us on this case, sir?' Dew asked.

Lestrade tried to loll, but lolling was a pleasure he'd have to forego for a while – that and scratching any part of the left side of his body.

'Precisely nowhere,' he muttered, looking intently at the bewildering array of pieces of paper on the wall before him. 'All right, gentlemen. Recapping by numbers. Walter – Murder One.'

'Murder One,' Dew clambered down from the chair. 'Four victims, Captain Orange, late of the Merchant service and his three nieces. Killed when the hames of their trap broke on a downhill gradient near Peter Tavy, Devon.'

'Clues?'

'A tall man seen near the Captain's house shortly before the trap left. He could have cut the harness.'

'And?'

'A broken mirror, we thought at first broken in the fall,

found in the Captain's breast pocket. Said mirror of Abyssinian origin.'

'Very well,' Lestrade nodded. 'Queux – Murder Two.'

'Murder Two, sir,' the detective cleared his throat. 'Janet Calthrop, fell downstairs at King's College, London, on the way back to the boudoir of her lover.'

'Cause of death?'

'Tripwire across the stairs. Fist in middle of back. Result – broken neck.'

'Clues?'

'Apart from the wirework on the nether limb and the bruising in the back consistent with the above theories, one Abyssinian mirror, found in said lover's boudoir.'

'Suspects?'

'No sign of a tall man, but my money is still on James Sparrow for that one.'

'You're entitled to your opinion,' Lestrade told him, 'within these walls. Murder Three. Bee?'

The constable was already combing the shoe boxes in search of dislocated victims of the Insurance Man, but, a prerequisite of the Met in those days, he was quite capable of doing two things at once. 'Juan Tomas de Jesus-Lopez, honorary major with the Sixteenth Lancers; body found under a collapsed floor of a ruined lighthouse near Beachy Head.'

'Clues?'

'Broken Abyssinian mirror. Officer of Sixteenth seen wandering – and apparently disappearing – at the cliff top. Presumably an attempt to make it look as though the Spaniard had committed suicide.'

'From which you deduce?'

'Er . . .'

'That our friend was buying time,' Lestrade helped him. 'He didn't want the body found too soon. All the police energies were concentrated at the bottom of Beachy, not three or four miles away where it *really* lay. Murder Four? That must be me. Victim – Sir Daniel Whiddon, gadget-fancier extraordinary. Done to death by a nasty little device for preventing peeing in the night. Spike through the staff of life, as a result of which he bled to death. An Abyssinian mirror under his pillow and he died near an ordinary English one at his home. He was visited, by an inventor calling himself Alvarez, on the day he died. Murder Five – Dew?'

'George Russell, brewer, drowned in a barrel of beer, caused by him falling into it having been knocked there by a shelf giving way.'

'Clues?'

'Abyssinian mirror, sent by post. Postmark unhelpful. No fingerprints of a suspicious nature. *But,*' Dew paused significantly, 'and here's the wrinkle, we know that the deceased's wife and the deceased's business partner conspired to kill said deceased by employing a professional killer. You know, guv, I'm still gobsmacked by that. I thought people like that just turned up in fiction.'

'That's right,' said Bee, *'The Dead Man Wore a Tutu* for example.'

'Bored to Death by Edgar Wallace,' said Queux. 'Mind you, his *Four Just Men* is better. Have you read it, Arnold?'

But before Bee could reply, Lestrade rapped on the desk with his good hand. Even so, it made his eyes water. 'Gentlemen,' he said, 'let me assure you that Mr Cotterell is a real enough character. I am living proof – thanks to Constable Queux here – of that fact. Walter, has Mrs Russell coughed?'

'Like a consumptive, guv,' Dew told him. 'We went through three dozen hankies, Metropolitan Police, Interrogations For The Use Of, but we got there in the end. It seems their torrid little affair began a year ago at the Brewers' Convention in Scarborough. Russell had to come back to London on some crisis in the firm and that was the signal for Mordecai to get his leg over. They planned the whole thing, lying alone in the darkness of Room 104 in the Lion Hotel. George Russell had been all right at first, but his night attire had got longer and silkier as the marriage progressed. Little by little it broke down – a little rouge here, a little lavender water there. As soon as he put lavender water *there,* her ardour cooled and she fell for what she called a real man. The last straw was Russell going off to some convention here in London – that must have been where he met David Runton. Mordecai wouldn't tell her who he'd hired to do the business. Only that a professional was being called in. Trapped in a loveless marriage, she was happy to go along with it.'

'And Mordecai's interrogation?' Lestrade had been in hospital at the time.

'Well, he took longer,' Dew remembered. 'Too manly to ask for a hankie. Even so, he's singing like a lark now. He read Cotterell's cryptic ad in the Chiswick Post Office. Apparently a friend of a friend had used him already.'

'Names? Places? Times?'

Dew shook his head. 'I didn't want to sidetrack him, sir.' Lestrade understood. 'He and Cotterell never met. They left messages at the Post Office as a sort of "poste restante". Half the money up front. The rest on delivery of the goods.'

'How much are we talking about?'

'A thousand quid.'

Bee and Queux whistled.

'Only somebody else beat them to it,' Lestrade said, attempting to chew his moustache before he realized it wasn't there. 'Right,' he staggered to his feet, 'we've got two names, gentlemen. Captain Charles Speedy – the tall officer Tenterden knew back in Abyssinia – and Señor Alvarez, inventor of rather dangerous personal accoutrements. Any luck there?'

'Adams is out on that one now, sir,' Dew said. 'Bee, you did something on this.'

'I found three Señor Alvarezes, sir,' the constable said, about to tackle his third shoe box. 'One of them – José – is in Abney Park, pushing up the daisies. The second – Geronimo – is confined to a wheelchair in a Home for Old Europeans in Chertsey. And the third – Miguel – is taking a five-year-long vacation at the expense of His Majesty at Strangeways jail, Manchester. All in all, rather disappointing, I thought.'

'And Speedy?'

'I was on that one, sir,' Queux said. 'Two likelies. Until you meet 'em, that is. One is a deaf old bell ringer who I think medically counts as a dwarf. To reach six feet five he'd have to commit murder up a stepladder. And the other is the nom-de-pen of an Alice McMalice, who writes for the monthly journal *So You Think You Can Do It Yourself?* She rightly pointed out that no one would trust a dovetail joint described by a female of the opposite sex, so she writes under the name Charles Speedy.'

Lestrade nodded as forthrightly as he could. 'Which leaves us with the view from this window behind me,' he said, 'staring at a brick wall.'

'Not quite, guv,' Walter Dew had been fidgeting all morning.

'You've been fidgeting all morning, Walter,' Lestrade had noticed too. 'Out with it, man. I'm booked in at The Blessed Release, Skegness at the end of July.'

'This came through earlier from Inspector Penrose of Q Division.'

'"Snotnose" Penrose?' Lestrade checked, 'I thought he was dead.'

'He is, guv. This is his son, "Toffeenose". Went to Oundle for a term.'

'Well, what is it?'

'It's a break-in, sir. Horniman Museum.'

'What?'

'The Horniman Museum, guv,' Dew beamed like the cat with the cream, 'London Road, Forest Hill. Somebody broke in last week. We've got some dabs.'

'I fail to see . . .'

'The Horniman Museum', Dew was enjoying his moment of triumph; he didn't get many of them, poor bastard, 'is a Museum of Anthr . . . Anthro . . . primitive old bits and pieces from primitive old foreigners.'

'So?'

'So, what do you suppose was taken?'

'King Rhameses' left testicle, Dew,' Lestrade bellowed, instantly regretting it. 'How should I know, man.'

'Four Abyssinian mirrors.'

'Four?'

'Four.'

'That's *it*,' Lestrade clicked his fingers and his eyes watered. '*That's* why there was no mirror found near Russell's body. The murderer had run out. His timing went to pot. He had to hit Russell on a Friday morning, at a time he knew he'd be alone in the tasting cellar. But he'd run out of mirrors. So he had to break in to this Horniman place to get some more. One he sent

167

by post to George Russell. Which leaves us with three. Well,' Lestrade's eyes swivelled all over the board, his blood up, his adrenalin flowing, 'well, at least we know our friend intends to kill three times more. That makes . . . eight. Why eight? What's the significance of eight victims?'

'Er . . . Snow White and the Seven Dwarfs?' Bee offered.

The others ignored him.

'George Russell the Brewer,' Lestrade muttered, his mind racing, 'George the Brewer . . . No, wait a minute. Walter, I can't read your writing. What did his sister call him? George Russell. What was the nickname she gave him as a boy?'

'"Bill",' Dew read the wall.

'Bill Brewer,' said Lestrade, 'Daniel Whiddon. Gentlemen, does any of this sound familiar?'

The others looked blank. Lestrade hobbled over to the wall. 'How many eyes did Juan Tomas de Spool have?' he asked.

'One,' said Queux.

'One,' said Lestrade. 'What was it Lieutenant Harkness of the Sixteenth Lancers said? "One eye", he said. "Used to be referred to as a 'piercer' in the old days. At least when my old pa was in the Sixteenth." And his English friends – and his lover – called him Tom. Tom Piercer. Not far removed from Tom Pearce, is it?'

'Tom Pearce?' Dew frowned. Perhaps the Insurance Man had done more damage to the guv'nor than was apparent to the naked eye.

'"Tom Pearce, Tom Pearce, lend me your grey mare",' Lestrade recited, '"All along, down along, out along lea. For I want to go to . . ."'

'"Widdicombe Fair",' Bee joined in.

'"With",' everybody but Dew chorused, '"Bill Brewer, Jan Stewer . . ."'

'Jan Stewer,' Lestrade halted the chorus. 'Queux, you were at the Polytechnic. What did you call a student who worked his bollocks off, morning, noon and night?'

'Er . . . A stewer!' Queux remembered.

'Right. Janet Calthrop was a model history student, having, by virtue of her gender, to work twice as hard as the men. That's our Jan Stewer.'

'"Peter Gurney",' Bee carried on with the song, even throwing in an attempt at pitch now.

'Not yet,' Lestrade shook his head. 'He's one of the three yet to come.'

'"Peter Davy",' Queux chimed, 'so's he.'

'No, he's not,' Lestrade told him. 'It's not the man. It's the place. The victim was Captain Orange, but the place is Peter Tavy. That's close enough for our man.'

'"Dan'l Whiddon",' Bee chirped.

'No play on words there,' Lestrade said. 'Straight from the shoulder, that one.'

'"Harry Hawke",' Queux chanted.

'Yet to come,' Lestrade said.

'"Old Uncle Tom Cobbleigh and all",' the constables bellowed, harmonizing in a Scotland Yard Glee Club sort of way, their hands clasped, their cheeks side by side.

'Yet to come,' Lestrade said again.

'I wish I knew what you blokes were talking about,' Dew looked lost.

'Widdicombe Fair,' Lestrade told him. 'Walter, you must know it. It's a traditional old English Ballad. Don't you see? All the names of victims so far come from that song. Oh, they're a little bit altered, but then the chances of our friend finding *exact* examples must be millions to one.'

'But he's out of order, guv,' Bee said, 'in more ways than one.'

'To throw us, I'd imagine. Bee, you know the tune – after a fashion. Get over to Charles Tenterden. Whistle it to him. See if that was the song Charles Speedy used to whistle constantly.'

'So all we've got to do now', Dew mused as the constable collected his jacket and boater, 'is to locate, identify and protect around the clock for the foreseeable future three people whose names are . . . er . . . Peter Gurney, was it?'

'Harry Hawke,' Queux added.

'And old uncle Tom Cobbleigh,' Lestrade ended it. 'A piece of cake, Walter.'

* * *

Peta Gurney checked her harness for one last time. In the pack strapped to her back were sixty-two square feet of silk. Below her, some three thousand feet below her, the angles of Alexandra Palace glinted in the sun. It was Lammas. 1 August 1906. And here she was, blonde, nineteen, beautiful. Her whole life before her. And the world at her feet. Abraham Knox tapped her on the shoulder as the balloon slid silently over North London. Up here, all was the rush of the wind and the creaking of the ropes and the wicker.

'Ready, Peta?' Knox shouted.

She was. Her heart thumping, she stood on the step inside the basket. She could just make out around the lake below the tiny pinpricks which were people in their hundreds. Grave old plodders, gay young friskers, the world and his wife had come to Ally Pally that hot, bright day to see Mr 'Opportunity' Knox pull off yet another miracle stunt. And to think of it – a double first. Not only was a closed parachute to be used in full view of the public for the first time, but the daring young parachutist was a girl – and a mere slip of a one at that. She knew her friend Gladys was down there, and the other girls from the Gaiety. And darling Letitia. And huge, handsome Harry. And best of all, that young Household Cavalry officer Gladys was always making eyes at. Well, after this jump, there'd be no contest. By tonight, she'd have won his heart and all eyes would be on her.

'Now!' she heard the impresario behind her order and she jerked forward with her legs, flying out into the currents of air, turning as the updraught caught her, twisting out over the world with her arms spread wide as a bird must.

'About now, Peta,' Abraham Knox said quietly to himself, 'never mind the fancy stuff.'

The men in the basket with him craned over the side.

'Now, Peta,' Knox's voice was louder. He wiped the film of vapour from his goggles. Then, his heart descended again. He saw the scarlet silk open above the falling girl like a rosebud, blossom and . . . What was wrong? His smile froze. It wasn't opening. It had sprung out of the pack, but that was all. Like a pastry whisk, it hovered over Peta Gurney, slowing her fall scarcely at all as she plummeted to the earth.

The watchers on the ground below were riveted to the scarlet speck, getting larger by the second. Letitia found her voice first, shielding her eyes from the sun, 'Harry. Is that right? Is that supposed to happen?'

But Harry had gone, pushing his way through the crowd, apologizing, buffeting, shoving. The murmurs and 'I says' reached a crescendo as he leapt the barrier. Like the good hundred-yards man he used to be, he raced forward, his boater gone, his tie streaming behind him, his shirt-tails flapping. There was a theory. Only a theory, mind, that if you could break someone's fall; if you got there a split second before impact and pushed hard enough, you might *just* save a life. It was only a theory. But it was all Harry Bandicoot had. And it was better than doing what the others were doing. Simply standing still and watching.

But Harry didn't understand physics. It had not been on the curriculum at Eton and for all that he knew his bullets and his guns in the hunting field, this wasn't the same equation at all. He'd also underestimated the crowds through which he'd had to fight every inch of the way. He'd left it too late. There were stewards running with him now, and all of them, it seemed to Letitia, back on the hill, running in slow motion. Where she was, there was no sound. The crowd had fallen silent. She was only aware of the girl Gladys's hand gripping her arm. Only aware of the horror on her lovely face.

Harry skidded to a halt, his shoes ripping and tripping through the spreading silk. He'd been that split second too late to put his theory to the test. And where he was, he'd heard only one sound. It was a sound he'd remember for the rest of his life. It was the sound of a neck, breaking.

8

The crowds had gone home, stunned by the tragedy, to Muswell Hill and Wood Green. The Bandicoots and their party, more stunned than most, had gone back to their suite at the Grand. Here they sat on that balmy summer's evening, Harry on the balcony watching the lights shimmer below him like dew-drops on some great black cobweb that met the pearl of the sky.

The talk was subdued, the mood sombre. People drank to forget, but they could not forget and the champagne Harry had ordered lay unopened in its bucket of ice.

There was a knock at the door. Letitia answered it and ushered in an apparition in bandages. 'Everybody, this is Sholto Lestrade, a dear friend of ours.'

'Sholto!' Harry left his perch and crossed the room to squeeze the man's hand. Lestrade winced. 'Am I glad to see you. But why here, of all places?'

'Duty, I'm afraid, Harry,' he said. 'Is there somewhere we can talk?'

'Of course. Letitia, mingle, will you, darling? Sholto and I will be in the bedroom.'

Harry Bandicoot had all the rakish good looks of his cavalry cousin, but none of the side. Tall, broad, voted Sportsman of the Year in 1894, he had served under Lestrade for one year and was now bringing up his old guv'nor's daughter, as though she was his own. 'Emma sends her love,' Bandicoot grinned, helping his erstwhile colleague on to the bed and for once reading his mind. 'I'm just damned glad the children weren't here to see this thing today.'

'The boys are well?'

'Fighting fit,' Harry had brought the brandy through and an

extra glass, like the perfect host he was. 'They've got Letitia's brains, thank God, and are both coping magnificently with old Underwood's Greek classes. Do you know he was at Eton in my day? God only knows how old he must be, but I remember he said he knew Aristotle inside out, so that must date him approximately . . . What do you mean, duty?'

'Miss Gurney,' Lestrade said, watching the amber nectar glow in the oil-lamp's light, 'and the parachute that didn't open.'

'Ah, yes, of course. Accidental death, I suppose. Still, I didn't think the Yard would be involved.'

'If it were accidental, no, we wouldn't.'

A strange light appeared in the eyes of young Bandicoot. He flicked up his coat tails and sat down on the bedside chair. 'Are you telling me this *wasn't* an accident?'

Lestrade nodded.

'Sholto, Peta Gurney was just nineteen. We celebrated her birthday last week in this very hotel. A lovelier girl you couldn't wish to meet – outside Gladys Cooper, that is.'

'Gladys Cooper?'

'Another of the Gaiety girls and I suppose you'd say Peta's best friend. She's in the other room, poor thing. Trying like the rest of us to put a brave face on things. Sholto . . . I don't like to pry . . .'

Lestrade waved his good arm and the brandy sprayed across Harry's shirt front. 'Oh, God. Sorry, Harry. You were about to ask about the bandages. It's a long story.'

'No, actually,' Harry mopped himself down, 'I was wondering how you got those carpet burns on your nose.'

They all told the same story. Peta Gurney was a lovely girl, destined for a glittering career on the stage. C. Aubrey Smith himself had asked her to play opposite him *and* he'd given her a part in his new show. Seymour Hicks had had his eye on her too, but then that applied to any woman under forty-five. No, there was no one special in her life. There was a young sub in the Blues who had sent her a Valentine and danced with her once or twice, but there was nothing in it. Her parents had died during a holiday in the Alps years before and she was the niece of the great physicist, the recently knighted Oliver Lodge. Lestrade raised an eyebrow at that, ever suspicious of the Masons as he was. No one knew of an Abyssinian connection or of any tall men in the dead girl's life. Lestrade talked to them, in ones and twos, until the early hours when the great hotel fell silent and the sad little party went home.

Only one of them stayed. She was sitting in the foyer, still wearing the garlands of the day. Only her eyes were sad. Only her hands were clasped.

'Mr Lestrade,' she said.

'Miss Cooper, isn't it?'

'Could I . . . talk to you?'

'Of course,' he said. 'Shall we walk? It's a lovely night.'

It was. The stars looked down on the detective and the Gaiety Girl, walking under the fitful moon. Only the odd stray cab clopping home to its stable, the last motor taxi coughing its way to the garage. A ginger and white cat had come from nowhere and curled itself around the girl's legs – skirts were shorter this year – and she stooped to pick it up.

'Aren't you adorable?' she said, tickling the thing under the chin. It lolled back in her arms like a baby, but it didn't take its yellow eyes off Lestrade.

'Let me see,' the Superintendent said, 'you're with George Edwardes's company, aren't you?'

'That's right,' she said. 'You know, I might make five pounds a week in time. We're working on the *Girls of Göttenberg* now. It's very exciting.'

'May I ask how old you are, Miss Cooper?'

'Gladys,' she said, her lovely eyes huge in the moonlight, 'you can call me Gladys. And yes, Mr Lestrade, you may ask. I am seventeen.'

Lestrade vaguely remembered being seventeen. He hadn't earned five shillings, never mind five pounds. And he didn't remember *anything* exciting. 'You had something you wanted to say to me?'

'Well, oh, it's probably nothing. And it's something I swore

I wouldn't tell a living soul, but well, poor Peta's dead now and I don't suppose you count.'

'Oh, thank you, Gladys,' Lestrade smiled.

'Oh, I'm sorry,' she held his arm, but it was his wrenched one and he winced. The cat flew from her arms, raking its claws down his shirt-front as it went. She looked at the dark eyes, sadder than her own, the white bandaged neck and the funny little nose with the carpet burns above the pale, tender-looking upper lip. What it was to be so old . . .

'No need to be,' Lestrade chuckled. 'What is it? This "something you wouldn't tell a living soul"?'

She looked serious suddenly, turning him to her in the gaslight. 'Peta had an admirer. Oh, lots of girls do. Lots of admirers. But this one, I got the impression was more serious than most.'

'Why didn't you tell me this in the Bandicoots' suite?'

'I couldn't,' she shook her head, 'not then. Not with all those people about. I'm not sure I should be telling you now.'

'Does he have a name, this admirer?'

'Charles. That's all I know. Oh, and I gather he was older than her. Much older.'

'How much older?'

'Old enough to be her father, certainly. Grandfather, perhaps. She was a little embarrassed about him, I think. Does . . . does this help?'

He put his good hand to her soft cheek, 'I don't know,' he said. 'But it might, Gladys, it just might. Come on, I'll walk you home.'

That summer Tsar Nicholas II behaved like the autocrat he was and dissolved the Duma. The intense heat, at midday breasting to ninety-three degrees, led to dissolutions of all kinds. Number One Court at the Bailey was like a boiler and Mr Justice Wunce broke the etiquette of centuries by disrobing. Mrs Wunce, who had ever called a spade a spade was quoted in the *Daily Mail* as saying 'That's a first'. The heat, too, gave rise to a plague of caterpillars in London's parks and a woman was fined half a crown for losing decorum sufficiently to kiss a uniformed constable. Only the lovely Patsy Montague stayed half-way cool by impersonating a living marble statue at the London Pavilion. It was all terribly tasteful of course and little boys attempting to blow away her fig leaves with pea shooters were cuffed around the ears by passing policemen.

It was one of those passing policemen who brought a note to Scotland Yard three days later – for the urgent and immediate attention of Superintendent Lestrade. But that officer was at the morgue, and grateful for the chill, by the time the letter arrived. The girl lying on the marble slab before him had been beautiful. Now her lips were dull and her eyes sunken, her pale auburn tresses that had been once so lovingly braided and teased lay spread across the slab. A green sheet covered her nakedness, but the severe bruising around her neck and shoulders told Lestrade all he needed to know. Peta Gurney had died as the police surgeon's report said she had, of a broken neck. She would have felt no pain he assured everyone who might have known the girl in life. No, thought Lestrade, but what of those moments as she had dropped like a stone to the earth that bore her? He had gone that way once, hurtling downwards in a balloon that somebody appeared to have burst. He had survived. She had not. It was all some ghastly lottery. A game of pitch and toss.

It was tea-time before he got back to find his shirt-sleeved, tieless team buried in depositions from those at Ally Pally who had witnessed the girl's fall.

'Letter for you, guv,' Queux passed it to him. 'Just a hint of lavender, I fancy,' and he winked.

'Haven't you got a kettle to put on or something?' Lestrade asked and the constable scurried away. Lestrade's eyes narrowed as he read the note's contents. 'You know what the manual says, Walter, about never going into an unknown situation in the dark, by yourself?'

'Hmm,' Dew nodded.

'That's where I'm going. I'll be at the Grand Hotel, the Bandicoots' suite.'

Walter Dew had worked with Harry Bandicoot. He'd got a lot of time for the huge Old Etonian with the heart of gold and the brain of lead, but he'd never really found him sweet. Still, he was bringing up Lestrade's daughter – and perhaps Lestrade was at that funny age old Gramma Dew had warned young Walter about all those years ago. In all the years he had served under Lestrade, chief inspector and boy, he had never wittingly accepted a sweet from him.

The Bandicoots' suite at the Grand had changed. The glittering lights had gone and only a solitary candle glowed eerily in the centre of a large oval table, its flame reflected in the burnished gloss of the burr veneer. Around it, once introductions were done, sat as odd a miscellany of people as Edwardian England could muster around such a table, on such a night, with such a purpose, to raise the dead.

On Lestrade's left, Letitia Bandicoot, radiant, calm, coping with whatever life threw at her, holding Lestrade's hand tight. On his right, the delicious Gladys Cooper with eyes a man could drown in, her low-cut bodice equally inviting of a dip. She held Lestrade's right hand, uncertain, nervous, her fingers wanting to be away, yet not daring to let go. Next to her, Harry, broad, handsome, resplendent as always in his black and white, smiling at his wife and the girl beside him. Beyond that a florid gentleman with a full, greying moustache and thin, slashed-over hair sat scowling at Lestrade. His name was Arthur Conan Doyle and he had recently been knighted. Completing the circle was another new knight, the renowned physicist Oliver Lodge, his huge, domed head like an egg in the ghostly light, his great beard nodding on his chest.

'I'm not sure about this, Olly,' Conan Doyle said. 'Science is against it.'

'Ah,' the physicist closed his eyes. '"There are more things in Heaven and Earth," Arthur. Trust me. I'm a Spiritualist.'

Now Lestrade had been this way before. In the macabre Case of Struwwelpeter, he had sat just like this, but short of lovely ladies, on a chill winter's evening in the heart of Warwickshire. And across the table from him then sat the great medium Madame Slopeski. That great medium had turned out to be a murderer. And so Lestrade was taking no chances now. Nor was that his only brush with the hereafter. In the Ripper Case, he had consulted the peculiar Robert Lees who had seen a man he knew to be the fiend sitting on top of a Number Thirty-eight bus from Hammersmith. His training, his logic, all of it told him that this was a waste of time. And yet. And yet . . . And yet he had been summoned by Miss Cooper. If no one else could help, her note had said, if no one else could shed light on the murder of an innocent young girl, why not ask the young girl herself?

'This is not ideal,' Lodge said, closing his eyes, 'we're a woman short. Still, Arthur's a man about town; he won't mind me holding his hand. Now. Everybody, concentrate. Squeeze. That's it.' His head lolled back so that his white beard pointed to the ceiling. 'Mr Lestrade, would you be so good as to blow out the candle. The departed, especially the newly departed, prefer the dark. It's a comfort for them. That's it. That's it. I feel . . . a presence.'

'Here in the room?' Conan Doyle looked alarmed.

'No, no,' Lodge's beard dropped to his chest. The rest of his head followed in quick succession. 'Nearby. The door.'

All eyes turned to it, except the physicist's. 'Is there anybody there?' he intoned, his eyes closed, his eyebrows wandering.

Nothing.

'If you can hear me, answer. Knock once for "yes", twice for "no".'

There was a double thump.

'No,' said Harry, the first to translate it.

'Utterly illogical,' muttered Conan Doyle. 'Time to stop this balderdash, Olly. It's preposterous.'

'Is anybody there?' Lodge tried again. 'Knock if you can hear us.'

There was another double knock. 'Is anybody there?' a muffled voice sounded.

The ladies leapt to their feet, shaking. Conan Doyle didn't look any too chipper, but then he was a mere silhouette against the curtains and the room still smelt of candle-smoke. Bandicoot was first to the door, Lestrade a shade behind because he had fetched his bad knee a nasty one on the table leg. Harry threw back the door, shoulders tensed, ready, in his public-school way for a dance or a shipwreck; it was all one to him.

'Hello,' a rather blowsy blonde lolled on the doorframe, 'I'm sorry I'm late, only gettin' a bleedin' taxi from the Strand's bleedin' murder. Oh. Have you started already?'

Conan Doyle had found some matches and relit the candle. 'Who the devil are you?' he demanded.

'I'm Queenie Blow,' she told him, rummaging in an outsize handbag, 'I've got me card 'ere somewhere.'

'What are you doing here?' Bandicoot asked.

She stopped rummaging and looked up at him, then back at the door, still ajar. 'This is the Grand, ain't it? Are you Mr Cooper?'

'No,' Harry said, 'my name is Bandicoot.'

'Lor'!' she giggled, 'that's a little furry animal, ain't it, native to Australasia?'

'Now, look . . .'

'As a matter of fact,' Gladys Cooper crossed to the light from the hallway, 'I sent for Miss Blow.'

'Mrs, Ducks,' the blowsy lady corrected her. 'My ol' man makes surgical appliances orff the Ol' Kent Road. But business ain't what it was now we've beat the Boers, so I do a bit o' night work.'

'Miss Cooper . . .' Oliver Lodge loomed over the Gaiety girl, 'I understood that *I* was to conduct this seance.'

Queenie pushed past him. 'No disrespect, Ducks, but you couldn't conduct a bus. 'Ere, can we 'ave some light on? Creepy in 'ere, ain't it?'

While Harry obliged by lighting the gas, Oliver Lodge proceeded to stand on his dignity. 'Do you know who I am, Madam?' he asked.

She squinted up at him, then began to lay all sorts of paraphernalia on the table. 'Yeah, you're that Sir Oliver Lodge.'

'What Sir Oliver Lodge?' Conan Doyle chortled, thoroughly enjoying this humiliation of his friend.

'That Sir Oliver Lodge what's professor of Physics at Birmingham University. You was awarded the Runford medal for experiments wiv lightning. You're a pioneer in electrolysis – 'ere, p'raps you can 'ave a go at me legs later. Got me ol' dad's legs, see. You're workin' at the moment on an electrical method of fog dispersal. Well, bleedin' good luck to yer, mate.'

Oliver Lodge sat down, his mouth hanging open.

'Oh, yeah,' Queenie turned back to him, 'you was Romanes lecturer at Oxford three years back, president of the Physical Society six years back and at the moment, president – or head snoop, should I say – for the Society of Psychical Research.'

'Bravo!' Conan Doyle clapped his hands, 'that's you demolished, Olly. Now, young lady, who am I?'

Queenie put a pair of ill-fitting pince-nez on her snub, cherry-coloured nose. 'You're the bloke what writes the Sherlock Holmes stories. You and that Dr Watson. Conan Doyle, ain't it?'

'It is,' the novelist shook his head. 'What else do you know about me?'

'You was born in Edinburgh,' the newcomer said, sitting down on one of the chairs and picking up the knitting she had taken out of her portmanteau, 'and practised medicine for a bit. I suppose you was tired of lookin' down people's froats all day, 'cos you took to writin'. You keep tryin', don't you?' she grinned at him and winked. 'All those 'istorical romances – Brigadier Gerard, Rodney Stone, the White Company. But all the great British public want is bleedin' Sherlock Holmes, ain't it? I can't see it, myself. Still, your 'eart's in the right place, doin' your bit wiv that field hospital in the Boer War. Now, let's get to business, shall we?'

No one moved.

'Look, do you want my services, or not?' she paused in the middle of her purls and plains.

'Yes,' Gladys Cooper sat down next to her. 'My friend was brutally murdered by person or persons unknown,' she said, her lovely eyes fixed on the disapproving face of Oliver Lodge. 'I sent for you, Mrs Blow, because your reputation goes before you. If anyone can solve this appalling crime, you can.'

'Well said, Gladys,' Letitia said and sat beside her, holding her hand.

'Right. Is he your husband, Ducks? That 'andsome one by the door?'

'He is,' Letitia smiled, well used to other women looking twice at Harry.

'Then you'll know where the drink is, sonny. Mine's a gin. Go easy on the water, only in this 'eat there's a shortage.'

Harry did as he was told while Conan Doyle sat down and Oliver Lodge grudgingly did the same. Only Lestrade still stood aloof.

'No, Mister,' Queenie Blow spoke to him for the first time, 'I ain't Madame Slopeski. She died last year of puerperal fever. No one's 'eard from 'er since. I'm who I claim to be – plain 'ol Queenie Blow from the Ol' Kent Road. You can pinch me if you like.'

'Who's he?' Conan Doyle was thoroughly enjoying this party game.

Queenie smiled quietly. 'He's the world's second greatest detective,' she said. 'His ol' dad was a copper; his muvver took in washin'. He's had some sorrow in 'is life, but then haven't we all?' she looked at Gladys, whose huge eyes were fixed on hers. 'You've got a little girl though, ain'cha? Apple of your eye an' the livin' spit of her muvver. Oh, she's all right, by the way.'

'My daughter?'

'Your wife. Sarah, ain't it?'

Lestrade nodded. He thought he ought to sit down.

'Would you like the lights off, Mrs Blow?' Harry asked, handing her the gin.

'Love you, no, Ducks. Ooh,' she sipped the glass, 'you pour a nice three fingers' worth, you do. No, we don't need to 'ave no candles. I leave all that to them Cafolics.'

Conan Doyle, sitting next to the medium reached out a hand. 'We don't need any more o' that, neither,' she stabbed him with a knitting needle, 'you dirty ol' man.'

'I'm sorry,' he bridled, 'I thought it was de rigueur at seances.' He looked accusingly at Lodge.

'It may be de rigueur to you, mate. To me it's a chance for lewd ol' men like you to fondle wot they ought not to be a-fondlin' of. You don't want to listen to them blokes from the SPR,' she flashed a glance at Lodge, 'they've got exposure on the brain.'

Suddenly she fainted. The glass dropped from her right hand, the knitting from her left. She lolled in the chair and had to be steadied by Conan Doyle. 'Good God,' the ex-doctor said, 'shall I slap her a bit? It's been years since I carried any smelling salts.'

'No, don't touch her,' Lodge was on his feet, 'Mrs Bandicoot,

I don't want to be accused of any impropriety. Would you place this feather under Mrs Blow's nose?' He produced one from his pocket.

Letitia looked questioningly at him, then at Harry, then at Lestrade. Finally she took it and tickled the little hairs that formed an unusually luxuriant growth on the medium's upper lip. There was no sneeze, no wrinkle of the nose, no movement at all.

'There you are,' said Gladys, sitting upright at the sensitive's side, 'I could have told you she was genuine.'

Lodge was unconvinced. With the speed of a deranged maniac, he whipped a pistol from his other pocket and fired it at the medium's head. Everybody except Mrs Blow jumped out of their chairs or their skins.

'You deranged maniac!' Harry shouted and snatched the gun from him, flinging it across the room to Lestrade, who missed it deftly and let it clatter to the floor.

'Only blanks, Mr Bandicoot,' Lodge said, grinning as Harry twisted the physicist's arm behind his back. 'Don't do that, there's a good chap. That's my electrolyzing arm. I had to be sure that Mrs Blow was not a fraud.'

'Let him go, Harry,' Lestrade said, pocketing the pistol, 'he's going a funny colour.'

'Dad, Dad,' it was Mrs Blow whose lips were moving, but it was not her voice.

Lodge sat down suddenly, his throbbing arm forgotten and his loss of colour had nothing to do with tangling with Harry Bandicoot.

'I don't like it here, Dad. It's dark.'

'Raymond?' Lodge whispered.

'Who?' Lestrade asked.

'His son,' Conan Doyle was suddenly serious. 'He has a boy called Raymond.'

'Where are you?' Lodge asked, blinking.

'In the trenches, Dad. There's water. It's cold. I can hear the rattle of the cans on the wire. There's somebody out there, Dad, calling my name. I can't reach him. I can't move.'

'Raymond! Raymond!' Lodge was shouting. 'What does she mean? Trenches? Wire? What's she talking about?'

Conan Doyle gripped his friend's shoulder. Queenie Blow's head came up from her ample breasts. Her eyes were open now, her grin fixed.

'I didn't do it, Dr Conan Doyle. As one physician to another, I ask you to believe that. Oh – and sorry about Louise, by the way.'

'Good God,' Conan Doyle stared transfixed.

'Indian,' said Letitia. 'She sounds Indian now.'

'What are you doing in here?' Queenie demanded with all the richness of the Bombay dialect. 'I've got absolutely nothing against horses and I categorically deny that I have ever molested one.'

'Good God,' Conan Doyle said again, 'Edalji. Dr Edalji. Is it you?'

'Could we have another take, please, Miss Cooper?' the Indian had gone and a rather raucous American sat in his place. Queenie had retrieved a knitting needle and was clamping it in her teeth like a cheroot, '*The List of Adrian Messenger*. Scene Twenty-six. Take Three.'

Queenie's head fell forward.

'Adrian Messenger?' Gladys Cooper repeated, 'who's he? I've never heard of him.'

There was a silence. Oliver Lodge sat stunned and still, the ghost-hunting gadgetry he carried with him untouched in his voluminous pockets. Conan Doyle's eyes bulged in his head and he rubbed his nose with agitation. Then the medium's head came up again and the knitting needle now rested lightly in her hand, its point against her right breast. Her knees sagged open and her neck stretched up. She looked serene. Regal. An odd light shone from her and her eyes were suddenly open.

'Charlie,' she said, 'my mirrors are broken. Who has broken all my mirrors?'

'Mirrors?' Lestrade stretched forward.

Queenie turned to him, the head twisting further than he'd seen anything twist since he'd spent that night in the Owl House in the Zoological Gardens in the Case of the Poisoned Pellet.

'I see all,' she said in a voice Lestrade had heard before. But he couldn't place it. It was stronger. Younger. He saw the blowsy woman's lips move but out of them came the voice of a young man. A young god. Who knew? Then there was a series of rattles in her throat and she began speaking in a tongue none of them knew. None of them, that is, except Lestrade.

'Abyssinian,' he said.

'Ooh,' Queenie was back as quickly as she'd gone, 'I'm sorry, Ducks, I appear to 'ave dropped me glass. Any chance of a refill?'

They could get no more out of her. Oliver Lodge's boy was still in his teens. He had dug a trench once in the garden of their home, but the connection with wire eluded the great scientist completely. He said nothing about this however. The blowsy woman from the Ol' Kent Road unnerved him. His attitude to the beyond would never be the same again.

'Sorry I wasn't any use,' she'd said, downing Harry's second gin, 'but that's 'ow it goes, ain't it? Oo do I send my bill to?'

'Me,' said Lodge. 'You seem to know a great deal, Mrs Blow. I'm sure you can divine my address.'

She smiled and patted his cheek, 'You bet I can, Mister. Oh, lor', look at that. Not content wiv droppin' me glass, I've dropped me stitches an' all. Wot a cluck.' She picked up her knitting and stuffed it in her holdall. 'Thanks for the gin, sonny. Lovely boys, you've got. You *will* look after them, won't you?'

Harry glanced at Letitia, knowing she was fighting down the urge to ring home and see if they were all right – her babies Rupert and Ivo. 'I'll see you out,' he said.

When he had, the company spread themselves, opting for the easy chairs away from the table. 'At least it didn't tilt,' Harry said, knocking the top for good measure. 'Look, is it me? Did *anybody* understand *any* of that? Sholto?'

The superintendent looked at Conan Doyle. 'Perhaps we could hear from the others first,' he said. 'Mrs Blow talked to you, Sir Arthur – by name.'

'And in an Indian accent,' Letitia agreed.

'You called . . .'

'The entity,' said Lodge, 'that's the phrase you're groping for, Superintendent. "The entity".'

184

'Thank you, Sir Oliver. You called the entity Dr Edalji. Who's that?'

'And who's Louise?' Gladys remembered.

A shadow seemed to darken the florid features, the square face. 'My wife,' he said. 'She had consumption. We moved to Surrey in search of fresh air, but it was no use. It is only always a matter of time with something like consumption. She . . . died last month.'

'Mrs Blow would have said "passed to the other side", doctor,' Letitia said.

The novelist smiled. 'Thank you, Mrs Bandicoot. If I could believe that . . .'

'What of Edalji?' Lestrade pursued.

'Ah,' the amateur detective in Conan Doyle resurrected itself. He's not a doctor – Mrs Blow must have her wires crossed.'

'The ether sometimes affects that,' Lodge commented. 'How long ago did he die?'

'Die?' repeated Conan Doyle.

'Yes,' the physicist was in full flow, 'you see, that would determine the level he is at. If his death was recent, he'd be in the first level, floating somewhere just above us . . .'

All eyes except Conan Doyle's looked inquisitively at the ceiling, as if the dead man was hiding in the chandelier.

'He's not dead, Olly,' the novelist told him, 'unless he's died of prison food. You must remember the case. It was three years ago. George Edalji is an Anglican clergyman. He was convicted of assaults on horses, sheep and cattle in Staffordshire.'

'Good God,' said Harry, 'that's appalling.'

'So, to some policemen,' Conan Doyle flashed a withering glance at Lestrade, 'is being the son of a Hindu. I have long believed that that is Edalji's only crime. Tonight has been something of an inspiration to me. I shall fight to clear the man's name.'

'Bully for you,' said Letitia, although Lestrade was less impressed.

'I do remember it now,' he nodded. 'The man's coat was found covered in blood and horsehair. Forensically, that's pretty damning, Sir Arthur.'

'There's nothing you can teach me about forensics, Lestrade,'

185

Conan Doyle riposted. 'If Sherlock Holmes hadn't existed, I should have had to make him up.'

'Sir Oliver,' Lestrade turned the spotlight of Scotland Yard on the great physicist, 'Raymond is your son?'

'He is,' Lodge said, 'but the woman's message was incomprehensible. Look . . . ladies and gentlemen,' the old lecturer in him was sneaking out, 'Mrs Blow is . . . well, I won't say she's a charlatan, but she defies all the rules. Full lights. No linkage of hands. Messages from the living via a seance. It's all pretty abnormal.'

'Are you saying she's wrong?' Lestrade asked. 'She seems to have been nearly right about this Edalji and the late Lady Conan Doyle.'

'Quite,' said Conan Doyle.

'Whose side are you on, Arthur?' Lodge snapped. 'Earlier this evening, it was all "stuff and nonsense" if I remember aright. You didn't want to come at all.'

'Well, that's as may be,' Conan Doyle said, 'but tonight has opened my eyes. Oh,' he caught the faces around the room, 'only to the *possibilities* of as-yet-indefinable laws of physics, of course. Don't worry, Lestrade,' he chuckled, 'I'm never going to see fairies at the bottom of my garden. Or anyone else's, come to that.'

'Trenches? Wire? Darkness?' Letitia said. 'Is your son in some kind of danger, Sir Oliver?'

'Of course not,' Lodge insisted, though his heart told him otherwise. 'The evening may have inspired and broadened you, Arthur, but it's been a waste of time for me. If it weren't for Edmund's memory . . .'

'Edmund?' Lestrade repeated.

'Edmund Gurney,' Gladys Cooper said. 'He was Peta's grandfather, Mr Lestrade.'

'And a founder member of the Society for Psychical Research,' said Lodge. 'He passed over in 1888.'

'I know,' Lestrade said, 'I was on the case.'

'You?' Gladys and Lodge chorused.

Lestrade nodded. 'A Brighton hotel,' he said. 'A murder disguised as a suicide. I hadn't made the family connection.'

'The only one who's mentioned Peta tonight is me,' Gladys

186

said suddenly, rushing to the window so that the others didn't see her tears. Letitia went with her, her motherly arms around the girl's heaving shoulders.

'That's not quite true,' Lestrade said. 'You see, there was a message for me tonight, and if we are to believe Mrs Blow, it came from Peta Gurney.'

All eyes turned to him.

'Which one?' Harry asked.

'The last one,' Lestrade told him.

'But that was gobbledegook,' said Conan Doyle.

'True,' Lestrade nodded, 'or it might just as well have been. What I want is someone who speaks Abyssinian like a native. And one more thing we know about Miss Gurney's death.'

'Oh?' sniffed Gladys, her friend.

Lestrade's stubbly lip took on a peculiar twist. 'It was all done by mirrors.'

Abraham 'Opportunity' Knox had had some disasters in his time. And such things, it had to be said, ran in his family. His father it was who had been the principal shareholder in the late Tay Bridge. An uncle of his, holidaying in Peking a few years back, had inadvertently wandered into the Forbidden City, made an unfortunate comment about slanty-eyed little gits and caused the Boxer Rebellion. And of course, Aunt Matilda, that much travelled dowager whose memories had gone through countless editions, happened to suggest to Father Gapon in Russia only last year that he really ought to go with three or four thousand unarmed peasants to the Winter Palace in St Petersburg and have a little chat with that nice Tsar Nicholas.

All in all, not a happy family. The man himself was every inch the impresario, his hair swept up à la Wilde into a Neronian frenzy, his bow tie dangling in a profusion of velvet, his Panama as wide as the canal. And to add to his air of theatricality, even his tan was not of the fierce August heat, but courtesy of Messrs Leichner, heavy on the five and nine.

'Look,' Knox was defensive, 'I have spoken to you chappies already, you know. I am naturally distraught about Peta Gurney, but that's the nature of the beast, I'm afraid.'

Even his Essex-man accent crept right over Lestrade's fuzzy moustache and up his nose.

'How did it come about, Mr Knox?' he asked.

'Well, as I told your Sergeant Adams, it's a promotional thing I've been running all summer. It's called "Abraham'll Fix It" and any member of Joe Public can write in to me and ask me to arrange a spectacular something-or-other they've always wanted to do. We had a chappie in May for example who'd always had a hankering to jump off the suspension bridge at Clifton.'

So had Lestrade, but he wasn't telling Knox that.

'And you arranged that?'

'Of course not. It's lethal. You can't jump two hundred and seventy-five feet and expect to live.'

'So you refused?'

'Of course. But he was so set on it, he did it anyway.'

'And?'

'And he died, Mr Lestrade, but you're missing the point.'

'I am?'

'I only take on sensible, practical projects. Oh, there must be an element of danger, certainly. We want those punters' hearts firmly in their mouths, those bums on the edges of seats, but nothing suicidal. I'd be drummed out of the SSS.'

'The SSS?'

'The Stupid Stunts Society. We have an international reputation now, you know. Matthew Webb. Blondin. To name but two.'

'But they're dead.'

'Only one of them by accident,' Knox defended his point. 'The only surprise is that Sir William Gilbert, the librettist, is a member. Still, I suppose he knows what he's doing. And anyway, with lyrics like his, I suppose a death wish is inevitable.'

'I understand that they are hurrying a Private Members' Bill through Parliament as we speak,' Lestrade said, 'about young ladies engaging in dangerous sports.'

'Yes, well, all members should be private in my opinion,' Knox bridled, 'but that's my strict Congregationalist upbringing for you. You've talked to Staveley of course.'

'Staveley?'

'General Staveley. Well, didn't Adams write any of this down? Do you not communicate at Scotland Yard?'

'Er . . .'

'They were . . . well, together, I suppose.'

'Together?'

'Yes. You see, I had worked with Miss Gurney for a week or so. Intensive training. The irony is that she'd made no less than six successful jumps using that very parachute,' he held up a section of the voluminous silk lying spread on the hangar floor. 'This is it. Careful how you handle it. I'm thinking of selling it to the more prominent members of Joe Public for a shilling a square foot. What do you think?'

'Appalling,' said Lestrade.

'You're right,' Knox checked himself, 'I had an uncle on my mother's side who was Scottish. Shilling a square yard it is.'

'Where does this Staveley come in?'

'Well, the first time, Peta Gurney turned up here with a bevy of luscious lovelies – Gaiety Girls – and some chinless wonder of a Household Cavalry officer. On the second and third occasions, however, this old fellow brought her.'

'An old fellow?'

'Yes. Well set up, mind. Body like a whip. But I'd be untrue to verisimilitude if I said he was a day under sixty-five. What these young girls see in coffin-fodder like that I'll never know.'

'And you say his name was Staveley?'

'That's how he introduced himself. Charles Staveley.'

'Charles?'

'Are you a little on the deaf side, Mr Lestrade? Aurally disadvantaged?'

'Eh?' said Lestrade, his timing, as ever, immaculate.

'I said . . . ho ho,' Knox scowled, 'very droll, Superintendent.'

'Tell me, Mr Knox, was this Charles Staveley tall?'

'Er . . . six foot plus, I would say, yes.'

'And what sort of relationship did he seem to have with the dead girl?'

'Well,' Knox closed to his man, 'I've seen this sort of thing before,' and he patted the side of his nose with his finger, 'as I'm sure you have. They pass themselves off as grandfathers, but in actuality, it's a bit of the dinky finger.'

189

'Dinky . . .'

'Yes, well, anything more vigorous would kill 'em. I shouldn'
think many sixty-five year olds can last more than an hour with
a Gaiety girl – although you could ask me again in twenty years
time,' he nudged Lestrade and winked.

'Did Staveley come up in the balloon with you?'

'No. Said he'd seen enough of observation balloons in his
time. He watched from the ground.'

'And on the day that Miss Gurney died, was he watching
from the ground then?'

'He must have been, though I'll confess I didn't see him.'

'Why "must have been"?'

'Well, Peta said that Charles had packed her parachute.'

'Charles had?'

'Yes.'

'Was that usual?'

'Not at all. The parachute may have been designed by
Leonardo da Vinci, Superintendent, but as a practical, working
piece of apparatus it's still very new. I wouldn't have though
Staveley would have known one from his elbow.'

'Well, didn't you check it?'

'We were running late. Any more delay and we'd have missed
the winds. I'd got nearly three thousand people on the ground
all their hot little sixpences in my hand. You can't disappoin
the crowd, Mr Lestrade. Robespierre, Danton, Louis XVI, they
all understood that.'

'So you went up anyway?'

'Look, Mr Lestrade, I have to admit that I don't care for
that tone of censure in your voice. I'm cut to the quick by
what happened. Emotionally gutted. All balloon flights were
suspended for the rest of the day after it happened. Miss
Gurney was adamant that Charles had packed her parachute
and that he knew what he was doing. So did she. She'd
done it for a week, for God's sake. Now, I'm a very busy
man . . .'

'How was it done?' Lestrade interrupted.

'What?'

'The tinkering with the parachute.'

'Ah, well, here, y'see. This cord should release all these ropes

190

All Miss Gurney had to do was to pull that and the thing should have opened.'

'She didn't pull it?'

'Oh, yes, she pulled it all right, but because someone had cut these ropes, it only opened partially. That's the really ghastly thing about this whole incident. The partially-opened parachute would have slowed her down just enough to prolong her terror. My, my, it doesn't bear thinking about, does it? Now, I have to be elsewhere. Can you keep this under your boater?'

'What?'

'There's a fellow over in France called Paul Cornu . . .'

'Right,' said Lestrade, 'I won't tell a soul.'

'I haven't finished,' Knox boomed. 'This Cornu is working on a new gadget – another one designed by da Vinci. He calls it a helicopter.'

'Really?'

'It's an aircraft like the Wright brothers', but – and this is what'll draw the crowds – it takes off vertically.'

'No!'

'As I live and breathe. Imagine that, Mr Lestrade – the thrill of hovering six foot above the ground. Man, it'll revolutionize getting to work. You'll be able to whizz over traffic jams.'

'But if we all have one,' Lestrade reasoned, 'won't that mean we'll still have traffic jams, but they'll be six feet above the ground?'

And with that imponderable, he left the obnoxious Knox to count his money.

'Oh, by the way,' the impresario stopped him in the doorway, 'who should I send this to? It was tied up in Peta's pack. Unfortunately it seems to have been broken in the fall.'

Lestrade didn't have to turn round to know that Knox was holding in his hand an Abyssinian mirror.

'Where's Adams?' Lestrade asked as the first nerve-jangling mouthful of Mrs Dew's lemonade hit his taste buds. His knuckles whitened on the desk top, his jaw crawled, the top of his head felt as if it had just bounced off the ceiling. 'Out buying sugar, I hope.'

'Wrote in sick, guv,' Constable Bee told him, fanning himself by the open window.

'Heat stroke?' Lestrade asked.

'Didn't say,' Bee said, 'but he'd be back as soon as he could.'

'Right. What have we got on Peta Gurney's family?'

'Parents deceased,' Queux said. 'Lives alone in St James' Street. Ward of Sidney Rowlatt.'

'Who's he?'

'Barrister-at-law. Lives in the Temple.'

'Anybody been round?'

'Adams was out on that,' Dew had just got back from the latrine on the floor below. The heat had warped the outside pipes and the whole of Scotland Yard was living on a sanitary knife-edge. No wonder the police had nothing to go on. 'How's the lemonade, guv? Going down a treat?'

'Delicious, Walter,' Lestrade managed through clenched teeth. He'd much rather it *was* going down a treat – anywhere but down his throat at that moment. 'Has he actually *been*, though. What with his off-sickness?'

No one seemed to know.

Lestrade's telephone jangled at that moment. He reached across for it, 'yes?' He sat bolt upright. 'Yes. When? I see. How? Where was this? Right. I'll be along.'

He put the receiver back and slowly stood up.

'Guv,' said Queux, 'you've gone as white as a sheet. Is it the sun?'

'It's Sergeant Adams,' Lestrade said. 'He's not coming in any more. He was killed this morning. By a tram. Dew, get your hat. We've got to say goodbye to a copper.'

9

The sun was at its height by the time Lestrade and Dew got there. For reasons of delicacy they had caught a cab rather than a tram and they crossed the North Metropolitan Tramway's yard to the relative cool of the sheds.

Killer tram Number 183, with its advertisements for Hudson's Soap and Okey's Knife Polish, was still being hosed down by an operative in waistcoat and shirt-sleeves. This was Finsbury Pavement, 8 August 1906. High noon.

'I don't know how it happened, guv,' the driver was muttering, slumped on a carton in the shade. ''E just stood there. I rung my bell. Bert, you'll be a witness to that. I rung my bell.'

'You did, Clement,' a smartly-liveried conductor sat down beside him, but on the other side of the carton, so that their feet were at right angles to each other. He eased his ticket machine aside, 'and yes, I will be a witness to that.'

'Where was this?' Lestrade asked, although he already knew the answer.

'Farringdon Street, guv,' the driver told him.

'What time?'

'Well, we was running late – you'll vouch for that, Bert?'

'Your vouch is safe wiv me, Clement, you know that.'

'We was runnin' late and it must of been . . . oh, arf past ten. Ish.'

'What happened exactly?' Lestrade folded his arms.

'Well, I'd just picked up from the station. We was pretty full, wasn't we, Bert – you'll subscribe to that.'

'Consider my subscription fully paid up, Clement,' the conductor said. 'Looked like a Methodist convention or I'm not an employee of the North Metropolitan Tramway.'

'What makes you think they were Methodists?' Dew asked, notepad at the ready.

'They all refused to pay,' the conductor said. 'I says to them "Pay up or piss orff out of it". Well, it's the only sort o' language they understand, them Methodists.'

'And what about the man?' Lestrade pressed the driver.

'Well, he was well away, guv,' the driver said. 'You'd put yer monica on that fact, Bert?'

'Wherever you'd like me to put it, Clement, me ol' mucker.'

'"Well away"?' Lestrade repeated, 'you mean drunk?'

'As a lord,' Clement confided.

'Why do you think that?'

'Well, he was rollin' about in the middle of the road. Sort of . . . totterage. I rang my bell, didn't I, Bert? An' I says to Bert, 'cos he'd come up front by this time, I says to Bert, "'Ere, it's a bit bloody early in the day, ain't it?" I mean, I like a larf. This bloke, 'e was just stood there. I thought to myself, "He'll move in a minute. Don't you worry, Albert Spivey, he'll move. Then you can shake your fist at 'im." Only we get lectures 'ere, don't we, Bert, on 'ow to treat annoyingly dangerous pedestrians. We get lessons in 'ow to shake our fists. Nothin' more, mind yer. In fact, for spittin' at people, we get fined, don't we, Bert?'

'We do, Clement. 'Ence the expression among us trammies – "Expectoration Equals Expulsion" – the three Ees.'

'But the man didn't move?'

'Nah,' Clement's eyes fell and he began to shake, 'He just . . . just stood there, sort of . . . smiling. I jammed on me brakes. Bert, you'll bear testimony.'

'As naked as nature intended, Clement,' Bert's loyalty was more than skin deep.

'What operates your brakes?' Lestrade asked.

'I do,' said the driver.

'Yes,' Lestrade saw the end of a tether looming, probably his own. 'But I mean, what stops the tram mechanically?'

'Oh, compressed air. I just pull the lever and the air is compressed.'

Bert motioned the Yard men aside, patting the driver's shoulder as he got up. 'That's what 'e's sufferin' from, guvs,' he said, 'acute compression. You dunno wot it's like, see. Out on the lines at eight, drivin' round an' round. It might look easy, but the tension is unbearable. You come 'ome like a wound spring. Now Clement, 'e's the salt o' the earth, 'e is. One of Nature's gentlefolk. 'E wouldn't 'urt a flea, unless it bit 'im first, of course. 'E's been gobsmacked by this. Might never drive again, you know. Terrible. Bloody terrible, I can tell you.'

'Yes,' said Lestrade, 'well, however wound up your driver gets at home time, at least he will be going home. That's more than can be said for the man he ran into.'

Emily Adams was a little woman, in apron and mob cap. If her family had come back from Mongolia with Marco Polo, they'd long ago lost all the usual racial characteristics. She just clung to the superintendent, her late husband's guv'nor, her knuckles white on his jacket sleeves, her face buried in his lapels. And she cried and cried. How long they stayed there in the bright little parlour as darkness fell, neither of them remembered in the years to come. The years that had a faded photograph of a sergeant of the Metropolitan police on the mantelpiece. The funny thing was that even when the Luftwaffe scored a direct hit on that little parlour in 1940 in a war which neither of them would have understood, the one thing to survive intact was that faded photograph.

There were no more words. And when she'd cried enough and the tears wouldn't come any more, he left her with her neighbours and her memories and the children whose daddy had not come home.

It was the one time in his life that Lestrade did not go to inspect the corpse. Adams had never been a friend, but he was a copper and, by his lights, a good one. And he had nearly saved Lestrade's life on that darkened stair in the house of Charles Tenterden in Peter Tavy, all those months ago. There was something about a thing like that. About a man who had stood with you, shoulder to shoulder, against death itself. Somebody else could identify him. Adams was a man Lestrade wanted to remember alive, not spattered the length of Farringdon Road.

So it was something of a shock to him to learn the cause of the sergeant's death.

'All I want to know, Freddie, is how much alcohol there was in his stomach.'

'Alcohol?' the police surgeon adjusted his spectacle chain. 'Why would you want to know that?'

'The driver and conductor of the tram that killed him both swore.'

'Well, that's the working class for you, Sholto. Good God, man, you've been a policeman long enough by now. They all do it, unless they're Methodists, of course.'

'I mean they swore that Adams was drunk.'

'Stone cold sober,' Freddie said.

Lestrade frowned. 'You're sure?'

The look on the police surgeon's face made it clear that his professional integrity had been impugned and one more such suggestion might well constrain him to put one on Lestrade.

'All right,' said the superintendent, 'sorry. But you see my diploma – I am supposed to explain to the man's widow and kids that their husband and father, the man who was their sole provider and won all the bread, was killed by an exceptionally careful and competent tram driver because at the age of forty-one he was standing in the middle of the Farringdon Road swaying from side to side in the face of an oncoming tram. And all this was done at half past ten on a Friday morning in broad . . . Oh my God!'

'Yes?' Freddie leaned back in his chair.

'"By Friday soon, or Saturday noon",' muttered Lestrade.

'What?' Freddie asked.

'Come on then, Freddie,' Lestrade snapped, 'out with it. You have all the hallmarks of a cat that's just learned to scoop the delicious bits out of a goldfish bowl.'

'*Oenanthe crocata*,' he smiled. 'That's Water Drop-wort to you.'

Lestrade was none the wiser.

'Hemlock, dear detective. The witches used to rub it on their skins. It entered their pores and produced an hallucination of flight. That's where the broomstick stories come in.'

Lestrade was in no mood for fairy-tales. 'You mean . . . Adams was poisoned?'

'Undoubtedly.'

'How?'

'Ah, well, there you have me. As you can imagine, the impact of a tram, albeit a braking one, on the human body, is not a pretty sight. I understand St Barts is bulging at the seams with witnesses to the accident, all of them traumata nervosa.'

The curious similarity of the witnesses' religious beliefs Lestrade would leave alone for now.

'The point?'

'The point is that I haven't enough of the body's externals to tell. He may have taken it orally, but it's difficult to disguise its bitter taste.'

'How long does hemlock take, Freddie?' Lestrade asked. 'It's a new one on me.'

'Can be as little as five minutes,' the surgeon shrugged. 'No more than an hour, I shouldn't think. His stomach showed little sign of it. Just lots of toast. That must have been breakfast. It's my guess he was stabbed.'

'Stabbed?'

'Hm. Stiletto. Something thin and sharp.'

'What would the symptoms be?'

'Lividity. Twitchings. Convulsions. Delirium. Coma.'

'So if witnesses say he was swaying about in the middle of the road . . .'

'Delirium. The poor bastard must have been livid and twitching already. Do we know his movements that morning?'

Lestrade shook his head. 'He sent in a note on Thursday to say he wasn't well. Could that have been the poison?'

'Unlikely,' the surgeon said, 'I've never known hemlock take twenty-four hours or more. How's his missus taking it?'

'Well, of course,' Lestrade said, 'she doesn't know about this. Cigar?'

'Hm. Thanks. Are you all right, Sholto?'

'Perfectly,' said Lestrade. 'Why?'

'It's just that I've known you now for what . . . eight years and in all that time, this is the first cigar you've given me.'

'Yes, well,' the superintendent scowled and lit a lucifer for them both, 'it's true I haven't been well. Mrs Adams said that her husband was working on something. He came home on Thursday afternoon very excited.'

'Why?'

'I've yet to find out. In the morning she thought he said he was going to the Temple to talk to the barrister Sidney Rowlatt.'

'Not much to excite anyone there, I wouldn't have thought.'

'Nor I,' Lestrade nodded, blowing rings over Freddie's microscope. 'But his movements on the Friday we just don't know. He left home a little before nine. And he was carrying his cuffs.'

'To make an arrest?'

'That would be my assumption,' Lestrade said. 'The point is – who?'

'Somebody with a knowledge of toxicology,' Freddie assured him.

'And somebody who knows about poisons,' Lestrade added.

'Oh, by the way,' the surgeon ferreted in a bag on the floor, 'you won't have had a chance to return belongings to the widow, but here they are.' He pulled out a pair of handcuffs, still darkened with blood. 'Oh, sorry, Sholto, I didn't have time to clean those.' And a bus ticket. And a little Abyssinian mirror, its glass shattered.

'Where was this?' Lestrade asked.

'In his pocket. Jacket.'

'Right or left?'

'Right. Why?'

'I don't know,' Lestrade clamped the cigar into his mouth, grimly, 'I really don't know.'

One by one they talked to the witnesses. That random cross-section of the British public who happened to be in the wrong place at the wrong time. Most of them, Freddie was quite right, spent the weekend at St Bart's hospital, too shocked to go out again. It was the usual story, as Lestrade and Dew and Bee and Queux listened patiently, and patted shoulders and offered handkerchiefs and held hands (with the distressed witnesses, that is, not with each other). Some had seen one thing, others another. It could have been Thursday. It might have been Wednesday. It was somewhere near Farringdon Station, or was it Blackfriars? One man swore blind it was on Thursday in Llandrindrod Wells, but clearly he wasn't going home after the weekend. Just a surreptitious transfer to the Royal Bethlehem. As the Salvation Army struck up all the tunes of God's glory in the little square by St Bartholomew's the Less, a core of hard fact was slowly beginning to emerge. As the tram had finally screeched to a halt, after the sickening thud of impact and a crowd began to grow, a man had pushed his way to the body claiming to be a doctor. What did he look like? Er . . . well . . . Was he old? Oh yes, quite old. Anything from forty-five to ninety-three. Tall? Definitely. He must have been seven foot, but he was kneeling down most the time. He'd said it was no use. The man was dead. What had he done? Only one of the witnesses was sure of that. He had felt for a pulse. And felt for it in a place where the witness hadn't realized there was a pulse. Inside the dead man's right pocket.

Lestrade didn't remember when he'd seen the Temple look so lovely. The heavy shade of the planes was welcome as he clattered over the cobbles that day in mid-August. Winston Churchill and one hundred other prominent people had only last week held a rally to protest against traffic noise. Here there was none. Only the dying cries of newspaper vendors and the happy chatter of trippers on the paddle steamers on the river. He looked across to the rooftops of King's College, empty as the building stood now in the summer vacation; to that place where Jan the Stewer had died at the foot of her lover's stairs all those months ago. And it gave him no comfort at all to know that he was no nearer catching her murderer now than he had been at the time. In a way, he felt he was further away.

A young man of diminutive stature opened the door to him. At least, unless he was a master of the stilts, this was not Lestrade's man. 'Sidney Rowlatt?' he asked.

'Thankfully, no.'

'Then may I have the pleasure?'

The young man blinked. 'You mean because I am not Sidney Rowlatt you want to dance with me? You're not a friend of Ramsay MacDonald, are you?'

'No, sir. I am Superintendent Lestrade of Scotland Yard.'

'Ah, a boy in blue. Well, once upon a time you may have been.'

'And you are?'

'In something of an early-thirties crisis, actually. Oh, sorry, do come in. Lemonade?'

'Er . . . no, thank you,' Lestrade's jaw ridged at the very prospect.

'I'm John Buchan, by the by,' the man said, 'I'm Rowlatt's devil.' He sounded too much like Abraham Knox for Lestrade's liking, except for the Lowland Scots twang. At least he was wearing his own hair. 'Tea, then?'

'No, really,' but Lestrade was grateful for the chair Buchan ushered him into. 'It's imperative that I see Mr Rowlatt.'

'Aye, well, that's a little problematical,' Buchan told him, closing a ledger of prodigious thickness. 'You see, the old bugger's away at the moment, on leave.'

'Where?'

'Senegal.'

'Ah,' Lestrade had no jurisdiction in Ireland. 'For how long has this been the case?'

'Oh, let's see,' he consulted a diary, 'middle of July. He's due back in early September.'

'Tell me, Mr Buchan, were you here on Thursday?'

'Thursday? Yes, I think so. Do you know anything about Chinese labour, Mr Lestrade?'

Clearly, here was a man obsessed. He'd already mentioned Ramsay MacDonald and now labour. Lestrade hadn't known about the native wing of the party however. In those days policemen were supposed to be apolitical. 'Not a thing, sir,' he said, 'but if you don't mind, I'd like to ask the questions.'

'Oh, that's rather good,' Buchan reached for a pen and notepad.

'What are you writing down?' Lestrade asked.

'That phrase of yours,' Buchan said. 'I should explain, Mr

Lestrade, that I am a man of many parts. A sort of huomo universale.'

Lestrade raised an eyebrow. The man was astonishingly frank, even for somebody's devil in 1906, 'or at least, that's what my wife says.' Lestrade was more confused than ever. 'You see, I was called to the Bar five years ago, but my heart's not in it. In some ways, my heart's in the Heelands, a-chasing the deer. But my greatest love is literature. You've read some of my modest collections of excellence, no doubt – *Sir Quixote of the Moors, Scholar Gypsies, The African Colony?*'

'Er . . . sadly, sir, in a busy life . . .'

'Oh, really,' scowled Buchan, slightly unbelieving that anyone could be *that* busy. 'Well, anyway, I want to branch out a bit. Write rattling good yarns that feature iron-hard young Scotsmen in plus-fours who save the world for democracy. You know the sort of thing.'

Thankfully, Lestrade didn't. 'Did a sergeant call here, sir?' he persisted, 'on Thursday?'

'Yes. Chap called Adams. Why? Checking up on him, are you?'

'In a way, sir. You see, Sergeant Adams is dead.'

'Dead? Oh dear. Accident?'

'Tram,' Lestrade nodded.

'Good Lord, yes. I read about that in the *Standard*. Farringdon, wasn't it? Frightful business, frightful. I didn't connect the name. I'm terribly sorry, Superintendent. Was he a friend?'

'No,' said Lestrade, 'but he was one of my men.'

'Of course,' Buchan nodded, his fingers to his pursed lips, 'no stone unturned, that sort of thing. You need say no more.'

'What did Sergeant Adams talk about, sir?'

'Well, like you he was looking for old Rowlatt. Like you, I told him he wasn't here. We got on to that poor creature whose parachute failed to open at Alexandra Palace a couple of weeks ago. She was old Rowlatt's ward by all accounts, although I'd never seen her around here. I don't have a forwarding address for him, you see, so we'll have to wait until he gets back.'

'Tell me, sir, how tall is Sidney Rowlatt?'

'Tall?' Buchan frowned. 'My word, but you chappies ask

some damned funny questions. I don't really know. Six foot two, three.'

'Tall, then,' Lestrade confirmed.

Buchan laughed. 'When you're five foot three, that's how everybody strikes you, Superintendent.'

'What else did Adams talk about?'

'Well, we got on to my African experiences.'

'Oh?' Lestrade was all ears.

'Well, you see, I was Lord Milner's assistant private secretary between 1901 and 1903. As such I ranged all over the Cape and the Transvaal. I won't say I ever got to like the Boers, but I do concede that they had a point. Look, Mr Lestrade,' Buchan lolled back with his feet on Sidney Rowlatt's desk, 'tell me if it's none of my business, but your Sergeant Adams wrote all this down last Thursday. Didn't he have time to pass it on before his tragic accident?'

Lestrade shook his head. 'It wasn't an accident, Mr Buchan, whatever the *Standard* said. Adams was pursuing his own line of inquiry. He was a good copper, but an over-ambitious one, I fear. Something he learned here on Thursday gave him a clue he had to follow up by himself. He broke all the rules – well, we've all done it – and took off after his quarry alone.'

'Something *I* said?' Buchan was intrigued. 'Oh dear, I hope the man wasn't killed because of something *I* told him.'

'What was it?' Lestrade leaned towards him, 'Milner? The Boers? *Think*, man.'

'I am, I am,' Buchan's feet came off the desk and his wide forehead creased with the effort of remembering. 'I had this damned piece to write on Chinese labour. I was only half concentrating. I remember we got on to Prester John.'

'Who?'

'Prester John. It's a legend as old as time, Superintendent. What can it possibly have to do with the case you and Adams are working on?'

'I'll let you know, sir,' Lestrade said, grimly. 'Who is Prester John?'

'Not *is*, Mr Lestrade,' Buchan corrected him, '*was*. Mind you, people like Alvarez believed him to be immortal, apparently.'

'Alvarez?' Lestrade was on his feet.

'Yes. Look here, are you all right?' Buchan looked up at his man. 'You've gone rather a funny colour. Would you like me to pick the lock on old Rowlatt's tantalus?'

'No, Mr Buchan,' growled Lestrade. 'Your conversation is heady enough. Who is Alvarez?'

'Again, *was*, I'm afraid, Mr Lestrade. Francisco Alvarez was a chronicler – the first to chronicle the great priest-king of Abyssinia.'

'Abyssinia,' nodded Lestrade, sitting down again, 'I knew it.'

'Well, if you knew it . . .'

'No, no, I don't mean I *know* it. Go on. Tell me everything you know about this priest-king.'

'Well, not a lot, really. Prester means priest or – bearing in mind my own antecedents – my dear old dad being a minister of the Free Church of Scotland an'a – Presbyter. Elder. Some say he was the John whose writings feature in the New Testament. Others that he was a descendant of one of the Magi. It was during the Crusades that the legend was born of a great Christian ruler who defeated the Muslims somewhere in Persia. His name is variously translated as Gur Khan or Kor Khan. From that, semantically speaking, we get the Hebrew Yohanan and the Latin Johannes. Our John. Apparently he wrote letters to the Byzantine emperor and to Frederick Barbarossa of Germany in 1165, claiming that he was ruler of a vast empire from Babylon to India and that seventy-two lesser kings paid him tribute.' Buchan chuckled. 'You must take all this with an awful lot of salt, Mr Lestrade,' he said. 'The only Empire that big in history is our own, God Bless It. I don't somehow see His Majesty Edward VII as a priest-king, do you?'

'How does Alvarez come into all this?'

'Well, as I said, he wrote the first book on the man. You see, by 1540, the area between Babylon and India had been explored by Europeans. And there was no Prester John. An area that had *not* been explored then was Abyssinia, so that became his mythical kingdom – a land at once mysterious, isolated and Christian. It fitted the bill perfectly.'

'Who is the current ruler of Abyssinia?' Lestrade had missed that lecture on Emergent Africa at the Yard.

'Er . . . Menelik II,' Buchan told him.

'And before that?'

'John, funnily enough. Oh, don't worry; not Prester John.'

'And before that?'

'Theodore III – Tewedros in the coptic dialect, I believe. He was the one who committed suicide in his fortress at Magdala.'

'In 1868?' Lestrade checked.

'That's right,' Buchan said. 'When Napier stormed the place. Ironic, really. Those pistols were given to the emperor by Queen Victoria, God Bless Her, and he blew his brains out with one.'

'Did or do any of these men have an obsession with mirrors?'

'Mirrors?' Buchan frowned, then smiled, 'no, no, you're back to Prester John again.'

'I am?'

'Yes. He had magic artefacts to help him rule his kingdom as no king before or since. Jewels that controlled temperature – I could do with one of those today. A glass church that could shrink or expand to fit any congregation. And most useful of all, a magic mirror so that he could see everything that happened in his entire kingdom at once. Handy, eh?'

'Indeed. And if the mirror should break?'

'Break?' Buchan sucked his teeth. 'You've got me there. I've never heard that part of the legend.'

'Oh, it's not a legend, Mr Buchan,' Lestrade shook his head. 'It's all too real. Tell me, what was the purpose of Prester John's mirror?'

'Well, I suppose to stamp out crime. Any wrongdoing anywhere in his kingdom and he'd know it instantly.'

'Unless the mirror was broken. That way he couldn't see it, could he?'

'Er . . . no, I suppose not.'

'One final question, Mr Buchan. Do you know, by any chance, a medium called Queenie Blow?'

'As a matter of fact, I do. I can't for the life of me imagine why I went now. Bit of a joke, I suppose. She was raising funds for our chaps in Mafeking and I attended one of her evenings. Why do you ask?'

'It's just that . . . I attended a seance of hers recently. Before

Adams died. She sat as a king would, the knitting needle in her hand like a sceptre. She was talking to someone called Charlie, asking why he'd broken her mirrors. Then she spoke in what I took to be Abyssinian. You don't know anyone called Charlie, I suppose?'

Buchan shrugged. 'I don't think so,' he said, 'but look here, Superintendent, I'm rather surprised at Scotland Yard taking this rubbish seriously. She told me the most arrant nonsense, advised me to keep out of bathrooms in Montreal. Well, I ask you!'

'Did you tell Adams all this?'

'More or less,' Buchan said. 'Why? Does it give you your murderer, Mr Lestrade?'

The Superintendent looked the man in his narrow, flinty eyes. He sighed. 'It just takes me back to Abyssinia,' he said, 'but I can be more precise than that now. I'm looking for a man who is mad as a hatter. And the road leads not to Abyssinia in general but to Magdala in particular.'

They buried Sergeant Adams that Wednesday, what was left of him. The Metropolitan Police formed the pall bearers and the guard of honour. Mrs Adams walked behind with her children, all of them proud, all of them erect, all of them glancing from time to time at the hollow-eyed superintendent on whose arm Mrs Adams leaned occasionally. He stared straight ahead at the flag-draped coffin and the bowler hat on top of it. Behind him, in black gloves and carrying canes reversed, Chief Inspector Dew and his constables, marching with measured tread. The blinds were drawn as they turned out of Adams's road and workmen tapping on tiles on the sizzling roofs nearby, stopped and doffed their caps and stood silent, like statues on their ladders. The cemetery bell marked time. Only the black stallions tossed their heads and pawed the ground. Mrs Adams had not wanted all this fuss, but the acting commissioner had insisted and there was nothing that the Morbid Major liked better than a jolly good funeral.

* * *

'It's about Magdala,' Lestrade heard himself saying for the hundredth time that morning. He looked at the littered wall across from his desk. 'Did they know each other?' he asked. 'Any of the victims?'

'No link we can find, guv,' Queux said.

'No,' Lestrade said. 'That's because the link is missing. He's a six-foot-five ex-intelligence officer who vanished in Abyssinia thirty-eight years ago. But now he's back. And he's killing people. Why? Why?'

'We've got him, guv!' Lestrade hadn't seen Walter Dew so excited since he thought he'd won the H Division sweep. Well, he had, but all he won was a free chimney-clean.

'Who?' Lestrade refused to let the chief inspector's enthusiasm become infectious.

'Charles Staveley.'

'Ah, Peta Gurney's sugar daddy.'

'Yes, but it gets better.'

'Oh?'

'He's a general now.'

'We know that, Dew,' Lestrade was tired of treading water and getting nowhere. He was no longer in the market for suffering fools gladly; Walter Dew not at all.

'Yes, but did you know he was a colonel then?'

'When?'

'In 1868.'

'Where?' Lestrade's eyebrows threatened to reach his hairline.

'Abyssinia!' all four men chorused.

Lestrade was on his feet. 'Bee, where's that stuff the police surgeon got from Adams's pockets? Did you give it to his wife?'

'The fifty quid you put there, guv,' Bee said, 'nothing else, I'm afraid. The cuffs were ours, so I returned them to stores. I didn't think the mirror was very tasteful, seeing as how the murderer put it there. Anyhow, it's evidence. And I didn't think she'd want an old bus ticket.'

'Brilliant, Bee. Remind me to have a word with the commissioner about you, when they get round to appointing one. Where is it?'

'Um . . .' the detective rummaged in shoe boxes various.

206

'Here we are,' he said, holding the ticket up. 'Why, guv? You can't use 'em again, you know.'

'Ah, but you can,' Lestrade laughed. 'That's the ticket! Come on, then, Walter. Let's show these youngsters a bit of sleuthing. You tell me where Staveley lives and I'll read what it says on this ticket. Or, as we used to say at Mr Poulson's Academy, "I'll show you yours if you show me mine".'

'Gray's Inn Road,' they chorused.

Lestrade grasped Dew's hand. 'Well done, Walter.'

'Fox Court, to be precise, guv'nor.'

'Fox Court,' Lestrade nodded, smiling. 'Well, the fox is caught indeed. Bee, Queux. Get your boaters. Walter, I want six of your biggest blokes.'

'Six, guv?'

Lestrade looked at his Number Two. 'He's already killed ten people, Walter. We're not doing a Benjamin Harry Adams and . . . going alone. My God.'

'What is it, sir?' Dew asked, fitting the ebony life preserver into his pocket.

'Go back a few years, Walter,' Lestrade ordered. 'Here was I, thinking Staveley was rattled by us getting too close. But he wasn't, damn him.' His fist thumped the desk and the teacups rattled too.

'I've gone back a few years, guv,' Dew's eyes were tight shut.

'Good. Now, what was slang for a policeman?'

'Er . . . copper. Miltonian. Esclap. Crusher. H . . .'

'Yes, Walter?'

'Hawk,' Dew said.

'"Harry Hawke",' Lestrade quoted. 'He beat us with Peta Gurney, finding a girl with the same-sounding name. Now he's beaten us with our own slang. Not a man called Harry Hawke, but a policeman called Harry. One of us.'

'Well, we've got him now, guv,' Dew rammed on his boater. 'Whoever Tom Cobbleigh is, he'll have reason to thank the Metropolitan Police by tonight.'

* * *

They went deliberately incognito. By bus rather than Yard despatch vehicle. The men with boaters, all of them sporting moustaches, one of them with a fuzz below his nose. Their names had already gone down in legend on many a London sportsfield. Six of the Metropolitan Tug-of-War team captained by Constable 'Juggernaut' Jenkins of L Division. They all sat on the top deck of the Number Thirty-seven, basking in the August sunshine, watching the world glide by.

'You never told me how you traced him, Walter,' Lestrade said.

'Miracle of modern science, really,' Dew said. 'The motor car was his undoing.'

'Oh?'

'First, the Vehicle Licensing Department by the Monument gave me one General Charles Staveley as recently having purchased one of these swanky new Rolls and Royce jobs. Silver Spook or something.'

'Ghost, Chief Inspector,' Queux felt he had to correct his guv'nor.

'And second?'

'Second – and you'll like this. No sooner had he bought it, but he ran into a police speed trap.'

'No!'

'As I live and breathe. Appears at Marylebone Magistrates Court next week.'

'And the Old Bailey the month after,' Lestrade nodded. 'Right, lads. Here we are. Jugger, are your lads all set?'

'Right you are, guv'nor sir,' the giant said, touching his boater. 'We take the front door, Atlas and me – orff its hinges if need be. Slammer and Pectorals take the sides. Killer hangs round the back with It. A spider won't be able to get out of there once we're in position.'

'Ooh, Jugger, I wish you wouldn't mention spiders. You *know* how I come over.'

'Pectorals, I gave you the choice. Now, look, you're starin' promotion in the face. Mr Lestrade is lookin' to you for a bit of weight. Now, it's just a figure of speech, all right? I don't suppose there's any spiders in there, anyhow.'

'You're sure?'

'No, I'm not one hundred per cent sure, Pectorals, no. But

seein' as how yer about four hundred times the size of one, does it really matter? Now, buck up, man, or it's back to the horse troughs for you.'

And they clattered down the spiral stairs and out on to the pavement.

Number sixteen Fox Court was a villa, unusually detached in that narrow enclave of streets and alleys. Bowler-hatted civil servants and Homburged solicitors rubbed shoulders with bewigged barristers on their way to and from chambers. Nobody noticed the ten, grim and purposeful, jostling their way along Chancery Lane and ducking surreptitiously round the corner. The big men paired off, loitering with intent at various corners. Slammer and Pectorals crouched by the drainpipes, on their opposite sides, the latter keeping a watchful eye out for any arachnoid movement in the alleyway. Jugger and Atlas noticed that the front door was slightly ajar and that there were sounds of singing coming from inside. In a little under three minutes, every orifice of the house was covered and unless Staveley chose to get away over the rooftops, in which case he'd almost certainly hit the concrete forty feet below, they'd got him.

'Now!' Lestrade brought his arm down sharply and winced anew, memories of his lucky escape from the Insurance Man rekindled in his sun-baked brain. Jugger and Atlas moved as one, their boots clattering on the cobbles, the ground shaking as they ran. They butted aside the door and vanished into the darkness. Lestrade and Dew were with them, Bee and Queux hanging back in case the demented old general were to leap from an upstairs window. The sound of singing came to an abrupt halt and turned to a falsetto shriek, which sent Jugger reeling backwards clutching his right ear.

'Get out, you great ape!' Lestrade heard a female voice shriek and saw Atlas go down with a broom across his cranium. The side door crashed back, letting the sunlight stream in and Slammer hurtled across the drawing-room, only to slip on the loose mat that said 'Welcome' and he ended up with his nose jammed against the skirting board. Pectorals on the other hand was pinned outside in the alleyway, a harvestman spider guarding the door like Horatius on the bridge. He felt the sweat trickle from his hairline, saw the world spin, the brickwork and the drains and plummeted forward as gracefully as you can when you're eighteen stone. The harvestman deftly jumped aside and, tutting to itself at the inconvenience, crawled over him.

'Not another step!' Lestrade obeyed. Dew did likewise. To one side stood the singer, in the black and white that was still de rigeur for downstairs maids, her deadly broom at the advance. To the other an elderly lady, well set-up and with fine bone structure, who had clearly once been very attractive. The twelve-bore shotgun she wielded was a beauty too and both its barrels stared at the policeman.

There was the crunch of glass somewhere else in the house, evidence that Killer and It had found their way in through the back.

'If that's the Dresden,' the old lady said firmly, 'there'll be hell to pay. Lie down on the floor. You, with the bovine face. You.' She waved the gun at Dew who dropped his hands and hit the carpet. 'Supine,' the old girl said, 'as befits one of your class. You.' Lestrade's hands instinctively rose higher as he felt the cold steel nudge his chin.

'Guv . . .' It was first into the hall.

'If this oaf is with you, tell him to lie down,' the old lady said.

'Er . . . thanks, It,' Lestrade's head was tilted back quite painfully. 'If you wouldn't mind.'

'Shall I just break her kneecaps, guv?' the constable asked.

'No!' Lestrade was a shade more falsetto than he would have liked in front of his inferiors, but now was not a time to stand on dignity. 'Do as the lady says, It – and now!'

It capitulated. Seconds behind him, Killer did likewise. Now there was a total of six policemen lying on the ground, two damaged, one unconscious and another with a shotgun up his nose.

'We are police officers,' Lestrade hissed, finding his current position particularly uncomfortable.

'Please,' said the old lady, 'I didn't come down with the last shower of rain.'

Lestrade edged his finger down towards his inside pocket. He felt the muzzle jam upwards under his nose and heard the hammer click at the same time. 'My warrant card,' he blurted, 'in my inside pocket.'

'Gertrude,' the old lady snapped to her maid. The girl lowered the broom, but wouldn't let go of it and gingerly slipped her hand inside Lestrade's jacket. 'Uggh,' she said, 'it ain't half sweaty in there, Mum.'

'In my day,' the lady said, 'only horses sweated. Are there any more in your gang?'

'"My gang", as you call it, is composed of police constables. And yes, there are others outside.'

The maid had found the warrant card and showed it to her mistress.

'Superintendent Sholto Lestrade,' she read aloud, 'good Heavens.' She released the catch on the twelve-bore and removed it from Lestrade's nostril. The air of relaxation in the room was audible.

'Right, on your feet, lads,' the superintendent ordered. 'Upstairs.'

'One moment!' the old girl's voice was authoritative enough to stop them all in their tracks. 'I demand to know the reason for this unseemly intrusion.'

'We are looking for General Charles Staveley,' Lestrade told her.

'Charles is not here.'

'Who would you be?' he asked.

'Given the choice, Good Queen Bess,' she told him, 'but that's immaterial. My husband may have been putting his new motor through its paces and run into one of your ridiculous, underhand and, I'm sure illegal, entrapments; but that does not give you the right to break and enter.'

'I'm afraid it's rather more serious than that, Madam,' Lestrade said, 'and any damage will be made good.'

'Indeed it will, Superintendent. Now, for the last time, the General is not here and I would like you louts to leave my house.'

He looked at her steady blue eyes and noticed that she cradled the twelve-bore like an expert. 'Mrs Staveley . . .'

'*Lady* Staveley,' she corrected him.

'Lady Staveley. We have reason to believe that your husband

may be involved in a series of murders. We must search the house.'

'Murders?' Lady Staveley was aghast and clutched her rope of pearls, 'Charles?'

'I'm afraid so.'

The next moment she was composure itself. 'Do you have a search warrant?'

'Dew,' Lestrade flicked his fingers.

'Er . . . no, guv,' the embarrassed chief inspector muttered 'I thought you . . . Bee! Queux!' he dashed back through the front door. Everybody stood around, waiting. Slammer started whistling until a ferocious glance from Lady Staveley silenced him. Then they listened in silence while snatches of conversation drifted back from outside.

'What the bloody hell do you mean?' they heard Dew scream.

'I thought you had one, guv,' another voice they recognized as Bee's.

The rest of it was fairly earthy and Lady Staveley balanced the shotgun against the sideboard before covering her maid's ears. There were various references to horse troughs and an awful lot of physical impossibilities. Moments later, Walter Dew dashed back into the passage. 'Er . . . might I have a word, Superintendent?'

'It is plain to me, gentlemen,' Lady Staveley said, 'that none of you has the requisite paperwork to search these premises. I demand, in light of that, that you vacate them immediately. And rest assured, Superintendent, as the door clicks behind you, I shall be on the telephone machine to your superiors. It is not merely your underlings, I suspect, who will be back on bleeding horse trough bleeding duty by tonight. Good morning.'

'I don't believe this, Lestrade,' Major Woodhouse was saying the next morning, the superintendent back where he often was, on the acting assistant commissioner's carpet. 'A new back door. Six priceless pieces of Dresden china. A recent photograph of the General along with a silver frame, suspiciously missing. Not to mention the appalling shock you gave those poor ladies . . .'

'Those poor ladies, sir, effectively demolished two thirds of my team.'

'It's as well they did, Lestrade,' the Morose Major emerged from his side of the walnut desk, 'I'm an army man and I've never seen bungling like it. You *are* a Superintendent, aren't you? I mean, you have a vague acquaintanceship with British law?'

'I . . .'

'I don't know how far my powers go, Lestrade,' Woodhouse interrupted him, 'but you may rest assured that I shall be trotting along to Mr Henry's office as soon as your back's turned. My recommendation is that you be taken off this case of yours and broken to . . . well, in view of your record, let's be generous and say sergeant, shall we? In Personnel.'

'Per . . .' Lestrade couldn't even bring himself to say the word.

'Did you say something, Lestrade?'

'I am *that* close, sir,' the still-just-about-superintendent told him, holding his thumb and index finger slightly apart, '*that* close to catching my man.'

'You still persist with this nonsense about Staveley?'

'It all fits, sir.'

The Major looked at his man. The sallow, rat-like features, the stiffly-held neck and arm. The bruised nose. The man was a physical and mental wreck. Well, not everyone could handle the stresses of the job. 'Does it?' he sighed.

'You've read my memorandum?'

'Of course.'

'Consider this, then. Peta Gurney, the sixth victim, had an elderly gentleman friend who goes by the name of Charles Staveley. It is he who packs the parachute on the day of her "accident" at Ally Pally – the parachute which killed her. The same Charles Staveley was a colonel back in 1868: part of Lord Napier's expedition to subdue the Emperor Theodore at Magdala.'

'Yes, yes, Lestrade,' Woodhouse threw himself down on the Chesterfield, 'I've read all this.'

'The only eyewitness account of anyone seeing a man who was probably the murderer is Kenrick, Captain Orange's man

at Peter Tavy. He describes the visitor to Orange's house as tal
Charles Tenterden says that Captain Charles Speedy was tall
six foot five or thereabouts. Don't you see, sir?' Lestrade ha
reached the end of his wit. It hadn't taken long. 'Either Speed
and Staveley are one and the same man – notice the similarit
of the names – or Staveley is pretending to be Speedy or vic
versa. What better ploy than to pose as a man who is missing
presumed dead?'

'But what's his motive, Lestrade?'

'He's mad, sir. If it *is* Speedy, something seems to hav
unhinged him. We know from Tenterden – and Dew checke
this with army records – that Speedy disappeared by the tim
the army had taken Magdala. And Tenterden says he wa
behaving strangely before that. Said he'd found something
out in the desert. Remember, he'd been made a general in th
Abyssinian army – spoke fluent Abyssinian.'

'Well, what had he found? A handful of mirrors?'

'No sir,' Lestrade shook his head, 'although I do believe the
came from there.'

'Where, man?'

'You've heard of Prester John?'

Woodhouse looked blank, 'I've heard of prestidigitation,' h
said. 'Any relation?'

'The mythical priest-king who for centuries it was believe
ruled an Empire the size of ours.'

'Oh. Really?' Major Woodhouse always contrived to loo
extra vacant when he didn't understand something. There wer
times when he positively took on the appearance of an empty
lavatory.

'Yes, sir,' Lestrade nodded, 'really. I believe Charles Speedy
found the kingdom of Prester John – or at least the remains o
it. What else he found – what drove him mad – I have yet to
discover.'

'I see,' Woodhouse drummed his fingers on the Chesterfield'
arm. 'Well, if it's Staveley you're after, you'd better get a
move on.'

'I've got Constable Jenkins watching the Fox Court address
sir.'

'I'm sure you have, Superintendent,' the Miserable Majo

scowled and crossed to his man, 'but that is somewhat reminiscent of horses and stable doors, isn't it?'

'Do you know where Staveley is, sir?'

'Vaguely,' Woodhouse nodded, 'and had you approached Lady Staveley – who is an utterly charming woman by the way – in a civilized manner, no doubt she would have told you. He's been rather upset, recently . . .'

'Tsk. Tsk,' frowned Lestrade, 'shame.'

'I won't have sarcasm in the Metropolitan Police, Lestrade. There's no place for it. When she'd finished demanding your resignation – or your testicles on a plate, she didn't want to cause any trouble – we got on to the General. Ever a keen fisherman, he's taking a little holiday, along the Thames somewhere near Mapledurham. And *if* you're going, keep reporting in. It may be, once I have talked to Mr Henry, we'll need to do some instant recalling. I'm not sure how many horse troughs they have in Mapledurham.'

The sun dappled through the elms that lined the road. Mallards quacked and moorhens fussed on the floating brown flotsam of the river. In the tall yellow grasses, long starved of greening rain, two men sat side by side in the buzz of the heavy, midday flies of summer, their rods at rest, their lines trailing in the water.

'Damn good of you to share your hamper with me like this,' one of them said, raising a glass. 'What do you call this drink again?'

'It's a cobbler,' the older man said, 'made from wine, lemon juice, sugar and ice. It's the ice that's all important. You're supposed to swallow the cube.'

'Really?' the other laughed.

'A vital part of the custom.'

'Very well,' and he did.

'In some parts of the country,' the older man said, 'it's known as a Cobbley. And sometimes, Tom Cobbley.' He raised his glass. 'Your very good health.'

10

The question 'Have you seen this man?' could often be heard along the upper reaches of the Thames in that long, dry summer of 1906. It came from the lips of tired, hot coppers whose feet ached and whose backsides rebelled at the thought of more hours in the saddles of regulation, black Raleigh bicycles hired from 'Lucky Larry of Lashbrooke' for three and six pence a week. There was much head-shaking too and assorted 'Now, let's sees' among the anglers and artists who regularly invaded Southern Oxfordshire when the days were long and the living easy.

And in those lazy, hazy, crazy days of summer, Super intendent Lestrade and Chief Inspector Dew sat under the striped brolly outside the Fighting Cocks at Sonning Eye and watched the brown river glide by on its never-ending journey to the sea. Their host, a rotund little man with swivel eyes, brought the two pints of the local brew on a silver-plated salver. Dew flashed him the photograph that Lestrade had liberated from Lady Staveley's when the old girl's trigger-finger had relaxed a little. He'd personally shown it to God-knew-how-many riverfolk and had had to listen to God-knew-how-many tales of the riverbank as a result. No reason why this one should be any different.

'Have you seen this man?' he squinted up at the white-aproned landlord.

'Some other blokes asked me that,' his host squinted back. 'Is there a prize or something? A newspaper stunt, is it? How much do you get if you find him?'

'We are police officers,' Dew said languidly, 'and the prize, if we find him, is to make the streets safe for women and children.'

He caught sight of the look on his guv'nor's features and instantly wished he hadn't said it.

'Have a close look,' Lestrade said. He wasn't quite prepared for the closeness as the landlord pressed the thing against the convexity of his glasses.

'Yes,' their host handed the photograph back, 'that's Mr Smith.'

The policemen sat up. Days of wandering the leafy lanes of Oxfordshire were forgotten. Even the flies stopped buzzing, anxious to catch the drift of the conversation.

'Mr Smith?' the Yard men chorused.

'All right, if you're nit-picking – General Smith.'

'General?' they repeated.

'Look,' the landlord turned round twice, 'is there an echo in here? Is there an echo in here?'

'I thought you'd already been shown this photograph?' Lestrade said.

'So I had,' their host said, flicking a wasp with a deft teatowel. It caught Lestrade a sharp one around the ear. 'Got him! No, I've only just got these glasses, see?'

'See' was patently something their host didn't do.

'Tell us about him,' Lestrade ordered.

'Who?'

'General Smith.'

'He was staying here, at the Cocks.'

'When?'

'Ooh, now you've asked me,' he took off the glasses and his eyes swivelled uncontrollably, red-rimmed and watering. 'Tuesday. That was it. It's in the ledger.'

'Show us.'

He led them into the cool recesses of the snug and to the bar, glittering with polished pewter. This was 1906 and refinements had reached the quiet river-pubs. There was no sawdust on the floor and no spitoons. Perhaps people were not expected to expectorate.

'Here it is,' the landlord said. 'Oh, no, that's the family Bible. Ha, ha,' a witticism suddenly struck him, 'it's been a while since Shem stayed here,' he chuckled, 'and we've never done such good business since the Israelites passed through.'

217

'General Smith?' Lestrade reminded him.

'Ah, yes,' he hauled out a heavy ledger from below the bar 'here we are,' and his head suddenly plummeted to the page 'I was right. He signed in on Tuesday.'

'And when did he leave?'

'Friday.'

'May I?' Lestrade swivelled the register to him. Like most Yard men he had the knack of reading things upside down but he had to be sure on this one. He read Mr Smith's address aloud, 'Menlove Gardens, Balham'. He frowned at Dew, 'Walter you're a walking gazetteer. Know that one?'

The Chief Inspector shook his head. 'Doesn't exist, guv. I'd stake a month's pay on it.'

'As I thought,' Lestrade nodded. If Walter Dew was prepared to put his money where his mouth was, there was no possibility of his being wrong.

'A fictitious name and a fictitious address.' He tapped the register. '*Mrs* Smith?' he said.

'Ha, ha,' their host tried to tap the inside of his nose, although he missed the first time. 'Actually a Miss Qualtrough.'

'Younger than Smith?'

'Could have been his granddaughter,' the landlord nodded 'or so Blodwen told me.'

'Blodwen?'

'My girl who does. From the Valleys. Bit of a rough diamond but very willing, if you catch my drift.' He glanced furtively – how else? – from side to side. 'And let's hope Mrs Mine Host never does, eh?' he attempted to nudge Walter Dew in the elbow, but only succeeded in hitting a beer tap and had drawn half a pint all over the floor before he realized and turned it off.

'Is Blodwen here?' Lestrade asked.

'Day off,' their host muttered, disappearing below the bar to mop up the damage.

'But she noticed Miss Qualtrough was on the young side.'

'Barely out of ringlets,' the landlord said.

'How do you know she wasn't really Mrs Smith?' Lestrade checked.

'Blodwen', their host wrung out his apron over a stone sink

got a curiosity on her like nobody's business. "Mr Frazer", she said to me, and he lapsed into the most awful stage Welsh, 'Look you, I couldn't help noticin' while dustin' Room six, that the name inside the luggage of the 'ooman purportin' to be Mrs Smith is actually 'Arriet Qualtrough." I can hear her saying it now.'

'Could be a maiden name,' Dew said, 'if they're recently married.'

'Yeah,' guffawed Frazer, 'and I could be in the rifle-shooting team in the next Olympics.'

Dew frowned. That was one gold medal we weren't going to get.

'We get a lot of this sort of thing along the river in the summer,' the landlord went on. 'I don't know whether it's the frogs and moorhens at it that brings them out. I don't give a bugger, really – as long as they pay up, Mrs Mine Host and I don't ask any questions.'

'All right,' said Lestrade. 'How do you know Mr Smith was really General Smith? It doesn't say that in the ledger.'

'No, I don't suppose it does,' Frazer nodded, 'Blodwen again – "I felt it incumbent on me, Mr Frazer, to dust 'is personal correspondence. Well, you know 'ow much dust, look you boyo, is inside envelopes, innit? Anyow, it transpires that the ol' codger we know as *Mr* Smith is a general – in the army, like" – and I am quoting verbatim here.'

'But the name Smith was on the envelopes?' Lestrade's eyes narrowed.

'No,' Frazer began polishing glasses, 'that was the peculiar thing. The envelopes were addressed – according to Blodwen – to a General Staveley, Fox Court.'

'And you concluded from that?' Lestrade asked.

'Well,' Frazer stopped polishing, 'it's obvious, isn't it? General Smith is such a mean old bugger he uses other people's stationery – cast-off envelopes and the like. It don't surprise me. I had a brother in the Oxford Light Infantry. Never had a good word to say about officers.'

'Tell me, Mr Frazer,' Lestrade said, 'did General Staveley – er .. Smith ... have any fishing tackle with him?'

'Yes.'

'So the General and Miss Qualtrough went fishing?'

'I don't know where they went,' Frazer told them, 'but the rod didn't go with them.'

'Oh?'

'According to Blodwen, it stayed in the corner of the wardrobe the whole time. Judging by the squeak of the bedsprings, the General and his lady had a different idea of messing about on the river.'

'Do you know where they were going when they left?'

'They turned right,' Frazer remembered.

'Right?'

'Yes, that would take them up river. If they followed it they'd go south-west, towards Mapledurham where they found that bloke.'

'What bloke?' Lestrade and Dew looked at each other.

'Well, that dead bloke', Frazer peered at them, wiping his glasses with his cloth, 'that they found by the riverbank. Well, I thought you being policemen and all, that's why you were here.' He handed them an ashtray. 'Peanut?'

Henley was murder at that time of the year. Every hotel was bursting at the seams as the well-to-do of Edwardian society basked in the sun and boatered and blazered young gigolos ferried well-heeled matrons up and down the river. Dew had never seen so many punts in his life. But it was not to the fashionable hotels and matchless lawns that the Yard men had gone. It was to Henley mortuary, a squat, ugly building to the north of the town.

Chief Inspector Rattray, the epitome of inter-force co-operation, stood with his foot tapping as Lestrade paid careful attention to the corpse on the slab in front of him.

'The bloke we're after did a runner,' Dew lolled against the green tiles.

'What? Killed an athlete, you mean?' Rattray asked.

'No,' Dew frowned, 'I mean he left the place he was staying at precipitously.'

'Where was that?'

'The Fighting Cocks at Sonning Eye.'

'Oh, yeah,' Rattray yawned, 'worst pint south of the Bedford Levels.'

'You'd better tell me again, Chief Inspector,' Lestrade didn't take his eyes off the body, although clearly it was going nowhere.

'Again?' Rattray moaned. 'Look . . . sir . . . I don't want to be rude . . .'

'Good,' Lestrade smiled coldly at him, 'that's an excellent maxim. And I wouldn't dream of forcing you to be otherwise. Let's have it.'

'His name is Arnold Howard. He was a Preparatory School teacher. I know that by the little patches on the elbows of his jacket.'

Lestrade wasn't interested in scoring points. He knew in his heart that what lay before him was chummy's eighth victim. He'd stop now – if that was physically possible for such a madman – if he was running true to the names in the haunting little song from the West Country. And he would slip away like a reed in the river, lost for ever, hidden from the light.

'Where and when was he found?'

'By the river at Mapledurham. It's a little village on the Oxfordshire-Berkshire border, but it falls in *our* patch.' Rattray was at pains to make the point. 'He'd obviously been fishing. His line was beside him. Pity, really. Got a fair-sized stickleback on the end of it.'

'Cause of death?'

'Doctor said poisoning. There were signs of a meal on the grass around the body. A few crumbs the moorhens hadn't got to. And a wine cork. A rather unassuming little Chablis the doctor thought, but then he's a pretentious old git so I let that lie.'

'What sort of poison?' Lestrade asked.

Rattray tutted. 'Look, this isn't Scotland Yard, you know. We haven't got the resources you blokes've got. I don't know, microscopes and cameras and despatch motors. Out here we make do with truncheons and bikes, mate . . . er . . . Superintendent.'

'In other words, you don't know what sort of poison?'

'No,' Rattray scowled. It was not the first time he had been in this position.

'Right,' Lestrade stood upright, 'it's my guess we're talking about a vegetable irritant. Hemlock, I would surmise.'

Dew broke away from the door frame. 'You mean . . . ?'

Lestrade frowned and shook his head. 'No one saw this man on . . . when did you say he died?'

'I didn't,' Rattray beamed, 'but it was . . .'

'Friday,' said Dew.

'Well, if you bloody well know, why ask?' Rattray snapped.

'Thank you for the unpleasantries, Chief Inspector,' Lestrade crossed to him, 'but Mr Dew and I are in rather a hurry. It may be that once this trail goes cold, it goes cold for ever. Did anyone see Arnold alive on that Friday?'

'Yes,' Rattray said, 'a courting couple saw him fishing at about eleven o'clock. He was alone then. We have another sighting at noon or thereabouts. He waved to a punter.'

'Still alone?'

'As a ranger,' Rattray nodded.

'But a cyclist at about one fifteen saw two men, sitting side by side with a picnic hamper at that spot.'

'Was one of them Arnold?' Lestrade asked.

'Well the cyclist is squeamish and refuses to view the body.' Rattray crossed to it and looked down at the blond, young man whose inane grin was lost for ever in death. 'Can't think why. This is nothing to the bloke we fished out of the weir last year. Had to put him on three of these slabs, we did . . .'

'Yes, thank you for "Post-mortems we have loved", Chief Inspector,' Lestrade cut the man short.

'Anyway,' Rattray was back to the point, 'from his description it was definitely Arnold. Stupid grin. Blond hair. Can't be two blokes looking *that* stupid on the river. Not on the same day.'

'Did your cyclist describe his companion?'

'My cyclist was alone,' Rattray explained.

'No,' Lestrade said, 'I mean . . .'

'Oh, yes,' Rattray smirked, no stone of non-co-operation left unturned, 'I see what you're getting at. Elderly chap. Long cravat. Old-fashioned wideawake.'

'How old-fashioned?' Lestrade asked.

'Well,' Rattray mused, 'how old-fashioned would you like it to be?'

'I thought *I* was asking the questions, Chief Inspector.'

'Well, I don't know. It's the sort of headgear my ol' dad used to wear.'

'Colonial?'

'I would think so. Not the sort of thing they'd raise an eyebrow at in Rangoon, I wouldn't think.'

'Tall?'

'The hat or the companion?'

'There *is* a limit to my patience, Mr Rattray.'

'He didn't say,' the chief inspector said. 'He was sitting down.'

Lestrade stood at Rattray's elbow, looking down at the late fisherman.

'You're sure about this man's name?'

'Oh, yes,' the Chief Inspector told him. 'He's been identified by his brother and sister-in-law; his sister and her young man; his headmaster; his old choirmaster; the vicar and his nanny. There's nothing like a sudden death to bring out the prurient sightseers, is there? It got silly in the end. I had to turn his window cleaner away.'

'And none of them came up with an alias?'

'Well, I didn't feel it necessary to go into their private lives – though I must admit I didn't like the look of the old choirmaster.'

'I am talking about Arnold, Mr Rattray.'

'Ah yes,' the local man was smirking again, 'of course. No aliases I am aware of.'

'Not Tom Cobbleigh, for instance?'

Rattray frowned, 'Tom Cobbley? I've heard that name somewhere. Or something like it.'

'Widdecombe Fair,' Dew told him.

'No,' Rattray shook his head, 'that's not it. Never been here.'

'No,' Dew persisted, 'not the place. The song. You know, "Tom Pearce, Tom Pearce . . ."'

Rattray muttered to Lestrade, 'is he all right? I mean, the heat, he flies . . .'

'He's fine,' Lestrade assured him.

'No,' Rattray clicked his fingers, 'I remember now. It's th
name of a drink. I knew that Chablis stuff was nonsense.
bet that's what killed him. It was a Cobbley. That must hav
finished him quickly. So quickly he fell on his little hand mirr
and broke it.'

For a long time neither of them spoke on the train back t
London. The smoke and grime settled on their boaters an
faces as they rattled through that Home Counties summe
Their jackets swung from the hooks they'd hung them on an
their striped shirts clung to their backs like a second skin. The
were alone in their carriage, but then, with armpits like their
it wasn't surprising.

'We've lost him, Walter,' Lestrade said.

'No, no, guv. The trail's still warm. Like this perishing day

'Don't patronym me, Dew,' Lestrade grunted. 'Our friend ha
struck at random. For the last three of his victims, it hasn't bee
the name we expected. Same sound, different spelling for Pet
Gurney. An old slang phrase for Harry "Adams" Hawke an
now this. The widest of the mark yet. He never intended t
kill anyone called Tom Cobbleigh. That was just the name c
his method. And now he's gone.'

'But we know who it is,' Dew said, 'and if he's running tru
to the song, he won't strike again. All we've got to do is fin
Staveley.'

'He's long gone, Walter,' Lestrade sighed. 'He'll have bee
on the boat train by last Saturday.'

'I don't share your gloom, guv,' Dew said, loosening his tie

'Well,' Lestrade stared at the dots in the yellow field
sweating with their harvest scythes under a merciless sur
'We'll give it one more crack. When we get back, I want yo
to spruce yourself up. And if you've got any humble pie, we'
both better have a slice.'

Jugger Jenkins had long ago run through his gamut of disguise
When Lestrade and Dew walked past him, he was an orga

grinder. It was not the most sensible of subterfuges. Irate neighbours had sent for the police and he'd been moved on three times already. Passing street urchins also complained because his monkey didn't appear to move around very much. Bearing in mind it had half a pound of best taxidermist's cotton-wool up its bum, that was hardly surprising.

Jugger was still on top of it all, though, so that when Lestrade casually raised his right eyebrow to enquire whether General Staveley had returned, he imperceptibly shook his head. When Lestrade raised his left eyebrow to enquire how many people were in the house at Fox Court, Jenkins raised two fingers at him. The superintendent did find the spitting a *little* superfluous, however. After all, he hadn't, in his Yard sign language, asked for the man's opinion of Acting Assistant Commissioner Woodhouse.

The door of Number sixteen opened warily and the maid Gertrude crouched there. Gone was the broom with which she'd been so handy days before. Now she clutched the infinitely-more-lethal Silber and Fleming Carpet-Beater in her red and scrawny hands. One sweep from that and she'd be looking squarely at a murder charge.

Lestrade's boater was off and in his hands in an instant. So was Dew's.

'Is the lady of the house at home?' the superintendent asked.

'Mum,' Gertrude wailed, never flinching from her place in the doorway for an instant, 'it's them. They're back.'

Lady Staveley swept down the stairs. Lestrade was glad to see she was not toting her husband's twelve-bore.

'Ah,' she said archly, 'you found the doorbell. Congratulations.'

'Indeed, Lady Staveley,' Lestrade smiled, 'but we have not found your husband. May we come in?'

The nozzle of the Silber and Fleming eased upwards in Gertrude's capable hands. Lady Staveley was at the girl's side. 'The suction on this', she patted it, 'is something else, gentlemen, I warn you. Besides,' she lifted a corner of her pink pelisse, to reveal the butt of a pistol, 'my husband's bull-dog. Like him, I have endured sieges before. Like him, I am a crack shot. You may come in, but you must sit down. I want to see your hands at all times. And I don't want you to break, steal or otherwise interfere with *any* of my property. Is that clear?'

'Perfectly,' said Lestrade. Even before she went for her bulldog, Lady Staveley was clearly calling the shots.

'Good. Now, Gertrude. Put that thing down and take some lemonade to that relatively nice young constable out there pretending to be an Italian. He must be terribly hot. If the General were here, he'd doubtless do him one of his infernal Cobbleys.'

'Cobbleighs?' Lestrade and Dew chorused as their backsides hit the sofa together.

'It's a drink,' Lady Staveley said, 'known as a cobbler in some parts of the country. Made from wine, lemon juice, sugar and a little ice. Very much a summer drink. The General's speciality.'

'Is it?'

'Kept them all going in Abyssinia, I understand, although the ice was in rather short supply.'

'It's about Abyssinia we'd like to talk, Lady Staveley,' Lestrade told her.

She sat opposite the Yard men. 'Really?' she said.

'I . . . feel I must apologize again for the conduct of my men on our last visit, Lady Staveley,' Lestrade flustered.

'Yes, well, let's just say I'm surprised to see you still on the case, on the Force and even on your feet. No doubt I am looking at two seriously demoted men.'

'Incurably,' Lestrade lied, 'I am now a detective-sergeant and Constable Dew here is just waiting to be fitted for his new blue uniform prior to returning to the horse troughs.'

'Excellent. Now, why are you back?'

'We are still unable to find your husband, Lady Staveley.'

'But that's preposterous. I told you. He's fishing somewhere along the Thames. You can't miss him. Tall chap. Wears a silly old wideawake. Terribly casually dressed, really; for a soldier, I mean.'

'We know where he stayed, Lady Staveley,' Lestrade explained, 'but he appears to have gone.'

'Lost his spoor, have you? Well, I'm afraid that's no concern of mine.'

'He hasn't been in touch?' Lestrade already knew the answer to that one. Jugger Jenkins still watched the house; Constable 'The Shadow' Royal followed the maid or the lady whenever they went out; and Constable 'Ears' McMullen was eavesdropping like the old hand he was while posing as a telephone operator.

'No. That doesn't surprise me. Charles is a free spirit, Sergeant. He often goes off for weeks at a time. He is a law-abiding citizen however. I am sure that if he knew you wanted to talk to him, he'd be only too pleased. The point is, Sergeant Lestrade, that neither you nor your superior, that rather lacklustre Major Woodhouse, has explained to me why you wish to talk to him. I cannot accept that this whole furore has been over his driving too fast. Especially since the vehicle in question is parked in the garage around the corner.'

'Indeed not, Madam,' Lestrade said. 'You may recall that I mentioned we were investigating a series of murders.'

'I do,' she nodded archly, 'I took that to be the ramblings of an idiot, Mr Lestrade. Did I take wrongly?'

Lestrade ignored her. 'We did trace your husband to a public house-cum-hotel in Sonning Eye, Lady Staveley.'

'Well, there you are, then.'

'Lady Staveley,' Lestrade braced himself, 'I hope you are prepared for what I am about to tell you. Your husband not only used an assumed name, he was there with a young lady who was posing as his wife.'

There was silence. The General's lady shifted position a little in her high-backed chair. 'Tell me,' she said, 'was this a young woman, blonde?'

'Young, certainly. I am unaware of the colour of her hair.'

'It will either be Hermione Wentworth or Harriet Qualtrough. Anthea Birley at an outside chance, although she is rather too aptly named for my husband, who tends to go for the willowy sort.'

'Y . . . you knew?' Lestrade and Dew chorused.

'He's very forward, isn't he,' Lady Staveley said of Dew, 'for a man about to return to uniform?'

'Very,' agreed Lestrade, 'I will have words with him. It was Harriet Qualtrough apparently.'

227

'Hmm,' Lady Staveley nodded, 'I'm not surprised.'

'Lady Staveley . . .'

But she cut the sergeant-superintendent short, 'Mr Lestrade, I am . . . well, never you mind how old. Let's just say I am a whisker past my prime. So of course is Charles – in fact he's older than I. But that's one of God's little injustices, isn't it? Since He made man in his own image and only created woman as a rather half-hearted afterthought, I think we can assume He shows a great deal of male bias. Accordingly he gave us women charms that fade, twinkles that raddle. Whereas you men . . . although, looking at you two, I doubt the veracity of my argument. The point is that Charles doesn't look a day over fifty-five, whereas I . . . well, the odd tuck here, the odd landslip there . . . My husband still has spring in his step, Mr Lestrade. He always has. And I'm ashamed to admit that he is not particularly discriminating – not since me, I mean. Why do you suppose Gertrude is such a dab hand at defending herself with various cleaning implements?'

'Er . . . the General . . . er . . . ?'

'Precisely. Makes advances on anything in a skirt. It's his military training, I suppose, advancing.'

'One of his conquests was Peta Gurney,' Lestrade told her.

'Really? I've read that name somewhere, although I'm sure I don't know her.'

'She was killed recently when her parachute failed to open above the Alexandra Palace,' the superintendent said.

'Of course. That's where I read it – in *The Times*. Just a moment – are you telling me that you believe that Charles had a hand in . . .'

'Her back-pack? Precisely, Lady Staveley.'

'Preposterous, Sergeant!'

He wiped his eye where the old girl's venom had hit him. Actually, he was very lucky. It could easily have been followed by her teeth. 'Tell us about Abyssinia,' he said.

'Abyssinia?' she repeated. 'Why?'

'Because I've asked you to, Madam,' Lestrade said.

'No, I mean, why do you want to know about Abyssinia?'

'I believe it is the common link that I am seeking in no less than eight murders.'

'Really? Good Heavens! Well, Charles was a colonel on the staff in those days – attached to old Napier. The old man apparently didn't like Charles; found him too casual a dresser and so on. The campaign was a rattling little success, like all Victoria's small wars – a nifty piece of advancing, by all accounts; but then the Abyssinian isn't a natural warrior. Spears and shields against the Maxim gun. Or was it the Gatling in those days? I really can't remember. Frankly, Sergeant, when you've seen one piece of ordnance, you've seen them all.'

'Did your husband mention a Charles Speedy?' Lestrade asked.

'Is this some sort of joke, Mr Lestrade?' the lady sat frowning.

'Joke?' Lestrade looked at Dew, who had paused in mid notepad.

'My husband did not have to mention Charles Speedy, Sergeant. I was engaged to the man.'

'To Speedy?'

'The very same. Striking fellow. Taller than Charles – Staveley, I mean. Charlie Speedy was six foot five if he was an inch. Clever, tough, resourceful, hung like a donkey. Unfortunately for him, he introduced me to my Charles and that was it – love at first sight.'

'Were you married to Colonel Staveley at the time of the Abyssinian campaign?'

'No. Charles wouldn't hear of it. He said he might not come back and wouldn't leave me a broken-hearted widow. We married on his return. Like the first Duke of Marlborough, he had me while still wearing his boots – I hope you aren't writing this down, young man!' she stabbed the air with her index finger. Nothing could be further from Dew's mind. He was still trying to spell 'resourceful'.

'So the Charleses – Speedy and Staveley – were not on good terms in Abyssinia?' Lestrade surmised.

'Well, it's difficult to say. They're both men of honour, Sergeant. I'm sure neither would do anything that would have upset the fine equipoise of the Mess.'

'And you never saw Speedy again?'

'Not a word. Charles said he saw him the day before they entered Magdala. He was a little odd then apparently.'

'Odd?'

'Preoccupied. He told Charles he'd stumbled across some thing that would change his life for ever. Something . . . strange Something dangerous.'

'What?'

Lady Staveley shrugged. 'He wouldn't say. Though he'd tolc the others, apparently.'

'The others?' Lestrade checked.

Lady Staveley chuckled. 'Oh, it was a joke with Charlie. He had this silly, irritating little song that he used to sing.'

'Widdecombe Fair?' Lestrade started to feel the hairs on his neck begin to crawl.

'That's the one. Silly little rustic piece without merit, of the sort that that equally silly and rustic little man Cecil Sharpe drools over. He's no loss at all to the Hampstead Conservatoire of Music; you take my word for it.'

'I still don't understand, Lady Staveley,' Lestrade said. '"The others". You said he told the others.'

'Why, yes, Mr Lestrade,' she sighed, 'I was coming to that Charlie Speedy claimed to know all those ludicrous people ir the chorus personally. All friends of his, he said. I think it was just a story he told the natives, so that they'd be more afraid o his magic. They followed him wherever he went.'

'The natives?'

'No, Sergeant,' Lady Staveley said, 'the people in the song – Tom Pearce and all those. Do please concentrate – and perhaps one day you'll make Inspector again.'

The constable wandered along the pavement that ran round Bloomsbury Square. The long, hot day had given way to a coolei night and the sun had set, a magic oval of fire over the brick skylines where one by one the twinkling lights went out. The uniformed man recognized the hurrying figure in boater and serge, the fuzz on his upper lip now filling out to something approximating a moustache again.

'Evening, Mr Lestrade, sir,' he saluted. 'Mind how you go.'

It was standard advice, but apt enough, because Lestrade missed his footing in the gaslight and caught himself a nasty one on Charles Tenterden's door-knocker. The door swung wide and the hall stood empty.

'Mr Tenterden?' Lestrade called, dabbing his eyebrow ridge with a regulation hankie. No reply. It was a silly thing. Lestrade had been about to call it a night at the Yard when he realized that before he died, Sergeant Adams had not reported back on his intended visit to Tenterden. He'd gone to ask him if the song that Speedy kept whistling had been Widdecombe Fair. He knew now, of course, that it was, but at the Yard, they left no tees undotted, no eyes uncrossed. It would just take a moment.

'I'm sorry it's late.'

'Who's there?' a voice called.

'Superintendent Lestrade,' he answered.

There was a silence.

'Can I come up?' Lestrade couldn't see in the darkness at the top of the stairs.

'Well ... It *is* rather late,' Tenterden said. He sounded strange, preoccupied, different.

'I know,' Lestrade said, groping his way in near darkness. 'It's just a minor point. I'd like to ask . . .' But he never finished his sentence. There was a thud, like furniture falling. Then a short scuffle and a gasp. Then what sounded like the creaking of a rope. He quickened his pace on the stairs, his heart pounding. He knew what those noises meant. God, let him be wrong. *Please* let him be wrong.

On the landing there were two rooms, to left and to right. Total darkness in both. Yet the creaking came from the right-hand room. He edged open the door, feeling it thud on an overturned chair. Silhouetted against the window hung the body of a man, his feet twirling two feet above the carpet. Lestrade was about to fumble for a lucifer when he felt a fist in the small of his back – the same fist that had pushed Janet Calthrop into oblivion down the dark stairs at King's College, that had slashed the harness of Captain Orange's trap, that had pulled the cork on the deadly elixir called Tom Cobbley. He stumbled forward over the chair, tapping aside the dangling feet as he went down. Then he heard the door slam and he looked up into the barrel of a pistol.

'Tenterden did it,' the voice said, 'or at least, that's how it will

231

look. Makes a good corpse, doesn't he? Your timing is rather unfortunate though. Not only have I not had time to forge a suicide note, in which the old reporter confesses all, but now I'll have to dispose of you as well.'

He heard the hammer click back.

'Just a minute,' Lestrade blurted, 'you didn't think I'd be daft enough to come here alone, did you?' He tried to make out the face, but in the blackness, it was impossible. Something gleamed dully round the neck, dark red, burning in the faint street-light. And the gun muzzle seemed to glow.

The man chuckled, deep, menacing. 'I've watched you since you entered the square, Mr Lestrade,' he said. 'You are totally alone. And why shouldn't you be? You haven't been closer to me than you have to the North Pole since this case began. Clueless have you lived and clueless will you die.'

Lestrade saw the gun come up as the arm straightened. 'You know my name,' he said. 'Might I not know yours?'

The deep, growling chuckle came again. 'You know my name, Lestrade,' he said.

'Staveley,' Lestrade guessed.

'Staveley!' the man in the darkness spat.

'Speedy, then,' Lestrade tried again.

'Well, now that introductions are over,' Speedy said, 'it's already time for our goodbyes.'

'Wait!' Lestrade's hand was in the air. 'Why? At least tell me that. Why did you kill the others?'

'The others?'

'Your friends from Widdecombe Fair.'

'Widdecombe Fair,' Speedy echoed. Lestrade could see the man was very tall. Judging from where the collar gleamed, at least six foot three, possibly more.

'But you changed the order, didn't you? If you'd started with Tom Pearce, I might have got to you quicker.'

There was a sigh. 'Very well, Mr Lestrade,' the voice said, 'I'll grant a dying man's last wish. I'll tell you how and I'll tell you why. In the meantime we'll let old Tenterden here dangle, shall we? As they do for an hour, I understand, after the hangman has sprung his trap. You will sit very still. Because one movement from you and I will blow your head off. Clear?'

232

'As a bell,' Lestrade nodded.

'Let me see. Where did it all start? Oh, yes, Captain Orange. He couldn't live, you see. I wanted to give myself as much distance as I could, between me and whatever infantile law enforcement came after me. So I hit upon the plan of a series of accidents. I went to see Orange. We chatted, about this and that. I pretended to be interested in buying property in the Dartmoor area. While he was fetching his nieces for their ride, I carefully cut through the straps. Just enough, of course, so that on the first curve, they'd snap.'

'But you killed three innocent girls,' Lestrade said.

'All human life is cheap, Lestrade, in the scheme of things. Anyway, I had other fish to fry. I guessed Orange's coachman had seen me at Orange's house. In King's College, I was determined that no one should.'

'Your other fish was Janet Calthrop.'

'Jan Stewer,' Speedy corrected him. 'I had of course inveigled my way into the History library under an assumed name. By careful listening and talking to the students, I discovered the little affair she was having with Sparrow. I found their revolting little lair. It was simple to rig up the wire and stay behind in the college after all the others had gone and the place was locked up. That, after all, is what she did. I hid in the shadows until she came out, then quickly put the wire in position, anchored with putty and when she reached the third stair, I pushed her. Like a dream.'

'Then there was the Spaniard?' Lestrade had given up on the man's name entirely.

'Indeed there was. Tom Pearce. Lieutenant Hedron, as well as being an utter rotter and a cad, had a mouth the size of the Blackwall Tunnel. I discovered his little blackmailing venture and realized, like James Sparrow, what a perfect little murderer he'd make. Sparrow might have killed the girl to hush up the scandal and Hedron might have killed the Spaniard because the Spaniard refused to pay up any more. I invited Tom of the one eye down to Beachy Head, nudged the roof on to him at the lighthouse and then made a big thing about appearing to jump off the top.'

'Hence the full-dress uniform?'

'A spare of Lieutenant Hedron's. I don't even think he noticed it had gone.'

'You wanted us to believe that the Spaniard had committed suicide?'

'It gave me time to organize my next little job.'

'You became Mr Alvarez, the inventor.'

'Correct. Sir Daniel Whiddon's obsessions were well known. I'd met his second cousin Lyall in Abyssinia years ago and he'd said the whole family were gadget-mad. But he knew too much. And he had to die. It wasn't difficult to alter the little appliance made by Heinrich Peschken to prevent nocturnal emissions – a little hole here, a little sharpened screw there. Admittedly, I wasn't sure that it would work, but it seems to have done the trick admirably. I made a point of helping the Misses Whiddon across the road to the park opposite their house and learned from them of Daniel's continuing little problem. Lyall had told me his little nephew wet the bed when he was three – it's funny what men will talk about under the searing sun and thousands of miles from home. But when the boy was forty-one . . . well, it was too delicious an opportunity to pass up.'

'And then you turned your attention to George Russell.'

'Bill Brewer,' Lestrade saw the dully-gleaming collar moving. The gun still held steady in the hand. 'I hadn't realized his strange dressing habits or the fact that his wife and partner were trying to kill him – what a gift that was. Like Sparrow and Hedron, I now had two more people to pin this one on.'

'But you'd been seen at Beachy,' Lestrade desperately played for time. 'Someone recognized you.'

'They did?' there was a shake in the voice.

'Yes, not as de Sesuj Olzep but as Pedro Alvarez. The knot was tightening at that moment, Captain.'

'Nonsense, Lestrade,' Speedy hissed, 'you came here tonight to talk to Tenterden, not to arrest me. You thought I'd died in Abyssinia years ago. Well, I'm sorry to disappoint you. Russell was easy. Everyone and his wife knew of his movements. It fitted "Widdecombe Fair" that he always went to the brewery early on Friday morning. All I had to do was to get there before him – the place was wide open – and loosen the screws on the shelf. The rest was gravity. Rather poetic, don't you think, that he fell into the vat? I was happy with that.'

'Then you turned your attention on Peta Gurney, posing as Staveley.'

'Correct. The bastard had taken my girl from me all those years ago. Why shouldn't I take his? You've seen her recently. How is Marjorie?'

'If you mean Lady Staveley, chipper as a bull-elephant.'

'That's my girl,' Speedy chuckled his baritone chuckle. 'Well, it was perfect. The young lecher – he couldn't keep his hands off women in Abyssinia – had become the old lecher. I was there that day at Alexandra Palace. I watched him pack her parachute, then, while they were canoodling and making sheep's eyes at each other, I unpacked it again. A snip here, a rend there and Bob's your uncle – death from three thousand feet. And that sent you scurrying after Staveley, which is exactly where I wanted you to go.'

'What about "Abou" Ben Adams?' Lestrade growled. 'Why him?'

'That was his fault,' Lestrade heard Speedy's voice falter, change range, then correct itself, 'I had plans for another, but he got in the way.'

'How was it done?'

'Hemlock, smeared on the tip of my umbrella. I did get a few odd looks on such a hot day – a man carrying an umbrella. I followed him for streets, then, when the press was thickest, stuck him like the pig he was.'

'He had a wife and kids,' Lestrade said, 'and Peta Gurney was just nineteen, just starting out in life . . .'

'Life?' Speedy screamed. 'None of them had any right to life. Not one of them. That babbling idiot by the river. I knew Staveley had taken another of his young things to a hotel nearby. It was perfect.'

'Hemlock again?'

'Unimaginative, but effective. It was in the ice cube in the drink. I insisted he swallow it. The concoction was a favourite of Staveley's. He used to mix it for us in Abyssinia. And now, Mr Lestrade, I'm afraid that your playing for time is over. Time itself, you see, has run out. I have yet to strike

235

one more time, though it spoils the pattern, of the song Goodbye.'

He saw the muzzle extend towards him and was grateful he couldn't see the finger tighten on the trigger. 'The mirrors,' he shouted, 'you haven't told me about the mirrors.'

There was a silence. 'Never mind those,' Speedy said, 'they're not important.'

'Yes,' Lestrade sensed the voice falter again, 'yes, they are. Why were they there? Near every body and always broken. You had to steal some more from the Horniman Museum.' He eased himself upright on to one knee. 'Answer me. Why are the mirrors always broken? Is it because he can't see you that way?'

'Who?' the voice was an almost inaudible whisper.

'You know who,' Lestrade slid his back up the edge of the fireplace. He was nearly standing now, aware that the muzzle of the gun had followed him every inch of the way. 'You know who, don't you, Mr Tenterden? Prester John.'

There was an explosion. A flash in the darkness. Lestrade felt a searing pain in his left arm, but he wouldn't have another opportunity. He lunged forward, aiming low to avoid the next shot and hurled himself at his assailant's feet. The man cried out, the second shot flying wide and shattering a window-pane. He'd toppled sideways and Lestrade was on him, grappling for the gun. Then his brass knuckles were out and crashing once into the man's face. Lestrade snatched the barrel and wrenched it out of the man's hand. Then he rolled clear and cocked the pistol at him.

'How did you know?' Tenterden lay panting in the darkness.

Lestrade fumbled with his matches, feeling his left arm stiffen and trying to keep the gun trained on his man. 'That you weren't Speedy? Well,' he looked up at the twirling body. It proved no more than a roughly-tied length of sacking, the sort of thing that kids threw on bonfires in confused homage to Guy Fawkes, 'I confess that I didn't – at first. I was so sure I was hunting Charles Staveley. Everything you told me made sense; tied up; except for one.'

He blew out his match. In that second, a younger, fitter madman might have lunged for him. But there was no fight in

Tenterden. He just lay there, blood trickling from a swelling lip. Lestrade found an oil-lamp and lit it clumsily, trying to steady the gun at the same time. Then he eased himself into a chair and tried not to shiver.

'What was that?' Tenterden asked, 'that one thing that didn't tie up?'

'The boots,' Lestrade told him, 'the Spaniard's boots. You took away his clothes and stashed them God-knows-where, but to pass yourself off as Speedy, you needed to be taller. That was all right at Captain Orange's house because you were wearing the special shoes you're wearing now.' He tapped them with his own, 'the ones I easily knocked you off balance in a moment ago. But at Beachy Head, you had to wear them again – and that meant leaving the Spaniard's boots behind.'

'I see,' Tenterden scowled.

'Even that I might have overlooked,' Lestrade said, 'but you buried yourself with that comment about the Misses Whiddon – that you'd helped them across the road and learned of nephew Daniel's continency problem. Slightly dotty they may be, but they'd known that nice, mad Captain Speedy. If he'd come back after all these years to chat to them in their dotage, I think they'd have told me, since he did crop up in conversation. But Charles Tenterden? Why should they mention him? No one was looking in his direction at all. Now, Mr Tenterden,' Lestrade stretched his arm, the blood pumping down his sleeve and dripping off his fingers on to the carpet, 'you will answer some questions of mine. What is that round your neck?'

'It's mine!' Tenterden's colour had drained and he clutched it.

'No doubt,' Lestrade said, 'but I want to know what lorry it fell off.'

'Lorry,' growled Tenterden. 'Peasant! Slave! You are not worthy to walk in the same sun. Do you know what this is?'

'That's what I asked you,' Lestrade said.

'In the Zulu dialect, it is Isetembiso Sami, the very sacred thing. It is a collar of rubies, Lestrade. Its worth cannot be estimated. If I put it on the open market now, they might as well close Kimberley.'

'Where did you get it?' Lestrade asked. 'No. No, don't answer that. You got it from Charles Speedy, didn't you? That was the something he'd found in the desert; the something that would change his life for ever. Is that what you killed him for?'

Tenterden didn't move for a moment. Then he nodded, his face glowing with a light of its own behind the dangling dummy. 'Yes, by God and I'd do it again. This is the Isetembiso Sami, the Ndhlondhlo . . . the collar of Prester John.'

Lestrade's mouth hung slack. He felt dizzy and sick. 'But he's coming for you, isn't he, Mr Tenterden?'

'No,' the man's lips were tight.

'Why?' Lestrade asked again, 'why did you kill those people?'

'They were his friends,' Tenterden muttered, 'Speedy's friends. He knew them all.'

'That was a joke,' Lestrade said, 'just his sense of humour, I suppose. They're not *real*, Tenterden. Even if they once were, they're not now.'

'Not now, no. Because I've killed them – Tom Pearce, Jan Stewer, Bill Brewer, Peta Gurney, Peter Tavy, Dan'l Whiddon, Harry Hawke, old uncle Tom Cobbleigh – they *were* friends of his. I thought they were out there. In Africa. When he talked, he sounded as if they were. I had searched high and low for all these years – Abyssinia, Eritrea, Somaliland. Then I realized they were here all the time. Here, at home. And they *knew*. They knew I had the collar of Prester John. They'd talk, Lestrade. They'd tell . . . him. Do you know? Do you know what it means to have the sacred power of John? Immortality,' he barely whispered the word, 'but the mirrors had to break. Without his magic mirror he cannot see me. Cannot see what I've done.' The grey old man staggered to his feet, blood from Lestrade's brass knuckles still bubbling from his mouth, trickling down on to the rubies that gleamed at his throat. 'With this, Lestrade,' he clutched the flaring stones convulsively, 'immortality.'

Lestrade's gun arm extended to the full.

Tenterden laughed, that deep, mocking laugh. 'Put that toy away,' he said, 'you can't hurt me with that. With anything.'

There was a creak on the stairs that rose into a measured tread. Tenterden stopped as though struck by lightning.

'He's here, Mr Tenterden' Lestrade said. 'You can hear him too, can't you?'

238

'No!' Tenterden screamed and the tread speeded up. 'No!' and he tottered across the room, his wild eyes staring at the open door. Lestrade flexed his arm and the gun shook. The room spun in his vision and he wasn't likely to hit a barn door. He saw Tenterden dash sideways and hurtle through the window, the sash disintegrating as he hit it. He was still screaming as his terrified body impaled itself with a thud and a squelch on the railings below.

A bewildered bobby put his helmeted head around the door. 'Oh, it's you, Mr Lestrade, sir,' he saluted, 'I could have sworn I heard a shot. Is that gentleman who just left by way of the upstairs window all right?'

General Charles Staveley fastened up his fly buttons, kissed Harriet Qualtrough au revoir and walked around the corner into Chancery Lane, then on through the bustle into Fox Court. A large man, who appeared to have one leg tied up behind him and a wooden projection below his knee, was begging on the corner. The General threw him a shilling, then marched in through his front door. Gertrude the maid kept a wary eye and a safe distance, but the General ignored her, crossing to his good lady wife and kissing her on the forehead.

'How was the fishing, dear?' she asked him.

'Not bad,' said Staveley, throwing his wideawake on to the table, 'not at all bad. And what's been happening here in my absence? Anything?'

'Oh, no, dear,' Lady Staveley smiled, 'it's been very quiet, hasn't it, Gertrude?'

In the offices of Sidney Rowlatt, John Buchan, bored out of his skull, reached idly for *The Times* and read of the events in Bloomsbury Square the night before, of the broken mirrors and of the collar of Prester John which they intended to donate to the Horniman Museum. And when he'd finished, he picked up a pen and a sheaf of paper and began to write – 'I mind as if it were yesterday, my first sight of the man. Little I knew at the time how big the moment was with destiny, or how often that face seen in the fitful moonlight would haunt my sleep and disturb my waking hours . . .'

'Well,' he said, half chuckling to himself, 'you've got to have a bit of artistic licence, haven't you?'

10/11   8X   7/12

Trow, M. J.

Lestrade and the
mirror of murder.

20.00

DATE			

X 6 - 4/07

10 X